REVOLUTIONARY ART AND POLITICS IN EGYPT

Political Communication and Media Practices in the Middle East and North Africa

The popular uprisings that rocked several Arab countries at the beginning of 2011, and the more recent ones in Algeria, Sudan, Lebanon and Iraq, arose, among other things, in the context of changing media practices and political communication in the region. Beyond visible actions by political elites and institutions, several of these movements were characterised by grassroots communication on social media, and many included creative practises by a diverse range of actors.

Books in this series critically engage with the complex and fluid relationship between politics, communication and culture in the Middle East and North Africa, taking into account the specificities of social and political local contexts, diverse political and media systems, media institutions, media and political actors and populations as well as differentiations along religious, sectarian, ethnic, gendered and racial lines.

Series Editors

Dina Matar, SOAS, University of London
Zahera Harb, City, University of London

Advisory Board

Omar Al-Ghazzi (LSE); Mohamed Zayani (Georgetown University); Gholam Khiabany (Goldsmiths, University of London); Marwan Kraidy (Northwestern University in Qatar); Adel Iskander (Simon Fraser University); Joe Khalil (Northwestern University in Qatar); Tarik Sabry (University of Westminster); Naomi Sakr (University of Westminster); Annabelle Sreberny (SOAS, University of London)

International Advisory Board

Loubna Skalli Hanna (University of California, Washington); Donatella della Ratta (John Cabot University); Reem Abou-El-Fadl (SOAS, University of London); Laudan Nooshin (City, University of London); Kevin Smets (VUB University, Brussels); Sophie Chamas (SOAS, University of London); Miriyam Aouragh (University of Westminster); Dounia Mahlouly (SOAS, University of London); Sadia Jamil (Khalifa University of Science and Technology)

Published and Forthcoming Titles

Revolutionary Art and Politics in Egypt: Liminal Spaces and Cultural Production After 2011, Rounwah Adly Riyadh Bseiso
The Political Economy of Egyptian Media: Business and Military Elite Power and Communication after 2011, Maher Hamoud
Digital Political Cultures in the Middle East since the Arab Uprisings: Online Activism in Egypt, Tunisia and Lebanon, Dounia Mahlouly

REVOLUTIONARY ART AND POLITICS IN EGYPT

Liminal Spaces and Cultural Production After 2011

Rounwah Adly Riyadh Bseiso

I.B. TAURIS

LONDON • NEW YORK • OXFORD • NEW DELHI • SYDNEY

I.B. TAURIS
Bloomsbury Publishing Plc
50 Bedford Square, London, WC1B 3DP, UK
1385 Broadway, New York, NY 10018, USA
29 Earlsfort Terrace, Dublin 2, Ireland

BLOOMSBURY, I.B. TAURIS and the I.B. Tauris logo are trademarks of Bloomsbury
Publishing Plc

First published in Great Britain 2023

Copyright © Rounwah Adly Riyadh Bseiso, 2023

Rounwah Adly Riyadh Bseiso has asserted her right under the Copyright, Designs
and Patents Act, 1988, to be identified as Translator of this work.

For legal purposes the Acknowledgements on p. xviii constitute an extension
of this copyright page.

Series design by Catherine Wood & Adriana Brioso
Cover image © Megapress/Alamy Stock Photo

A catalogue record for this book is available from the British Library.

A catalog record for this book is available from the Library of Congress.

ISBN: HB: 978-0-7556-4475-9
ePDF: 978-0-7556-4476-6
eBook: 978-0-7556-4477-3

Series: Political Communication and Media Practices in the Middle East and North Africa

Typeset by Deanta Global Publishing Services, Chennai, India

To find out more about our authors and books visit www.bloomsbury.com and
sign up for our newsletters.

For my parents,
Mona Salim Bseiso & Adly Riyadh Bseiso,

To whom I owe everything, and without which I am nothing.

CONTENTS

FIGURES

PREFACE

The Egyptian revolution of 25 January 2011 was set against a background of ongoing police brutality, widespread government corruption, high rates of poverty and the possible succession of then-president Hosni Mubarak's son Gamal as an extension of his father's thirty-year rule. In the aftermath of Hosni Mubarak's ouster, I decided to travel to Cairo to see for myself what a post-Mubarak Egypt looked like, as he unquestionably represented the dominant visual symbol of power; from the images on billboards and street signs and buildings to the front page of every state-owned newspaper to the government propaganda posters plastered on the streets, Mubarak's image was an integral component of the Egyptian cityscape which I had become unknowingly accustomed to since my frequent visits starting in the early 1990s. The prevalence with which his name and image appeared in the media and within the everyday visual landscape was a clear symbol of his political dominance and unrelenting hold on the Egyptian presidency. Mubarak was Egypt, and Egypt was Mubarak – or so state media would have you believe. As *New York Times* reporter Neil MacFarquhar wrote,

> cataloguing every public use of the Mubarak name would require an effort not unlike constructing the Pyramids. It was plastered across schools, libraries, hospitals, clinics, bridges, roads, squares, airports, stadiums, ministry buildings, industrial complexes, dormitories, scouting centres and various national prizes. You name it . . . The president was the namesake for 388 schools, compared to 314 for the three previous presidents combined . . . the profusion of Mubarak rooms, photographs and statuary in the National Assembly rivalled that of Julius Caesar in imperial Rome. In fact one marble bust that media reports said cost around $30,000 gives the former president a passing resemblance to the Roman emperor. (MacFarquhar, 2011)

For the first time since my earliest memory of visiting Egypt nearly twenty years prior, I could no longer see images of Mubarak inundating every street corner or beneath the front-page headline of every newspaper on every street stall. Instead, images and messages calling for a communal spirit and a sense of ownership became pervasive in public spaces, and not just in downtown Cairo. Female college students collecting money (and, to my surprise, people happily donating) in the streets to buy paint for a 'beautify Cairo' campaign without getting harassed and groups of schoolchildren randomly sweeping and collecting garbage off the streets and repairing street signs represented an incredible turn of events, and on a personal level I felt that Egyptian society had been significantly transformed. Notices the like of which I had never seen before in my own apartment building in my twenty-some years of living and travelling to Cairo (see Figures 0.1 and 0.2) called for a 'clean, civilized society' and urged people to volunteer in cleaning up the streets. In that particular time and place, it truly felt like Egyptians were attempting, in a very real and visible way, to reconfigure their environment as a different one to their lived reality under almost three decades of Mubarak's rule. Had I not lived and travelled to Cairo for the majority of Mubarak's rule, perhaps I would not have truly understood the extent to which the deconstruction of his domineering name and image meant at that specific moment in time. It was, truly, a momentous – and wonderfully hopeful – feeling.

During my first trip back to Egypt since the revolution, in April 2011, I decided to take a walk in a district of Cairo, called Nasr City, with my father, Adly Bseiso, a veteran journalist and media consultant, and my dear late uncle, Amer Bseiso. Figures 0.3–0.6 are only a small sample of the many photographs that I took during my first experience of seeing the kind of revolutionary art which had gained traction and visibility after the initial eighteen days of the revolution. They encapsulated very real and symbolic feelings of fraternity, patriotism, solidarity and optimism in the beginning stages of the revolution in the aftermath of Mubarak's ouster. Recurring revolutionary symbols and images illustrated in these visual artefacts embodied the early feeling of victory and national pride people experienced when Mubarak was ousted, such as fists raised in defiance and unity, as well as signs of peace, chains breaking and the Egyptian eagle proudly spreading its wings. Images encouraging unity and civic duty (such as keeping the streets clean) as well as patriotism ('Proud to be Egyptian') are a reflection of what Salwa Ismail (professor of politics at the School of Oriental and African Studies) described as a form of active citizenship understood beyond simply a legal sense, to one which 'signifies a normative orientation towards a certain kind of civic self that assumes responsibilities as a member of a collective and that seeks to reconcile individual interests with the interests of that collective' (Ismail, 2011: 990). In this sense,

Figure 0.1 A sign posted in my apartment building in Nasr City, Cairo (April 2011) that says, '*A Clean Society = A Civilized Society* [my translation]'. *Source*: Photo by Author.

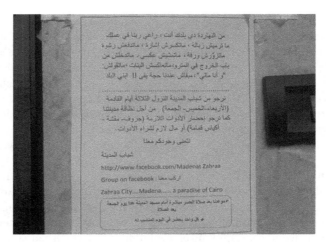

Figure 0.2 A sign posted in my apartment building in Nasr City, Cairo (April 2011), which says, '*From now on, this country is your country, be conscious of God in your work, do not throw garbage, do not cross a red light, do not pay a bribe, do not forge a paper, do not walk the opposite way, do not enter from the exit door in the Metro, do not harass girls, do not say "Why should I care", or we will have nothing left! Build your country. We urge the youth of the City [Madenat Zahrah] to go down for three days next week (Wednesday – Thursday – Friday) in order to clean our City. Please bring your own necessary tools (shovel, broom, garbage bag) or money to buy the necessary tools. We hope you will join us. Shabab [Youth] Al Madina *We will meet immediately after afternoon prayers in front of the Madina mosque tomorrow, on Friday, after prayer. Everyone come at the day which is suitable for them* [my translation].' *Source*: Photo by Author.

Figure 0.3 On the Egyptian Media Landscape, with the words 'Free Media' on the left, taken in April 2011, taken in Ahmad Al Fakhry Street, Nasr City, Cairo. *Source*: Photo by Author.

Figure 0.4 'Egyptian & Proud', taken in April 2011 on Ahmad Al Fakhry Street, Nasr City, Cairo. *Source*: Photo by Author.

Figure 0.5 'Cry for freedom', taken in April 2011, in Ahmad Al Fakhry Street, Nasr City, Cairo *Source*: Photo by Author.

Egyptians 'performed' their citizenship by taking it upon themselves to regulate traffic, protect one another and clean the streets, among other things. By doing so, they disrupted the normative, everyday relationship between the state and the public from one of *ihana* and *mahana* (humiliation) to one of national dignity and regaining a sense of civic identity and duty in the running of one's country (Ismail, 2011: 991). The formation of subjectivities which situate themselves in a place of power, instead of subversive to power, that is, the 'oppositional self' (Ismail, 2011:

Figure 0.6 'We are Egypt', alongside an image of the Crescent and the Cross, taken in April 2011, taken in Ahmad Al Fakhry Street, Nasr City, Cairo. *Source*: Photo by Author.

Figure 0.7 My father (bottom, centre) and uncle (bottom, far left) felt such pride and kinship towards the Egyptians' resilience and success which led to Mubarak's ouster that they wanted to take a picture with a group of Egyptians we met as we were viewing revolutionary art on Ahmad Al Fakhry Street in the district of Nasr City, Cairo. *Source*: Photo by Author.

990), was performed not only through civil and political conduct but also through cultural forms of expression witnessed in public spaces during the revolution, which, as Ismail argued, are acts which are intrinsically 'linked to imaginaries of modern citizenship and the subjectivities through which it is performed' (Ismail, 2011: 990).

It is, therefore, not entirely surprising that the celebratory and optimistic tone of revolutionary art – combined, of course, with the more subdued art commemorating and honouring the martyrs of the revolution – represented a form of mediated sociopolitical discourse of the actions of the revolutionaries in Tahrir and throughout Egypt, which emphasized both individual and collective responsibility and power, along with a concomitant sense of duty and patriotic sentiment. It was these images, and the elation of the revolution which they captured – along with the liberating notion that anyone could now pick up a marker, spray can or paint brush and freely write or create art in previously patrolled and restricted public spaces – which initially captivated my attention and sparked my interest in exploring revolutionary art further.

ACKNOWLEDGEMENTS

First and foremost, I am eternally grateful to my parents, Adly Riyadh Bseiso and Mona Salim Bseiso, whose constant encouragement, guidance and support are the driving force in my life. I would also like to thank the rest of my family for believing in me and supporting me throughout my academic and professional career – Sido Riyadh Bseiso and Jido Salim Bseiso, Tata Radiya Bseiso and Teta Fatima Malhas, my aunts Maysoon Bseiso, Amtoe Boshra, Noha, Abeer and Majida Bseiso, and my uncles Kareem and Amer Bseiso, and of course, my brothers, Riyadh and Saleem Bseiso and Zaid Taha, my sister-in-law Dana Chit and my wonderful nephews and niece, Adly, Eissa and Leena Bseiso.

I would also like to thank Dina Matar, whose constant supervision and advice have consistently motivated me to become a more inquisitive scholar. I also sincerely thank Rory Gormley, Yasmin Garcha, Mohammed Raffi and Benedict O'Hagan at I.B. Tauris, for their patience, genuine support and guidance in the process of publication.

This book would not have been possible without the valuable input from those I interviewed, the men and women mentioned in this book who – regardless of the difficult circumstance in Egypt at the time – openly shared their life experiences, memories and dreams with me. Without them, this would not have been possible. I hope that one day the economic, political and social justice ideals that they had fought so hard for in 2011 becomes a reality in Egypt.

Finally, I would like to thank my husband, Khalid Al-Fulaij, for his love and support, as well as my three wonderful boys, Yousef, Nasser and Bader Al-Fulaij, who are my daily motivation in life and whose endless curiosity constantly inspires my own.

INTRODUCTION

... little consideration has been paid to the 'cultural' as a terrain for doing politics, or engaging with the 'political', partly because of a narrow, instrumentalist definition of politics, and, in the Arab context, partly because of elitist interpretations of culture that dominated Arab intellectual thought for much of the twentieth century.

Dina Matar (2012b:125)

25 January 2011 – The people want the overthrow of the regime

Art is one of the many ways in which the Egyptian revolution of 25 January 2011 was experienced, contested, described and narrated as the revolutionary process unfolded. If we are to start taking the 'practice of politics seriously' (Haugbolle, Bandak, 2017: 191) outside of its more formal understandings, this necessarily 'means that we pay attention to what revolutionaries do – their repertoires of contention – as much as we pay attention to what they say and write as they seek to create a new political world' (Haugbolle, Bandak, 2017: 191). As we look back and reflect over a decade after the initial revolutionary moment in January 2011 and attempt to make sense[1] of the events which occurred, one of the ways in which we can most effectively do so is to look at *what* people *did* and *why*, and what it meant to them in that particular time and place. Highlighting the importance of lived experience in terms of how people responded to changing political events provides critical and necessary insight into the different ways people 'do' politics outside of formal understandings to top–down processes of the state and its institutions. This notion of politics does not capture the myriad ways in which people actually practice politics in meaningful ways on the ground.

In this book, I focus on one particular political and cultural event – the Egyptian revolution of 25 January 2011 – which witnessed the magnificent emergence of Tahrir Square in downtown Cairo as a location and platform for popular politics, with its simultaneous manifestation of solidarity, conflict, resistance, defiance, peace and struggle. This was paralleled by a surge of cultural production, artistic performances and art works emerging from unconventional – and most importantly previously policed and highly controlled – public spaces,[2] such as the *Mogamaa*,[3] walls, streets, sidewalks, squares and alleyways across the capital, Cairo, and in several other large cities in Egypt such as in Luxor, Ismailia and

Mansoura, to name a few. Creative forms of expression paralleled political dissent, with the proliferation of public performances and practices of artists and non-artists alike, solidifying a narrative that this momentous historical event was not only a 'political' revolution but also a 'cultural' one.

Romanticizing the revolution

Western commentators tended to romanticize and glorify the Egyptian revolution as a phenomenon that emerged seemingly out of nowhere, inundating media headlines on Egypt devoid of context,[4] as part of the problematically[5] labelled 'Arab Spring'[6] led by formerly apathetic[7] youngsters. While there is no doubt that the Egyptian revolution produced a visible surge of large-scale political and cultural performances in public spaces, dominating narratives depicted the North African nation of Egypt as a politically and culturally dormant country and, while doing so, ignored the underlying (and extraordinarily rich) historical political undercurrents of the revolution's emergence and existence.[8]

In manufacturing this particular image of the revolution as arising seemingly out of nowhere, Egyptian filmmaker Philip Rizk argued in an excellent article – aptly entitled '2011 is not 1968[9]' – that Western media outlets and the internet contributed to compartmentalized explanations of the origins of the 2011 Egyptian revolution. The reality, argues Rizk, is that the revolution was decades in the making through civil disobedience, worker's strikes, protests, and spurred by 'structural dimensions of injustice' (Rizk, 2014), the roots of which lie in the uncomfortable reality of existing 'neo-liberal policies promoted by the likes of the IMF, the EU and the USA in deepening the stratification between poor and rich [which] made you forget that it is out of these structures of injustice that the desire for social justice is born in the first place' (Rizk, 2014). Instead, what was presented in mainstream media and the internet was a 'hyper-glorification' (Rizk, 2014) of the familiar, with easily digested slogans that the revolution was 'only an act against dictatorship', an 'individual cry for freedom' or the oft-repeated 'demonstration for democracy' (Rizk, 2014). These Western ideals of modernity embedded within sanitized slogans, argues Rizk, led to 'dominating narratives – the narratives of domination – [which] localized the problematic, for instance, to that of a homegrown dictatorship. By isolating the crime and highlighting the corruption of individuals, these accounts helped set the neocolonial stage for the now empty shells of the old regime to be replaced by another that maintains the same logic of governance'[10] (Rizk, 2014).

Rizk argues that one must look beyond these 'familiar' and decontextualized narratives mainstream media seeks to perpetuate in its recycled linguistic repertoires used for the convenience of Western audiences, and instead, to critically examine the revolution beyond a surface-level analysis in order to be able to recognize that the reality is grounded within the nuanced, the messy and the unfamiliar. That it was, in actuality, a violent revolution rooted within a long history of dissent, and that although the face splattered all over the media was that of the social media-savvy English-speaking middle-class Egyptian, the revolution was carried on and propelled by the majority Arab-speaking 'underclass', the 'unemployed' and the 'workers' (Rizk, 2014), who were the predominant forces on its front lines. These grounded realities were largely ignored, and instead, argues Rizk,

> [a]cademia, film, art; the world of NGOs relied on us as the ideal interpreter of the extraordinary. They all eventually bought into and further fuelled the hyper glorification of the individual, the actor, the youth subject, the revolutionary artist, the woman, the non-violent protestor, the Internet user. All this took place in the undercurrent of an unrelenting need to identify, validate and valorise the role of the familiar. (Rizk, 2014)

The goal of this, according to Rizk, is for outsiders, the onlookers of the revolution (primarily those in the West), to fabricate an image of the Egyptian revolution which fits a bite-size and oversimplified narrative global audiences can easily digest,[11] conveniently ignoring local histories focused on the structural and political roots of injustices, many of which are rooted within the inconvenient reality of the West's complicity and support of Mubarak's regime.[12]

'Representation of a revolution'

If the revolution's recycled political narrative was that it was a conflict against a dictator or a fight for democracy, then the dominant cultural narrative at the time was that art was simply acting as a 'representation of the revolution' and was a sign of a 'cultural awakening'. The pervasive discourse pushed forth by academia and mainstream media was reinforced by international cultural festivals showcasing these 'new' artistic activities from 'newly revolutionary' countries such as Egypt as evidence of a primitive awakening to Western modernity. Ilka Eickhof, assistant professor of sociology at the American University in Cairo (AUC), noted that art festivals such as the annual Shubbak Festival in London and the 2011 Venice Biennale helped reinforce these narratives because they 'problematically us[e] art as a code word for proper consciousness or modernity. Representations of the educated, modern, graffiti-spraying rebel do not challenge global structures . . . rather, the assumed anti-position of the Arab artist fits into the Euro-US ideal of the progressive individual who breaks with tradition, closely allied to the rise of the bourgeoisie in modern Europe' (Eickhof, cited in Gribbon, 2014).

Sociocultural anthropologist Jessica Winegar (professor of anthropology at Northwestern University), who has written extensively on the cultural politics of Egypt, urged researchers to avoid perpetuating these recycled narratives of Egyptian revolutionary art. In a Facebook post in 2014, she pleaded with

> art writers and curators who go to Egypt to check out the scene there: the scene is much more complex and much more interesting than the same 5 artists and

3 galleries that everyone else before you 'discovered'. (No offense to those artists
and galleries, of course). Try a little harder. At least get a translator so you can
speak to some artists not fluent in English or French. Challenge yourself with
other visualities that don't necessarily fit your definition of 'critical art'. And
stop asking artists to represent a revolution. Thank you. (Winegar, 2014)

Another vocal participant to comment on these problematic discourses was
Ganzeer,[13] a local and internationally recognized artist who created iconic works
associated with the revolution in 2011, such as 'Tank vs. Bike' and 'The Mask of
Freedom'. Ganzeer argued that since the revolution in January 2011, 'mainstream
media has focused on the rise of street art in its very superficial sense: art on the
street protesting the regime. At the same time, it has overlooked the qualities that
are very specific to Egyptian street art: void of the artist's ego and tackling concerns
of your average Egyptian' (Ganzeer, 2014b). The advent of the Egyptian revolution
and the artistic creativity that poured into public spaces showed that art in Egypt
could be a non-elitist endeavour in that it does not require one to hold formal
credentials such as an art degree to participate, require a formal cultural space to
be showcased or need the presence of an interlocutor to translate and interpret its
meaning to the audience. Art should be inherently connected to one's political and
social climate and thus relevant to the Egyptian people, as Ganzeer argues:

> there are a bunch of thirty-something artists in Egypt today who think of
> themselves as cutting edge for adopting a 1917 [citing Marcel Duchamp's
> 'Fountain' as the example] art form that most Egyptians do not relate to – they
> adopt it anyway out of an urge to appeal to art institutions centered in Europe
> and the USA. Such an art form has no place in Egypt's revolutionary climate.
> Although many Westerners may want to believe that Egyptians revolted against
> our regime out of a desire to adopt more 'Western' values – or Western products,
> as was suggested by French author Guy Sorman in a public debate with me in
> 2011 – in fact Egyptians were revolting against a bad regime that had taken
> much of its legitimacy from other world powers while simultaneously revolting
> against the conformist traditions of older generations. What the Egyptian people
> sought was independence in its truest form. Although Egyptians have obviously
> failed badly at achieving that (for now), it does not mean that the effects of the
> revolution should not find their way into art and culture. Conceptual Art in
> Egypt, with its compass oriented to point north-west, proves itself to be a rather
> anti-revolutionary art form. (Ganzeer, 2014b)

To understand Ganzeer's disdain for an art which caters to a Western lens and is
seemingly devoid of any relevancy to Egyptians, during my interviews, the words
'bland' and 'lifeless' were the most common depictions of the cultural field in Egypt.
Many of those I spoke to, such as artist Radwa Fouda,[14] described the art found within
gallery walls as intentionally 'empty', because 'part of what was happening before
the revolution was the art inside the exhibition . . . was an art that had nothing to do
with what was actually happening . . . Or maybe it was, it was actually representing

the numbness, the numb state we were at' (Radwa Fouda, Cairo, pers. comm., 13 August 2014). Radwa noted that this 'numb state' was a direct result of the lack of collective action in the sociopolitical field, in that 'the public were not moving so as an artist I am a mirror of the public of what is happening around me. So when that doesn't happen, when that is not existing I only draw my own world, that reflected that each of us were in our own bubble, so we did not know that each other existed' (Radwa Fouda, Cairo, pers. comm., 13 August 2014). Mubarak's image domination in the media, the streets and billboards, which regurgitated official party lines, coupled with his party's (the National Democratic Party – NDP) domination of the cultural field, which ensured 'appropriate', controversy-free art through strict state censorship – helped propel what professor of political science Lisa Wedeen termed the politics of 'as if',[15] which argues that politics, far from just being about controlling material interests, is about effectively monopolizing symbolic space in order to ensure the public's compliance. The politics of 'as if' means that there is no genuine loyalty to the authoritarian regime or its ideological beliefs, but that the public 'performed' obedience 'as if' they believed the authoritarian regimes fabrications, and this politics, if done effectively, simultaneously works to isolate citizens from one another (Wedeen, 1999: 6) to discourage – and prevent – the formation of a genuine political-public.

Many thus praised Ganzeer for his call to revolutionize art to the wider Egyptian public through the notion of Concept Pop – an amalgamation of Pop Art and Conceptual Art – which is inherently connected to the Egyptian political and social climate and is 'about' something. This notion of popularizing art to make it 'about' something connected to the public's everyday reality is in parallel with the belief that much like the political field, the cultural field in Egypt has remained for far too long a largely elitist endeavour. However, others such as Adham Selim, an Egyptian architect, suggested that art should remain autonomous from politics and that Ganzeer promoted a reductive binary logic wherein the choice lies between pro- or anti-revolutionary art, while others, such as Shehab Fakhry Ismail, argued that instead of art imitating life through what he calls 'the facile aestheticisation of the revolutionary moment and . . . political sloganeering, artists would do better to revolutionize the vocabulary of their art, which in no way precludes treating political themes in a more radical manner. Perhaps then will art do what it can actually do best: shake us away from the complacency of unthinking' (Ismail, 2013).

Surti Singh, assistant professor of philosophy at the AUC, weighed in on the debate between Ganzeer and Selim in an article published in December 2014 entitled 'Historical Realities of Concept Pop: Debating Art in Egypt'. Singh argued that although Ganzeer's notion of Concept Pop 'ekes out a new and vital political role for art at this particular moment in Egyptian history, a moment suffering from an absence of politics', it 'risks embracing an overly simplistic equation of aesthetics with politics' and also had a danger of 'becoming a mouthpiece for the *status quo*; instead of remembering suffering . . . aestheticizing suffering into an object for enjoyment or pleasure' (Surti Singh, 2014).

Singh argues that although the public may identify with art work which embraces ideas and themes familiar to them, this identification only leads to validation of their present sentiments, absent of critical reflection or thought. On the other hand, argues Singh, while Selim wants to 'protect art from its reduction to a political tool, his view of the subject that simply enjoys art without concern for politics is equally superficial. Both Ganzeer and Selim neglect the role art can play in transforming the subject instead of simply appeasing it' (Singh, 2014). For Singh, an art which is not self-absorbed into obscurity or an art which is simply a mirror of one's reality is not the solution; what is needed is an art that can 'provoke and unsettle the subject' and 'cause the subject to shudder at its concrete historical reality' by 'refusing rather than promoting reconciliation with a false reality' (Singh, 2014).

Notwithstanding the significance of the emergence of these debates in the aftermath of a revolution in a country in which the cultural field is predominantly within the purview of state institutions (discussed in greater detail in the following chapter), this book intends to take an alternative approach to Egyptian revolutionary art as it draws on the anthropological framework of liminality to examine why and how people – specifically, those who, for the most part, art was a central practice, but in which street art was a completely new field – create art during different temporal registers, or liminal moments, of a major political. This framework allows us to look at the 25 January revolution as not just one unified bloc of time but as several blocs – or moments, in time – each defined by different revolutionary events and contexts which produced creative forms of political and artistic practices and communicative strategies. The main objective of this book is to provide a more nuanced approach to the art which emerged as a result of the Egyptian revolution by examining how this art adapted and responded to shifting political conditions over time. The art which emerged from the Egyptian revolution should not be seen as a stagnant, homogeneous, entity – rather, it was constantly evolving as the events of the Egyptian revolution unfolded.

Liminality and the Egyptian revolution

It is imperative to provide a brief explanation as to what liminality is and why it can be useful in studying human behaviour during moments of political rupture such as revolutions. The term liminality (from '*limen*', meaning threshold) originates from Dutch–German–French anthropologist and ethnographer Arnold van Gennep's *Rites of Passage* (1909), which describes a transition stage between the three main phases (separation, liminal period and re-assimilation) of a rites of passage. However, it was Victor Turner, a British cultural anthropologist, who elaborated on the three stages which could be applied to all rituals, and expanded specifically upon the term 'liminality' primarily in two major works, 'Betwixt and Between: The Liminal Period in *Rites de Passage*', from *The Forest of Symbols: Aspects of Ndembu Ritual* (1967), and 'Liminality and Communitas', from *The Ritual Process:*

Structure and Anti-Structure (1969). Turner characterized the liminal period as being a state of 'betwixt and between' (1969: 95), which describes a temporary phase characterized by the suspension of the normative order (i.e. the structure) of society, a state of anti-structure that is both a 'realm of pure possibility whence novel configurations of ideas and relations may arise' (Turner, 1967: 97) as well as a potentially destructive[16] (in its inherent ambiguity and unpredictability) time. During this period of 'in-betweeness', sociopolitical and cultural categorization and distinctions are essentially non-existent, and individuals are at the peak of heightened self-awareness and consciousness (1974: 255). This meant that the liminal period was not only marked by its enormous transformative possibilities and the importance of agency but also characterized by a utopian society of sorts, described as communitas. Communitas, according to Turner, is a 'relatively undifferentiated . . . community, or even communion of equal individuals' (1969: 96) characterized by 'an intense feeling of . . . social equality, solidarity, and togetherness experienced by those who live together in a site in which the normal social statuses and positions have broken down' (Peterson, 2015a: 6). It is important to note that the liminal period is intended to be a temporary state, as it is a passageway from one structure to the next. In other words it is a transitory period, yet also a time of limitless possibilities and potential.

Although Turner did 'hint' (Thomassen, 2012: 679) at an application of ritual studies and liminality theory towards major political transformations – what he called 'macropolitics' (Turner, 1988: 91) – as well as 'social drama' (1969), a concept used to understand major transformative events, it was other scholars, such as Szakolczai (2000, 2009), Thomassen (2009, 2012, 2014, 2017) and Armbrust (2013), who have specifically articulated the need for an anthropological approach to understanding political revolutions by applying the framework of liminality beyond the concept of rituals.

The call for an anthropology of political revolutions is embedded within the demand by scholars (Thomassen, 2017) to recognize the importance of an ethnographic perspective of political action and change from below, from everyday forms of political behaviour to extraordinary demonstrations of resistance, rebellion and revolutions – a period of 'in-between' time, similar to a ritual. From looking at the importance of revolutionary symbols such as Tahrir Square within contested narratives of the revolution to the possibilities of the formation of new subjectivities, as well as imagining different ways of being in the political and social sphere, liminality is a way for us to better understand the evolution of political and artistic practices, events and narratives during the 25 January revolution, and how these were shaped by different moments. These different moments necessarily called for 'different narrative understandings about the event', and so '[m]any narratives, discourses, analytic frameworks, best practices, and so on, are anchored in specific temporal registers. They shape, and are shaped by, what actors do and what they understand to be happening' (Schwedler, 2016). The 25 of January 2011 was not the same as 25 January 2012 or 25 January 2013; though arguably all were within a revolutionary time frame, they were different liminal 'moments' in revolutionary time which necessitated different political and artistic tactics. This book investigates the ways in which the revolution – a fluid, unstable, constantly changing historical/political/cultural moment in time – was experienced through revolutionary artistic practices – themselves political communicative strategies – and how these practices and strategies evolved over different liminal periods of time during the Egyptian revolution. In this way, this book intends to highlight the importance of 'human reactions to liminal experiences' and the significance of 'tying together thought and experience' when looking at the ways people practice politics from below (Thomassen, 2012: 688).

In the next chapter, I provide context on the Egyptian political sphere and its relationship to the cultural sphere in order to illustrate the extent to which cultural policy is controlled and directed by political motivations and interests and entrenched within government institutions. The significance of emphasizing the extent to which the political field monopolizes the cultural field is to understand that any type of unfiltered cultural expressions outside of the confines of state institutions and particularly in open, public spaces is – in and of itself – radical and revolutionary simply for existing outside these stringent barriers.

Chapter 1

CULTURE AND THE EGYPTIAN STATE

A BACKGROUND

At the heart of the contest within the visual field lie questions of
representation, authenticity, identity, modernity. Who will represent Egypt?
And how will Egypt be represented? The historical development of modern
art in Egypt is entangled in the history of colonialism and the subsequent
visual construction of the modern nation. It is therefore no surprise that
the state has taken it upon itself to become the patron of modern visual
production on both the academic and curatorial levels. Such patronage has
meant the institutionalization, surveillance, and control of the visual field
in order to instil and produce a national image of 'modern Egypt': at once
modern but authentic, secular but traditional.

Samia Mehrez (2008: 208).

Hosni Mubarak's image was ubiquitous – on the front page of daily newspapers,
billboards, street signs and the evening news – which served as a consistent
reminder of the extent of political capital he and his crony capitalists regime
enjoyed throughout his nearly three-decade rule. Yet Mubarak's visual domination
and its reproduction within the public sphere was certainly not a sign of the
population's consent or adoration. The underlying sentiment (which was generally
self-censored) on the streets towards his presidency was, for the most part, one
of derision and scorn.[1] Ongoing police brutality, high rates of poverty and crime,
corruption, repeated incidents of electoral fraud and violations (which saw
presidential and parliamentary elections unsurprisingly[2] garner the lion's share
of votes), censorship and surveillance, the three-decade long emergency law,
crumbling infrastructure and a shrinking middle class are just a few of the many
reasons why Egyptians had a disdain for Mubarak and what they ridiculed as a and
one-[3]party state. Almost everyone I interviewed described the atmosphere under
Mubarak's rule as one of faux compliance, a situation similar to the politics of 'as
if' mentioned previously by scholar Lisa Wedeen in her work on Syria in the 1990s
where people act 'as if' they revere their leader (Wedeen, 1999: 6). El Teneen,
one of the anonymous Egyptian street artists I interviewed, described this as a
'beautiful schizophrenia' (El Teneen, Cairo, pers. comm., 30 April 2014). In this

state of affairs, there was a detachment between internal sentiments and external sentiments, in that 'the reality did not matter, it was disgusting, the difference between what we saw and what people felt, there was no compatibility ... everyone hated Mubarak, yet they put his pictures everywhere' (El Teneen, Cairo, pers. comm., 30 April 2014).

When I asked Egyptians to explain why they believed this sort of 'beautiful schizophrenia' prevailed for so long, there were several responses ranging from people's resignation, to fear, to indifference, however, all these emotions stemmed from their awareness that the so-called 'consent' of the public for the regime was actually the result of a mutually reinforcing situation, one described as seemingly inescapable. This type of 'as if' behaviour does not imply acceptance but rather, acting as though one consents with the status quo. This behaviour, according to Marxist philosopher Antono Gramsci, is understood as a complex mental state, a "contradictory consciousness" mixing approbation and apathy, resistance and resignation' (Lears, 1985: 590).

Many said initiating this compliance began at a young age while they were at school, as it did not provide them with innovative and critical ways of thinking. Instead, their education involved a rigid, unidirectional system of teaching which discouraged independent thought. Yet others complained that the poor education they received was compounded by a real sense of fear which they internalized and justified as part of the 'way things were'. Mira Shihadeh, a Palestinian yoga instructor, who has resided in Cairo almost all her life, and who was never involved in politics or art prior to the revolution, articulated the ways in which people subconsciously adapted to Mubarak's repressive police state, adding that self-censorship due to fear was a 'normal' condition that you did not question:

> There was a consciousness you had to keep and you were terrified, you were scared [during Mubarak's time]. All this makes you think it is a police state and we got used to it, and I wasn't aware – I was aware that there were things to be scared of and I shouldn't show my opinion but I didn't think twice about it I just thought it was normal. Then there is a friend of mine who turned out to be an amazing activist. . . . I remember the conversation we had, he's like 'Mira you know we are in a police state', and for me it is like what is a police state, because this is all that I have lived in, do you understand? I was so indifferent . . . but then when he told me what he was getting up to, I . . . I could go to jail for knowing this guy. I was also very aware of that, but not thinking how absurd it was, how outrageous it is. We're numb. (Mira Shihadeh, Cairo, pers. comm., 30 April 2014)

This condition of always being aware of injustice, yet unaware of the degree to which it became a normative condition one unconsciously – or consciously – 'got used to' was a situation Radwa Fouda described as being akin to 'living in a box your whole life' (Radwa Fouda, Cairo, pers. comm., 13 August 2014). Keizer, an Egyptian anonymous street artist, added that the pervasiveness of this numb state due to the fear Mira spoke of is intentionally spread within Egyptian society from the top to the bottom through deliberate scare tactics by the authorities – 'fear comes straight down from the government, through intimidation, bullying, blackmailing. Mubarak has planted this seed' (Keizer, Cairo, pers. comm., 29 April 2014).

Keizer argued that this penetration of the state's influence from the top to the bottom created multiple manifestations of Mubarak, or 'mini Mubaraks', as he labelled it, which could be found in 'one's home, school, supermarket, wherever' (Keizer, Cairo, pers. comm., 29 April 2014), and so one could not escape the repressive state because it was everywhere, continuously reasserting itself within society. This is akin to the way that Gramsci envisioned the hegemonic state not only as a set of political and social institutions and apparatuses which ruled by force, but that the state was also reflected within everyday societal relations (Gramsci, 1971).

Ganzeer set forth a completely different argument – that the fault did not lie with the state, but with one's own self, in that

> during Mubarak's time we would self-censor, we would say I am not going to do that and you would come up with reasons not do to it, but then after [the uprising] you would come up with reasons to do it as opposed to reasons not to do it, it has to do with the self, it has nothing to do with the regime. (Ganzeer, Cairo, pers. comm., 26 April 2014)

Ganzeer's comments illustrate the ways in which hegemony is not only external but is also internalized, creating a form of self-policing of one's own self which only strengthens the authorities' hold on power (Wedeen, 1999: 6). This level of control extends not only to the political but also to the cultural field, and so the cultural field in Egypt, much like its regional counterparts (see, e.g. Wedeen, 1999; Cooke, 2007), has been predominantly controlled from the top. Although a private sector does exist – boasting independent art galleries and nonprofit cultural organizations – they remain under the regulative control of the state. For the purposes of this book, it is significant to provide a brief explanation on how the cultural field is politically constituted in Egypt (Winegar, 2006: 138) and the ways in which the state directs cultural policy for its overarching political goals.

Nasser's establishment of the modern Egyptian state's cultural institutions

The beginnings of the establishment of modern national culture in Egypt date back to the late nineteenth century (Gershoni, 1992), and owes its foundations to the Ottoman viceroy Muhammad Ali (who ruled Egypt from 1805 to 1849), as he 'instated various institutions responsible for the production and dissemination of modern cultural products in the cultural sphere . . . with a serious effort to forge a national Egyptian image and culture'[4] (Gershoni, 1992: 209). As several writers have noted (Armbrust, 1996: Karnouk, 2005; Winegar, 2006; Mehrez, 2008), the emergence of a 'modern' Egyptian state brought with it questions and struggles over how to develop a 'modern' (a word identified as a Western construct) Egyptian cultural field while retaining the *asala* (authenticity) of the Egyptian identity. Although the roots of the modern national cultural industry began well before the turn of the twentieth century, I use Gamal Abdel Nasser's socialist rule as my historical starting point, as it was under his reign that the current centralized cultural structure was established.

Nasser's rule as Egypt's second[5] president (1956–70) in the aftermath of the 1952 revolution saw the end of the Egyptian monarchy under King Farouk.[6] One of the main tasks of the new regime, which had inherited a feudal system and the remnants of European colonialism, was to institute a new direction for cultural policy (Awad, 1968: 143–61) that would embody and symbolize the newly founded Egyptian republic. In order to accomplish this goal, a centralized system was created to regulate cultural production towards serving (and legitimizing) these nationalist goals via the establishment of state cultural institutions such as the Supreme Council for the Development of Arts and Literature in 1956 (Winegar, 2006: 143), as well as the Ministry of Culture and National Guidance in 1958 (Winegar, 2006: 144).[7] While the council 'coordinated, instituted and expanded arts activities and programs in several areas' (Winegar, 2006: 143) the Ministry of Culture's role was essentially to set the nationalist parameters under which artists would work to promote the new state and its activities, such as the construction of the High Dam in Aswan. The Supreme Council, along with the Ministry of Culture, together 'expanded and centralized state arts support even further' (Winegar, 2006: 144). The establishment of these two major state cultural institutions ran parallel to the government's establishment of museums, as well as the Egyptian Academy of Arts in 1960 (Winegar, 2006: 144) and the creation of hundreds of 'culture palaces' in small towns and villages, which were created with the intent to spread art to the public and act as a launching pad for many lower-class artists. This was considered a significant step in reducing elitist barriers into the cultural field, and so not only were these palaces intended to 'bring arts to the masses', they also served to expand the spaces in which artists could exhibit (Winegar, 2006: 144).

Under Nasser, the main policy frameworks guiding the state centralized cultural field were instituted, elevating the state to the position of being 'patron, promoter, and protector of the arts' while the nation acts as the 'conceptual frame . . . for evaluating artistic practices and policies' (Winegar, 2006: 145). Pahwa and Winegar argue that although Nasser's rule ended over half a century ago,

> the major goals at the time [still] remain central to the Ministry's mission today: to define the nation and national identity; to protect cultural patrimony; and to uplift the so-called masses by exposing them to the arts. To these ends, the Ministry employed legions of artists [such as singers Umm Kalthoum and Abdel-

Halim Hafez] and literati [such as writers and journalists Mohamed Hassanein Heikal and Ahmed Bahaa el-Din] who often did works in line with nationalist goals of the regime. (Pahwa, Winegar, 2012)

Although Nasser invested a great deal in establishing a modern cultural field which was primarily restricted within the parameters of the national goals of the 'new' Egyptian republic, it is important to note the context under which this cultural field emerged and the reasons behind the dominant nationalist overtones of cultural works. Egypt was under a British mandate until 1922, yet British occupation still continued in the early 1950s, with forces still remaining in Egypt during Nasser's reign. The beginning of Nasser's presidency saw him involved in a conflict between colonial 'Israel', France and the UK, who invaded Suez in 1956 in light of Nasser's announcement that he would nationalize the French–British-controlled Egyptian Suez Canal.[8] This situates Nasser's cultural policy precisely within the Egyptian state efforts to promote and maintain the revolution's core ideals in which culture acted as an essential tool to resist foreign aggression, as well as those who continued to maintain their loyalty to the *ancien regime* of King Farouk. In a speech given at the Festival of Science in December 1961, Nasser 'himself set the general mood for the events of the next decade' (Crabbs, 1975: 386), when he declared:

> The cultural revolution puts itself at the service of the political and social revolution. We are on the way to building a society based on self-sufficiency (*kifāyah*) and justice. We must have a cultural revolution which will be hostile to imperialism, hostile to reaction, hostile to feudalism, hostile to the domination and dictatorship of capitalism, hostile to all forms of exploitation – a cultural revolution which aims at [letting] the people know their rights, their [true] gains, their hopes, and finally who their friends and enemies are. (Anis, 1967, cited in Crabbs, 1975: 387)

Nasser's pan-Arab, pro-socialist message – highly influenced by the political events of the 1950s (as mentioned, the Suez Crisis) and 1960s (such as the Six-Day War, the third war between colonial 'Israel' and the Arabs) – significantly influenced the Egyptian tone of the cultural field during his rule, in line with his political vision of Arab unity and a fully independent, economically and militarily powerful, Egyptian republic. The cultural field, albeit in line with dominant nationalist agendas restricting oppositional voices which did not adhere to the state's overarching goals, still showed a 'promising beginning'[9] (Pahwa, Winegar, 2012) during Nasser's era, with. However, after Nasser's death in 1970, the cultural field took a complete turn and 'devolved into decades of disappointment' (Pahwa, Winegar, 2012) with Anwar Sadat's rule.

Sadat: Infitah *(open-door) policy and the marginalization of culture*

Anwar Sadat became Egypt's third president after Nasser's death in 1971 until his assassination in 1981. Sadat's regime was characterized by a complete shift in political, economic and cultural policies, which was adequately dubbed as 'de-Nasserization' (Cull, Cullbert, Welsh, 2003: 18) for its almost total reversal of Nasser's policies. Nasser restricted the Muslim Brotherhood's operations and jailed its members in light of an assassination attempt, operated a more 'closed door' (Weinbaum, 1985: 206) policy through a socialist economy which included land and wealth redistribution, as well as the nationalization of key industries while promoting an Arab nationalist political ideology intent on ridding the country of foreign domination. Together, these policies were dubbed 'Nasserism'. Sadat, on the other hand, allowed the Muslim Brotherhood to operate more freely,[10] embraced neoliberalism and pushed for an open-door (*infitah*) economic policy which saw a large influx of foreign goods and investors into Egypt.

Sadat's turn towards Western policies and foreign investment saw him adopt unpopular recommendations by the World Bank and the International Monetary Fund (IMF), such as the termination of state subsidies on basic foodstuffs which led to the infamous 'bread riots' of 1977. This event saw massive protests is over high prices of basic foodstuff spread across Egypt, where people chanted slogans such as 'Thieves of the *Infitah*, the people are famished' (Bohstedt, 2014: 17). The riots ended with military intervention and the return of state subsidies, however, they created a severe setback to the legitimacy of Sadat's political and economic leadership. In line with Sadat's political vision was his attempt to 'radically change cultural policy' – a policy which was 'met with tremendous opposition. Sadat not only re-imprisoned many leftist intellectuals and student activists but also called for the dissolution of the Ministry of Culture under the slogan "Culture is for the Intellectuals"' (Winegar, 2006: 150). This led to policies intended to cut resources and remove art subsidies through an even more intensive centralization and downsizing of the arts administration. A Supreme Council for Culture that reported directly to Sadat was formed and charged with running any remaining arts programmes to bring cultural policy in line with political policy (Iskandar et al., 1991, cited in Winegar, 2006: 150). Winegar quotes one of the artists she interviewed as saying that Sadat was a 'catastrophe [*nakba*] for the cultural movement in all of Egypt, because the political idea was *infitah* and consumerism. We changed to a consumerist society' (Winegar, 2006: 151). The interconnectedness of cultural policy with economic and political policy, in which cultural aspects of Egyptian culture were marginalized in favour of foreign investments and open markets, led to

> major shifts in political, economic, social and cultural policies, over less than a
> decade, [which] produced a series of new realities on the ground: an accelerated
> immersion in a global capitalist market, the deregulation of a socialist economy,
> the collapse of the state cultural apparatus, the increasing visibility and influence
> of Islamic fundamentalism, the exodus of many members of the cultural field
> (professors, journalists, critics, writers, artists, painters) and the advent of
> foreign investors in several domains. (Mehrez, 2008: 210)

When Sadat was assassinated in 1981 by members of the Egyptian Islamic Jihad, what remained as the legacy of his regime was a 'contradictory set of realities'

(Mehrez, 2008: 210), which saw Egypt left with essentially a non-existent cultural field, a destabilized economy almost completely reliant on the West and financial packages from the United States, and a slew of opposition from leftists to the Muslim Brotherhood, the latter of which had abandoned its support for Sadat when he refused to implement *sharia* (Islamic legal system) law and signed a peace treaty in 1979 with colonial "Israel".

Mubarak: Using culture to curb political Islam

After we renew what is authentic in our culture and tie it to what is useful from our modern lives, we must disseminate this civilization among the people . . . cultural elements are diffused in society from above to below.

(Extract from a high-school science text in Egypt, 'Abd al-Gawwad and Amir 1988, cited in Armbrust, 1996: 25)

Hosni Mubarak's (1981–2011) three-decade presidency was marked by an increasingly stifling bureaucratic system, crony capitalism, police brutality and the repressive emergency law (in place without interruption since Sadat's assassination in 1981) which gave the state unprecedented powers and curbed basic freedoms (Reza, 2007). Mubarak's attempt to quash the rise of political Islam (see Winegar, 2009) saw him reinstate the Ministry of Culture in 1981 and use the cultural sphere to counter 'the rising Islamist wave and recaptur[e] a modern secular image' (Mehrez, 2008: 210) in order to 'thrust the marginalized and dominated cultural field into the centre of the political one' (Mehrez, 2008: 6–7). The 1980s and 1990s were thus marked by a 'massive increase in monetary, institutional, and discursive focus on culture in the Mubarak period [which] coincides with the spread of the piety movement and Islamic activism' (Winegar, 2009: 190) which 'can be directly traced to the early 1990s, when Islamist groups launched violent attacks against intellectuals, government figures, and Western tourists . . . It is clear that *thaqafa* [culture] – as defined in particular ways and created through certain government institutions and discourses – has become an important feature of state projects to manage Islamic practice and identifications' (Winegar, 2009: 190).

The defining feature of Mubarak's cultural policy was to curb the rising influence of Islamist groups which had become increasingly radical in the aftermath of Sadat's assassination, while using Islamic symbols in the effort to declare the state as 'the sole moral and religious authority' (Mehrez, 2008: 3). One of the main ideas set forth by officials at the Ministry of Culture was that 'put simply, the loss or decline of a strong national Egyptian identity is understood to lead to a problematic rise in religious activity. But the rise in religious activity is also frequently presented as a cause of Egyptian national culture loss' (Winegar, 2009: 192). This preoccupation with ensuring 'more' culture to essentially reduce the influence of 'wayward religion' was so 'dominant among state officials and among intellectuals generally that it is rare to find a critique of the state's culture project outside of its terms' (Winegar, 2009: 193). The state's efforts under Mubarak's patronage to counter increased religious activity through its 'enlightenment project' was embodied by then Minister of Culture (from 1987 to 2011) Faruq Husni's 'barn/fair' strategy, which ensured the compliance of intellectuals – and marginalized those who did not follow suit – to stick to the political script[11] by keeping them under the state's financial wing (Naji, 2014). This was the 'barn' aspect of the strategy, which turned the lacklustre Ministry of Culture into councils that issue bonuses and salaries for Egypt's intellectuals and elite class, thereby integrating them into the state apparatus and the regime's control schemes (Naji, 2014).[12]

The 'fair' part of the strategy was 'crafted to render Egyptian culture into one of museum pieces and folkloric scenes . . .[t]his was done by promoting all that is museum-ready, reflecting Egypt's distant past (which, not coincidentally, is what the West in general imagines when thinking of Egypt)' (Naji, 2014).[13] Mubarak's era thus witnessed a heavily controlled, inefficient and bureaucratically bloated cultural field – a reflection of the political field – whose primary intent was to endorse the image of a secular, modern Egyptian state. Mubarak himself (and his wife, Suzanne) played a heavy role in funding cultural palaces[14] and promoting cultural fairs and projects, all of which provided the illusion of widening the margins of freedom in the cultural field through its increased activity despite remaining heavily regulated by the state and its censors. Although there was a large influx of funds to the cultural field which promoted its activities – 'behind the façade of state prizes, awards, stipends and costly public events in the fields of literature, theatre, music, dance, film and visual arts lurks the ghost of censorship, at all levels including self-censorship, that ensures the political field's domination and control over the cultural one' (Mehrez, 2008: 212). It is for these reasons that almost everyone I interviewed described the cultural field during Mubarak's rule as an area awash with nepotism and corruption, and considered 'gallery art' during that time as a derogatory term for the art which was approved by the censors. This made both public and private art galleries, according to those I interviewed, devoid of genuine artistic creativity and critical reflection, and many expressed their outright contempt for private galleries and exhibition spaces, but the particular focus of their ire was what they described as the bureaucratic and sterile Ministry of Culture, which I will address in the next section.

The Ministry of Culture and the 'Independent' art scene – one and the same?

Egypt arguably, probably, has the biggest cultural impact in the Arab world, I think. Even with a very horrible, very inactive Ministry of Culture, so one would imagine what Egypt would be capable of culturally if the Ministry was actually effective and actually active. Now of course most of the artists in Egypt create with pretty much no funding and with very little resources, but they are still able to produce amazing stuff. On the other hand, the Ministry

of course has government money that is not really spent on producing art
. . . and at the end of the day you have the most boring sterile stuff produced,
and they are not even using all the resources, like the majority of cultural
and art palaces across the country are just like shut down, theatres are shut
down . . . it's horrible obviously.

Ganzeer, Cairo, pers. comm., 26 April 2014

Without any exception, all of the comments addressed towards the cultural field
– which, to most of those I spoke to, was representative of the Ministry of Culture
– were negative, especially from a few who had the most direct experience with
them. This stemmed from what they saw as the Ministry of Culture's 'corruption',
'thievery', 'failure', and the fact that it dedicated the vast majority of its resources
to paying salaries to their large network of, what the respondents told me, were
ignorant and corrupt officials who were not interested in promoting cultural
activities or cultural production, only in getting promoted. However, their
disenchantment with the Ministry was also largely based in what they saw as its
exclusionary nature and its role as legitimizing certain forms of cultural production
and completely subverting others. On this point, Egyptian expressionist artist
Hala El Sharouny (or, 'Boshou', as she is known) added that this formed the basis
of their exclusionary policy, in that

> . . . all the Ministry does is spend a fraction of its budget on cultural activities
> and the rest of the budget goes to a small group of people who are benefiting
> and at the same time the money is getting swallowed, so in the end if an artist
> does not follow the book of the Ministry or the mindset of the government then
> goodbye, you have no place with us. (Hala El Sharouny, Cairo, pers. comm., 18
> August 2014)

Most of the artists I interviewed said control over who could exhibit and what
they could exhibit was not an exaggeration and was based largely on whether
or not they were well known; if they had no connections and their work was
considered unconventional or too inappropriate (politically and/or socially)
which failed to abide by modern art 'trends', they were not able to enter the
formal cultural field.

Hala's disdain of the Ministry of Culture stems from her unfortunate
experiences prior to the uprising, with what she called corrupt Ministry employees.
One particular incident she recalled during one of our conversations was when
an official at the Ministry pushed her for a bribe which she refused to give and
then threatened to make things more difficult for her should she ever apply to the
Ministry again for any kind of funding. Yet this conception of the official cultural
field as being exclusionary, selective, restrictive, and awash with nepotism was
the same sentiment echoed in regard to the independent cultural scene, in which
several of those I interviewed described as also being restricted to a tight-knit
group of cultural elites who had pre-determined criteria for the art they coveted in

their galleries, and that their concern was primarily based on profits, not creative cultural expression:

> There is a gang, and certain criteria that they have [independent galleries]. I had a friend that tried to submit his artwork to a gallery and they told him 'it is not our thing,' and even when he amended his art according to their criteria they told him they are not interested. So everyone insults government galleries . . . the government is closed off on itself and restricts itself to a gang [of the same people] . . . private galleries just want things that can sell for more. They care about money. So they sign monopoly contracts with certain people – like Safer Khan will do a contract with an artist for five years. It is impossible for a private gallery to take you because they already have the artists whose work they are selling the whole year round, so there is no opportunity for the work of young artists to be showcased. The Zamalek Gallery showcases for an artist named Gamal El-Sagini[15] [an Egyptian painter, sculptor, and medallist]. This guy has been dead for over forty years and his sculptures sell for 200,000 Egyptian pounds – fine, keep your exhibition of El-Sagini, but also leave a section next to it for the smaller, up and coming artists to get a chance to showcase their work. Encourage people! No, they still showcase the same people, Gamal El-Sagini, Rabab Nemr[16] [a female Egyptian artist], what is his name, the former Minister of Culture? Farouk Hosny. Even when he was Minister, he never gave a chance to the youth. (Hala El Sharouny, Cairo, pers. comm., 18 August 2014)

Saiko Maino, an Egyptian street artist, graphic designer and junior calligrapher, told me that his friend Riham was not allowed to sing on the topic of women and harassment in *Sakiet El-Sawy* (El-Sawy Culture Wheel, which is a cultural centre in Zamalek, a wealthy area in western Cairo), which tends to be the platform for relatively more open forms of unhindered expression, because the organizers told her they did not want any 'politics' in the music, even though she said she had zero political content in her work and that she was simply addressing a pervasive social issue (Saiko Maino, Cairo, pers. comm., 26 August 2014). Sad Panda, an anonymous Egyptian artist and aspiring DJ, also lamented that artists not only faced restrictions in government institutions and formal private galleries but also even more in 'independent' galleries such as Townhouse Gallery, considered to be a pioneer of the contemporary art scene in Cairo, were equally restrictive because they were also constrained (though less visibly so than official government cultural institutions) by the politics of the state:

> When we were younger, the art places and spaces wouldn't take our work to present it because we had no name, so a lot of people, me for example and Aya Tarek [Egyptian artist from Alexandria] in Alexandria, we started on the premise that ok you don't want our work to be showcased in galleries we don't want our work showcased in your galleries. First of all, they [private galleries] would say who are you, you are in still in school or university and you want to showcase your work? Secondly, this is a part of them from the beginning not

even accepting your work but even if they did they say let's talk about what you draw and what work you do, this is a form of censorship. . . .. In late 2009, I wanted to do an exhibition in Townhouse here in downtown Cairo, and I went to the people and showed them my work. The guy told me . . . we can't showcase your work here because of the politics and the state and they will close the place down and things like that. He said there are already artists working with them in Townhouse, and that I could come and bring my work and they would tell me what I should remove and what I should add. I told them let them do it themselves, why should I be there what is my role? This is added to the fact that they might not even accept you even after you make the changes they want. There are several reasons that lead you to say that you are going to revolt against the art institutions in that I am going to take my drawings and throw them in the street so that everyone can actually get to see it. (Sad Panda, Cairo, pers. comm., 28 April 2014)

This latter comment would act as an important precedent to understanding one of the underlying motivations for doing street art during the revolution, as this type of interference was common during Mubarak's rule. According to Hala, this was what she described as the typical whitewashing and censorship of 'real' (i.e. uncensored) art not only by the Ministry of Culture but also by private galleries and festivals alike. She recalled her own experience of censorship during, ironically, a Graffiti Festival she participated in before the uprising:

In 2008 I joined a Graffiti Festival, sponsored by the government. . . . Graffiti did exist before the revolution, it was not wide spread and you could not say anything powerful – they brought us a canvas to work on, and this itself is outside the concept of graffiti itself, and most of the artists did not consider that we were doing graffiti, just regular murals . . . they just called it graffiti because they thought it sounded trendy . . . anything to do with politics, sex, and religion was not allowed. Of course regardless of that myself and others did works which had political commentary. This was before 2011, and of course people were bitter and angry, so I went in and I did a mural of beggar children wearing *jellabiyas* [a traditional dress like garment, typically worn by *fellahin*, peasant farmers, agricultural labourers] and torn up clothes who were all giving a military salute and I wrote under it in Arabic 'We are all yours, Pasha' and I stamped it with the Eagle [the symbol of the Egyptian republic] (see Figure 1.1). They told me that Salah Al Mulaigy [the Head of the Museums and Galleries] says you cannot insult the government in a government place, so you have to make . . . adjustments. So I told them if I do any changes to the mural I will paint it all white and leave. So they asked me if I minded if they amended the mural for the government catalogue, so I told them change it however they want, and of course they completely defaced it, they made the sentence into scrambled, separated letters, they amended the Eagle and they left the beggar children as is. It no longer had any meaning. (Hala El Sharouny, Cairo, pers. comm., 18 August 2014)

Figure 1.1 Halal El Sharouny's original mural, which the authorities censored for being 'insulting to the government'. *Source*: Hala Al Sharouny.

It is this type of interaction with the cultural field which seemed to have led most of those I interviewed to express the belief that this was the reason why 'standard official gallery circles . . . are discredited' (Ganzeer, Cairo, pers. comm., 26 April 2014). Most of the cultural producers I interviewed also emphasized that this is not an isolated problem unique to the cultural field but that it reflects 'the problem of Egypt' as a whole in which

> the official bodies and the real deal are so detached from each other . . . the Ministry of Culture are completely detached in my opinion from people inside and as well as outside the country, it is completely detached from everything. They are catering to what they want, and so they are only relevant somehow to each other and to the government sponsored guys. (Ganzeer, Cairo, pers. comm., 26 April 2014)

It is important to note that this sense of detachment, according to Ganzeer and many of those I spoke to, applied also to opposition groups. According to Radwa, even if a legitimate intellectual opposition did exist, it was completely detached from society and their language intentionally obscure much in the same way (as mentioned in Chapter 2) the Egyptian Art & Liberty Group was accused of being.

> The opposition have to get off of their ivory tower. They are very cultured, they have so much information that it is for the good of the people – whether they be Revolutionary Socialists, Socialists, Marxists, whatever. Their diversity is good for the people to know that we have this diversity, but they are very cultured, they are very much secluded in their ivory tower, so even when they write something

people don't understand it. For example, even the terminology – there are a lot of terminologies, like transcendental. It is very conceited, there is a word and there is an upper word that is beyond our consciousness. Explain it to people in a way they can understand. But they do not – they got used to the fact that this is something normal for them and this is their own language and that people have to adapt to their level, and not that they have to make their language accessible. (Radwa Fouda, pers. comm., 13 August 2014)

This sense of detachment from the government and the opposition alike towards the people will form an important precursor to understandings and approaches to art as something that is accessible to the public, as mentioned earlier regarding Ganzeer's emphasis on the importance of an art that is relevant to Egypt society. Most cultural producers argued that because the political field (Mubarak's regime) was corrupt and instituted failed policies on all levels (political/economic/social), this was also reflected in the cultural field which operated along the same lines, as 'the Ministry of Culture is from the regime, and the people in charge are failures, so there is no art in its real meaning' (Hanaa El Degham, Berlin, Skype interview, 29 November 2013). An art field devoid of 'real' art, which paralleled the political field devoid of politics.

I was surprised to find that even non-artists were aware of the state of the cultural field even if they did not participate in cultural activities or had any contact with official cultural institutions, but were simply observers. For example, Diaa Al Said said that although he was interested in experimenting with graffiti years before the uprising because he thought it was 'cool' (Diaa Al Said, Cairo, pers. comm., 27 July 2014), especially hip-hop graffiti, he only ever went twice to an art gallery, once in a gallery named Safer Khan in the upscale Zamalek neighbourhood and another named Darb 1718, a contemporary art and culture centre in Old Cairo (Diaa Al Said, Cairo, pers. comm., 27 July 2014). Dia explained that the cultural institutions he visited never felt like genuine places for artistic creativity, because for him, his conception of 'real art' is art which necessarily exists outside the political and economic processes and calculations of the state, and since the only type of art that was promoted and exhibited was based on the state's criterion and parameters for 'acceptable' cultural production (even those in the independent culture scene) which could then be viewed and consumed as a valuable commodity (as part of the neoliberal character of the state), it could not be considered real art (Diaa Al Said, Cairo, pers. comm., 27 July 2014).

Rather, it was described as a monopolization of heavily promoted commodities which served a political and economic function for the interest of the 'nation-state of businessmen' (to use Hala's description):

Galleries aren't the only place where art exists and it shouldn't be considered as the only place where 'real' art exists. Art is lost in this country . . . there is no art in this country, there is only a monopolization of art which is the whole contemporary art environment. They don't want more people to join them because they want to be a small group of elite contemporary artists so they can make more money. It is a hegemonic monopoly. (Diaa Al Said Cairo, pers. comm, 27 July 2014)

This antagonism towards 'gallery art' tended to reflect a criticism of the overall control of the cultural field by the Ministry of Culture and by the cultural elite (curators, art critics, formal artists, wealthy buyers and an audience that came from a certain socio-economic class) at the expense of the marginalization of those who were not privy to enter this field and forced to exist on the (invisible) margins. Keizer described the exclusionary art field to me as follows:

> The art scene before the revolution was extremely secluded to an exclusive club of people that had money to enter these places, sip a few wine bottles, and point and decide what art was. That's the problem, when they get to dictate what art is, that is a huge problem, I think that is when art died in this country, when they tried to define it and gave it value and turning it into an expensive commodity, when it could be just because that person is part of that exclusive circle. There was loads of nepotism. (Keizer, Cairo, pers. comm., 29 April 2014)

In light of these unfortunate experiences, recurrent phrases I heard to describe the state of art and the cultural field by most of those I spoke to was that art was 'lost', there was no 'real' art and art 'died', as an effect of its monopolization through control the distribution, content, and form, of art, and indeed, even who could be visibly (and legitimately) recognized as an artist.

This had deeper repercussions beyond the fact that the state controlled cultural production for its own immediate political interests and economic benefits or that it marginalized artists. It involved deeper questions which are implicated in questions over 'what is made visible, who sees what, [and] how seeing, knowing and power are interrelated' (Hooper-Greenhill, 2000: 14). It is in this sense that French philosopher Jacques Rancière not only asks us to question the self-evidence of what is seen but simultaneously asks us to question what (and why) things are rendered invisible in the perceptible order of things. For the majority of the cultural producers, it was politics (i.e. the state) par excellence which ensured the existing arrangement and legitimized certain art forms – thus rendering them perceptible – while simultaneously marginalizing those which do not contribute to the common ordering of things, because the state wanted to promote not only a certain way of seeing things but also of legitimating understandings (through political and economic means) over what is considered art and who can be considered an artist. Legitimacy was tied to visibility, and cultural producers (artists and non-artists alike) were very aware of this situation, and how it was all tied into a larger narrative involving political control and economic interests.

Therefore, although many of those I spoke to complained of an inactive ministry, the deterioration of the cultural field and its production of sterile art, as well as the exclusionary practices towards artists located outside of the state's nepotistic circle, independent artists – those who are excluded from private galleries and government funding – still found ways to try to exhibit their work. Welsh cultural critic and theorist Raymond Williams asserts that even though hegemony is constantly reasserted, it is also at the same time, constantly 'resisted' and 'challenged' (Williams, 1977: 112).

For example, one of the artists I spoke to, Mohammed Alaa, a performance artist, had tried to submit a video performance in 2010, one year prior to the revolution, entitled 'A Piece of Bread'[17] to the government, which was rejected with no reason given. That experience made him realize that he should have never relied on official cultural institutions to exhibit his work, and instead, decided that he would no longer concern himself with official cultural spaces and their governing authority, that is, those 'people in control who say we can't exhibit this here because this is political . . . I think people should be outside the track and exhibit independently in unofficial, unconventional spaces, which would create a crisis for the regime' (Mohammed Alaa Cairo, pers. comm., 12 August 2014).

Other artists who tried more direct forms of expressing dissent under Mubarak's regime were discouraged from ever trying it again due to fear of being caught by the police. In June 2010, Amr Nazeer who had never been interested in art or politics until Khaled Said's murder, attempted to experiment with creating political graffiti prior to the uprising (in October 2010) with a relative in their upscale neighbourhood in Maadi. They recorded themselves at dawn spray painting the logo of the April 6 movement[18] in the streets and wrote 'yes to change, the youth of April 6' (Figure 1.2) beneath the logo. Less than 15 minutes after they had completed the graffiti, the police had already mobilized in the area and a patrol car parked right under the stencil, with a booth set up with a police officer inside keeping watch (Amr Nazeer Cairo, pers. comm., 9 March 2014). Nazeer said he was discouraged to try graffiti again, lest he be caught the second time around.

This was also the reason why Hany Khaled only experimented once with political graffiti prior to the uprising. He told me that he was interested in trying

Figure 1.2 Logo of the April 6 Youth Movement, founded in 2008.

graffiti – which he knew nothing about – after he saw a friend of his brothers do it (Hany Khaled, Cairo, pers. comm., 11 August 2014). In November 2010 he wrote 'Down with Mubarak the Corrupt' on the wall of the Belgian ambassador's home, near his own residence. He said he was shocked at how quickly the police came to the scene, and that they closed off the street and were asking everyone questions about who sprayed the graffiti:

> The people in the coffee shop knew it was me but they didn't say anything, the police did not even bother to arrest the people who were doing drugs in the coffee shop right in front of their eyes. Their only interest was to arrest the person who drew this graffiti. When they did not know who it was, they wiped over it and left, and I did not bother to do anything since then until the uprising, because I became a bit scared and I was still in university, I don't know what would have happened if they caught me. (Hany Khaled, Cairo, pers. comm., 11 August 2014)

During Mubarak's rule, those who were more formal artists recalled experiences of being excluded from the cultural field as a whole – from the government to private galleries to the independent cultural scene – and those who were not artists and that attempted to create any form of critical graffiti were starkly aware of the consequences of attempting such a feat twice. It was this restrictive environment in which cultural producers operated which undermined any form of unconventional expression, therefore, when the uprising occurred it formed the basis of a rupture which would have repercussions not only in political performances and acts but also in creative cultural ones. Thus, the violence of the state was not relegated to the physical field – but also the symbolic and creative one.

The irony of the abject failure of the cultural field to nurture the ambitions of young artists, promote a participatory environment, and encourage independent cultural activity comes through more clearly in light of a document (published on the tenth anniversary of Mubarak's rule) outlining Egypt's 'enlightened' cultural policy, entitled *Culture: A Light Shining on the Face of the Nation*. The document advocated, among other things, such as 'cultural democracy . . . the youth as the barometer of the art movement . . . and non-centralization' (Winegar, 2006: 154–5). A clear propaganda piece, two important examples within the public eye embodied the failure of this cultural policy in fostering and retaining a genuine intellectual and culturally diverse environment. The first came at a meeting between intellectuals and Mubarak, at which the late prominent human-rights activist Dr. Mohammed El-Sayed Said presented a 'political reform program based on political pluralism, strengthening civil society, separating the head of state from the head of the ruling party, and enacting a new constitution' (Khodr, 2012). According to one journalist, 'Mubarak immediately chided him and called him an "extremist"' (Khodr, 2012), a label he initially reserved for political Islamists, yet later used as a tool against any opposition groups or activists to discredit them. In another example, leading novelist Sonallah Ibrahim publicly refused – on the podium of the Cairo Opera

House and in the presence of then Minister of Culture Faruq Husni – the Arabic Novel Award prize in 2003 given by the Ministry of Culture, because 'it is awarded by a government . . . that lacks the credibility of bestowing it. . . . We have no theatre, no cinema, no research, no education. We only have festivals and conferences and a boxful of lies' (Mehrez, 2008: 212). He also refused the prize on the grounds of 'the oppression of the people by the Egyptian political system' (El Attar, 2009).

These examples demonstrate the contradictions within the cultural field, in which the state heavily subsidized brochures and book fairs which manufactured an image of a culturally 'modern' yet 'authentic' Egypt, yet in reality, there was no substantive, independent or critical intellectual activity other than a form of cultural window dressing situated within an increasingly repressive political system. The Ministry of Culture's incapacity to support artists beyond a minority elitist group 'approved' by the regime strengthened the role of civil society organizations which, in the 1990s and 2000s, saw a proliferation of private artistic and cultural institutions in Cairo, such as Townhouse Gallery (an independent art space founded in 1998), Karim Francis Contemporary Art Gallery (founded in 1995), Al Mawred Al Thaqafy (translated literally to Culture Resource, a nonprofit organization founded in 2004 which seeks to promote artistic activity), Darb 1718 (a contemporary art and culture centre in Cairo founded in 2008) and the CIC (Contemporary Image Collective, a cultural institution founded in 2004). Established commercial galleries in Cairo such as Mashrabia Gallery of Contemporary Art (founded in 1990), along with newly established institutions, pleaded for quality in art and independence from the corrupt state system, to no avail.

Despite the growth of independent cultural groups and organizations, the Ministry of Culture remained (and remains) the principal promoter, distributor and sponsor of culture, and intellectuals which did not (and do not) follow its political agenda were ostracized. Samia Mehrez (Egyptian professor of contemporary literature), notes that although the presence of these alternative cultural spaces are significant, one could not forget that they operate within 'a certain illusion of autonomy vis-à-vis the state' (Mehrez, 2008: 214). According to Sonallah Ibrahim, the reason why intellectuals were primarily marginalized during Mubarak's era was due to a 'deliberate distinction between what is cultural and what is political, rendering the opinions of intellectuals in politics invalid, and limiting the role of intellectuals in political organization' (Ibrahim, cited in Ahram Online, 2012).

The Ministry of Culture during the optimistic revolutionary years (2011–12)

In the immediate aftermath of Mubarak's ouster in the wake of the initial 18 days of the Egyptian revolution, questions immediately arose regarding the Ministry of Culture's role and how it could be 'imagined' differently (Elwakil, 2011) or whether it should be abolished altogether. This was indicative of the public's awareness that any substantive political change would need to effectuate a substantive change within the cultural field, ruled under Faruq Husni for over two decades. The nomination and later appointment of Mohamed El-Sawy (founder of El-Sawy Culture Wheel, a cultural venue in Cairo established in 2003) in February 2011 received immediate outcry and led to organized protests from revolutionaries and members of the cultural community alike, who argued that El-Sawy was 'not qualified enough to be the minister. He is a businessman' (Hamdy Reda, photographer and owner of Artellewa centre, Taher, Metwally, 2011). Other major grievances against his appointment at the time were that El-Sawy was a close ally to Mubarak's former regime, that he was not adequately qualified to hold such an authoritative post as he was not considered knowledgeable enough in matters of culture and that he 'exercised excessive control over many artistic productions presented at the centre' (Mohamed Hassane, an Egyptian scriptwriter, cited in Taher, Metwally, 2011). Therefore, his poor reputation as a businessman and stringent bureaucrat who excessively censors the artistic community in his private cultural venue led to public resistance which manifested in several protests outside the Ministry of Culture in late February 2011. El-Sawy resigned in early March of 2011 along with Ahmed Shafik (a former minister of civil aviation under Mubarak's regime) and his much-derided interim cabinet for their ties to the former regime. El-Sawy's successor was Emad Abou-Ghazi, who, unlike his predecessor, was highly welcomed by the intellectual community for his academic and professional credentials. However, in a setback to the cultural community, Abou-Ghazi resigned in November 2011, in protest at the violent tactics used by the Supreme Council of the Armed Forces (hereinafter SCAF) against protestors during clashes in Tahrir Square.

A conference held in February 2012 at the El-Sawy Culturewheel entitled 'The Future of Culture in Egypt' attempted to address pressing questions of cultural identity, cultural production and the effectiveness of cultural institutions within Egypt, in which the Ministry of Culture's role was attacked for its 'passive and insufficient performance as simply a "censor of" instead of as an "enabler of" cultural development' (Montasser, 2012b). However, although this conference set off a healthy and much-needed debate regarding the role of the state in culture, repeated calls for the decentralization of the Ministry of Culture so that its role would be reduced to funding rather than producing culture remains unrealized.

Culture under Morsi: Brotherhood domination

SCAF ruled on an interim basis in the aftermath of the Egyptian revolution, until Mohammed Morsi, a member of the Muslim Brotherhood, was elected president in June 2012. Although Morsi's presidency was brief (it lasted from 30 June 2012 until 3 July 2013, when he was forcibly removed by the military), his economic, political and cultural policies polarized the Egyptian public (Hellyer, 2013). Morsi's intervention in the cultural scene was swift, and many activists accused his amendment of the constitution as something that 'threatens freedom of expression and creativity' for privileging religion over the law and civil society (Shaw, 2013). The accusations of the 'Brotherhoodization' of the Egyptian state and the cultural field (El Nabawi, 2013) continued in the aftermath of then Minister of Culture Saber Arab's resignation (in protest at the mistreatment and violence against protestors after the second anniversary of the revolution), who was replaced by Alaa Abdel-Aziz, a Brotherhood member.

Abdel-Aziz removed prominent members of the cultural community[19] and replaced them with Brotherhood members, arguing that he needed to 'inject fresh blood in the cultural scene' (Metwaly, 2013a). His removal of Inas Abdel Daïm, the head of the Cairo Opera House (the largest performance venue in Egypt), proved especially controversial and led to Egyptian artists halting all performances for three days. This provoked a flood of statements by cultural organizations which accused the Brotherhood of wanting to 'destroy the Egyptian culture' (Metwaly, 2013b), and resulted in the spread of widespread protests, sit-ins and dance protest performances outside the Ministry of Culture. During these protests, calls for the decentralization of the Ministry of Culture were repeated and one of the protestors argued that the Ministry of Culture should no longer retain its role as 'producer, executor, and distributor' of culture, but remain only as a 'funder and sponsor' (El Nabawi, 2013). These protests illustrated the divisive issues faced by the Ministry of Culture, with artists from the independent arts scene arguing that the Ministry was redundant and should be removed as its role would always be to 'advance the state's agenda' (Jacquette, 2013). According to writer Muhammad Aladdin, 'The Ministry of Culture is the same as it was under Mubarak, just with new faces. It still has a narrow and opportunistic understanding of Islam and culture. The real problem with the Ministry of Culture is the idea that culture can enlighten the masses, because funding can be used to push their agenda or ideas' (Jacquette, 2013).

Morsi's unpopular rule was met with continuous protests, and according to Ahdaf Soueif, the Egyptian novelist and commentator, this was because '[Morsi] failed to honour every one of the promises he made in order to be elected. He basically behaved as though he had somehow legitimately inherited the old Mubarak regime with a veneer of piety' (Soueif, cited in Abdel Kouddous, 2013). In response to overwhelming public anger at Morsi's performance as president, in April 2013 a grassroots movement entitled *Tamarod* ('rebellion') was founded by members of the Egyptian Movement for Change (also known by its slogan Kefaya, or 'Enough') and set as its main goal the collection of signatures in order to call for early presidential elections.

On 29 June 2013, *Tamarod* announced 22 million signatures (their original aim was 15 million) had been collected and on 30 June 2013, millions of Egyptians called on Morsi to step down. The next day the military gave the president a 48-hour ultimatum to solve the current crisis otherwise, as Abdel Fattah El-Sisi (who was a general in the Egyptian military at the time) stated in a television address: 'If the people's demands are not met, the military, which is forced to act according to its role and duty, will have to disclose its own future plan' (Bradley, Abdellatif, 2013). On 3 July 2013, the military intervened and forcibly removed Morsi as president where he was taken into military custody, overruled the amended constitution and installed an interim government until the next presidential elections, which Sisi won by a landslide in June 2014. Sisi is the sixth, and the current president of Egypt.

Creative closures under the rule of Sisi

'If Egypt's cultural elite had hoped that the overthrow of Islamist President Mohammed Morsi in 2013 would usher in an era of creativity and freedom of expression, they must be deeply disappointed', journalists Ghada Tantawi and Mariam Rizk lamented under Sisi's presidency (Tantawi, Rizk, 2016). An atmosphere of repression and intolerance to criticism of Sisi came into being even before his ascendancy as Egypt's sixth president officially began on 8 June 2014. On 9 May 2014, Ganzeer was accused by a famous television personality named Osama Kamal of 'terrorism' in his support for the Muslim Brotherhood after launching a revolutionary art campaign with the hashtag #SisiWarCrimes. The show, entitled 'The President and the People', (*Al Kahera Wal Nas*, which translates to 'Cairo and its People') was broadcast on a television station known for its staunch support of Sisi. In response, Ganzeer wrote a blog post addressing the television host's claims against him:

> Dear Mr. Osama Kamal, I should point out to you that what you're doing is in all actuality not in Mr. Sisi's best interest. What you're doing makes him come off as a man who is very afraid of the impact of art. Rather than see us as a threat to the State, critical artists should be seen as a source of information to the State. By paying attention to what we do, perhaps the State can better understand popular grievances and adjust its policies and governance accordingly, rather than invest so many resources into trying to shut us up (see Figure 1.3). (Ganzeer, 2014a)

This blog post, published on 15 May 2014, in which he declares that Sisi is 'very afraid of the impact of art' came several days after an official tweet on 12 May 2014, by the @AlSisiOfficial Twitter account, which stated: '#AlSisi: Egypt needs its intellectuals and its thinkers and its writers to play a very major role during the upcoming phase, on the basis of national responsibility and judged by national interests' (my translation).

Using social media to mobilize cultural intellectuals to 'play a major role in the upcoming phase . . . according to national interests' (the phase referred to the lead-up to the presidential elections at the end of the same month the tweet was posted) is, according to Huda Lutfi, a Cairo-based artist, a familiar method used by the regime to make 'strategic alliances with cultural élites to bolster national pride and to crack down on "undesirable" and opposition art' (Lutfi, cited in Guyer, 2014). In the years since Sisi has been in power, cultural events have been arbitrarily cancelled, cartoonists, singers, writers and poets have been jailed, and prominent cultural centres such as Townhouse Gallery and the Merit Publishing House have been raided and temporarily shut down (Amin, 2015; Kennedy, 2015; Tantawi, Rizk, 2016).

According to one journalist, 'rights advocates lament that the space for free artistic expression and creativity has diminished in Egypt' (Amin, 2015), and public cultural events which were borne out of the revolution, such as El-Fan Midan (Art is a Square) which was initiated by the now-defunct Independent

Figure 1.3 Ganzeer, 'Who's Afraid of Art?'. *Source*: Guyer, 2014.

Culture Coalition, was shut down by security forces in 2014 in a move which, according to the Arabic Network for Human-Rights information, was indicative of the 'the mounting police interventions and violations against the freedom of art and creativity' (Shoureap, 2014). Although El-Fan Midan was only one of many cultural activities initiated in the public sphere, it was one of the earliest initiatives in the immediate aftermath of Mubarak's restrictive rule on the political and cultural sphere. As Lewis writes,

> El-Fan Midan seemed to be an ambitious step to unfetter art from closed halls and elitist alienation to thrive in public spheres already bustling with revolutionary vigour. Organized in various public squares across Egypt by volunteers from the Independent Culture Coalition, and supported through donations from its members and other interested people, the monthly free-of-charge event cracked a hole in a long-enduring cultural siege laid by the Egyptian government, whereby artists and intellectuals were subject to 'play the game,' and the public sphere was largely inaccessible due to security measures. (Lewis, 2014)

For some, the closure of such a celebrated – and public – cultural activity that was formed in the wake of the revolution was representative of a general and disturbing trend of the complete subversion of the indepedent cultural field scene in the aftermath of the revolution. More established cultural institutions that had existed prior to the revolution, such as Al Mawred Al Thaqafy (Culture Resource), aslo closed down in the light of increasingly restrictive laws on civil society which led them to relocate their headquarters to Beirut 'due to the increasing antagonistic state attitude toward civil society' in which 'the fate of the programs and activities run and funded by Al-Mawred, founded 10 years ago by a group of Arab artists and intellectuals . . . remains unknown' (Lewis, 2014).

For many, this indicates a trend since Sisi's rule not only of using a heavy hand to restrict any oppositional voices and signs of political dissent for unpopular decisions but also of severely restricting cultural production, halting creative practices and re-appropriating the public sphere back under the government's full control. As Lewis writes,

> such events [the closure of El-Fan Midan and the decision of Mawred Al Thaqafy to close its Cairo office due to repressive new civil society laws] strike at the very core of the cultural scene. On the one hand, they have resulted in a complete takeover of the public sphere by the authorities, a space that had been forcefully reclaimed by the revolution. On the other hand, the recent laws intend to decrease the margin of cultural production, even inside elite circles, and to dry up the already scarce funding resources that have thrived in the past decade due to the Mubarak regime's relatively liberal policy toward foreign funding. . . . As it takes up the reins of the public domain – of political activism, the media, universities, economic activity and even religious institutions and civil society – the Egyptian state seizes artistic and cultural territory, robbing them of all potential. (Lewis, 2014)

As such, while Helmy El-Namnam, a former Minister of Culture, once said that 'Egypt's future is its cultural future' (El-Aref, 2015), cultural producers find themselves negotiating and operating within an increasingly restrictive environment. Indicative of the tumultuous period between February 2011 and January 2018 was the appointment of eight Ministers of Culture, the eighth – and most recently appointed – being Inas Abdel Daïm.[20]

Although the current political climate in Egypt has not been conducive to the independent cultural scene, creative manifestations of public expression and unconventional cultural acts still continue under increasingly difficult circumstances (Alfred, 2014; Jankowicz, 2016). Independent cultural actors continue to face severe intimidation, yet there are 'still the handful of artists, cartoonists and writers . . . willing to push the boundaries to experiment and challenge the public with their creations' (Amin, 2016). The lack of pervasiveness of the visibility of cultural expressions is not necessarily indicative of failure even if it is a sign of extremely difficult times for creative acts in all their forms – as Tripp notes, 'the more vigorously the authorities try to put a stop to this by arresting artists and singers, closing down plays, raiding art exhibitions and seizing artworks, or blacking out graffiti, the clearer it becomes that they have failed to establish their own version of the truth' (2013: 261).

Keizer's hope is that the continued process and existence of revolutionary art can lead to 'alternative ways of thinking which can lead to alternative modes of living, and maybe we are part of it now without realizing it as revolutionary artists, but I think that is a huge part of what we are doing' (Keizer, Cairo, pers. comm., 29 April 2014). The potential of revolutionary art as a fluid form of cultural expression may sustain new modes of engagement in the cultural field which may creatively constitute new ways of understanding the sociopolitical potential of art and its role and spark a necessary debate regarding its role in the aftermath of a revolution.

Chapter 2

SETTING THE STAGE FOR A POLITICAL
AND ARTISTIC REVOLUTION

A HISTORY OF DISSENT

> this sudden gaze towards revolutionary art could be interpreted as part of the Western euphoria in analysing the Arab Spring as an ahistorical, unprecedented and sudden revolt. While the January revolution mesmerized the world . . . such analyses that focused on the Facebook revolution often ignored the long cumulative history of political struggles, demonstrations, and numerous protests that took place prior to 2011. The same could be said about the long-established traditions in the field of art and culture in the Arab world.
>
> Mona Abaza (2016: 318)

The 25th of January 2011 should be seen as an outburst of sorts, a manifestation of political and cultural acts of dissent which came before it, of which Egypt has a rich history. This section, far from being an exhaustive account of this history, situated the Egyptian revolution of 2011 within a larger history of contemporary key moments of political and artistic acts of dissent.

A history of political dissent

Outlining any particular date[1] to discuss the history of dissent in Egypt is nearly impossible, yet for the purposes of this chapter I will begin my discussion within the last decade of Mubarak's presidency, as it is within this decade of his rule in which it was clear that Mubarak did not intend to relinquish his hold on the presidency, and that he was grooming his youngest son Gamal as his successor. In light of this reality, political and economic dissent[2] intensified within all levels of Egyptian society, from youth movements to labour workers and Muslim Brotherhood members, with many of their grievances and demands overlapping.[3] On 28 September 2000, in the immediate aftermath of the second Palestinian uprising (*intifada*), thousands of Egyptians took to the streets in solidarity with Palestinians, which, according to journalist Hossam El Hamalawy, 'soon gained an anti-regime dimension . . . [t]he president, however, remained a taboo subject, and I rarely heard anti-Mubarak chants' (El Hamalawy, 2011). However, this began to change in the early 2000s when resentment at regional wars from Palestine to Iraq inspired local activists to channel their anger at these injustices towards the source of their own domestic injustice, which saw protestors chanting slogans such as 'Hosni Mubarak is just like [Ariel] Sharon' to burning down a billboard of Mubarak in Tahrir Square (El Hamalawy, 2011). This would then lead to the emergence of the grassroots Egyptian Movement for Change, or *Kefaya* (Enough), in 2004, which focused on protesting Mubarak's presidency and the possibility of extending his rule to his son Gamal. Although this movement eventually lost momentum shortly after its founding (see Oweidat et al., 2008) due to internal strife and a failure to 'create a mass following among the working class and the urban poor' (El Hamalawy, 2011), it still remains one of the best examples of a grassroots coalition movement which saw a diverse membership base of activists, as such it was seen as a 'cross ideological force' (Shorbagy, 2007: 39). Kefaya's 'use of both social and mainstream media helped shift the political culture in the country. Millions of Egyptians, while sitting at home, could watch those daring young activists in downtown Cairo mocking the president, raising banners with slogans that were unimaginable a decade before' (El Hamalawy, 2011).

Mahalla strikes

Within the background of the emergence of broad political coalition forces came a turning point in political dissent against Mubarak's presidency in December 2006, when over 20,000 workers at the Misr Spinning and Weaving Company in the industrial Nile delta town of Mahalla El-Kubra went on strike due to unpaid bonuses which 'followed two decades of a lull in the industrial struggle, caused by repression and by an aggressive neoliberal programme that had the blessing of [Western financial institutions] the IMF and the World Bank' (El Hamalawy, 2011).

These strikes were renewed in the company in 2007 and 2008, and they gained traction and strength over the years (Beinin, 2009, 2012). This had a dramatic impact on the increase in public shows of dissent from 2006[4] until 2010 – the 'snowballing protests spread from factory to factory, mill to mill, one here, another there, until they practically became a general phenomenon in Egypt. The number of social mobilisations has increased from 266 in 2006, to 614 in 2007, and to 630 in 2008. In 2009, we witnessed around 609 protests' (Abdalla, 2012).

The economic grievances of striking workers gained a political dimension when their demands went beyond unpaid bonuses to the larger and overarching neoliberal structure imposed on by Mubarak's regime, and so in April 2008 a much more visible and direct attack – dubbed the 'Mahalla *intifada*' (El Hamalawy, 2011) against Mubarak's rule took place, with protesters taking down Mubarak's posters, battling the police troops in the streets, and challenging the symbols of the much-hated National Democratic party. Soon after, a similar revolt took place in the city of el-Borollos, north of the Nile delta. Though these uprisings were quelled, the country continued to witness almost on a daily basis strikes and sit-ins by workers, and smaller demonstrations by activists in downtown Cairo and the provinces. (El Hamalawy, 2011)

The intensification of the Mahalla uprising was one of the key events which served as a turning point towards interest in local protest movements for many of those I interviewed. When I asked Saiko as to when he started to gain interest in local politics prior to the uprising, he informed me that it was when he became more aware of internal dissent from the coverage of the Mahalla strikes through social media,

> it was only in high school when I heard about the train flipping over, the ship that sunk . . . I started to realize how, internally, we had so many problems. In 2008 when I saw the workers strike in Mahalla[5] (see Figure 2.1) and they were holding up Hosni Mubarak's picture and hitting it with slippers, I started to understand that there truly was oppression all around us. (Saiko Maino, Cairo, pers. comm., 26 August 2014)

Hany Khaled also started to become more interested in local politics in 2007, when his friend sent him a video of a microbus driver being brutalized and sodomized with a stick by an officer. He said before then, he was just a 20-year-old kid who played around and got his allowance, but that after that, he became more interested in what was happening around him, though he admitted that although he cared, he was still not 'a political person' (Hany Khaled, Cairo, pers. comm., 18 August 2014).

Figure 2.1 Protestors stepping on Mubarak's picture during the Mahalla strike, 6 April 2008 (*Source*: ElSharnoubi, 2013).

This is an interesting point – in that many cultural producers had an awareness of the '*balawee* [problems] which you see everywhere you look' (Far3on, Cairo, pers. comm., 17 August 2014), but this did not necessarily translate into political involvement – quite the opposite, in fact. For some, it led to a disenchantment with politics. Sad Panda, who (even after the uprising) was not interested in politics, said that during Mubarak's rule, he realized that politics was a dead-end, that it was an area in which there was no space to act and that any involvement in politics simply reinforced the status quo when the authorities intervened and simply was a continuous show of the state's power:

> I don't like to waste my time on hopes that I know for a fact that nothing will change . . . a long time ago on Twitter, in 2009, it was like a comedy show during a protest. People would write 'Guys, we are getting arrested and they are taking us to so and so on prison, we need a lawyer fast', two tweets later, 'Mohamad Abd Al Salam the lawyer is going now to release I don't know who', two tweets later, 'Mohammad Abd Al Salam the lawyer was arrested we need a lawyer to release Mohammad', it is so stupid. And this happens until now, that lawyers go to release people and they get arrested, so you need to get a lawyer to release the lawyer so that that lawyer could release the person originally arrested. In all this madness, I personally don't want to be a part of it. (Sad Panda, Cairo, pers. comm., 28 April, 2014)

For others, personal experiences may have led to a disillusionment with political action, but later spurred them to become more involved in underground tactics. In a story recounted to me by Amr Nazeer, an Egyptian business developer at Axeer Studio,[6] his first political act of dissent (prior to the uprising) was to stand in silence as part of the 'We are all Khaled Said'[7] campaign. Although the protestors were non-violent, it ended with a violent clash downtown Cairo between police, *baltageyeh* (plain-clothed thugs paid by the regime to suppress and break up protests using violence and rudimentary weapons such as sticks or batons) and the protestors. Therefore, regardless of the protestors adherence to the *qanun al tagamuh* (law of public assembly) and the non-violent nature of the protest, the regime's brutal suppression of the protest led Amr to conclude that one cannot 'have nothing to do with politics – you can't enter politics with people who have weapons, with *baltageyeh*. If I say something, they will beat or kill me, so this isn't politics, I won't kid myself' (Amr Nazeer, Cairo, pers. comm., 9 March 2014). For Amr, the word 'politics' essentially loses all meaning because the understanding of politics is an absence of being able to 'do' politics – in the sort of meta-politics Rancière defined as a disavowal of politics, in that it is a way to 'to achieve politics by eliminating politics' (1999: 63).

This contradiction – of a politics with no politics – reflects one of the most common sentiments I heard during more informal discussions with the cultural producers I interviewed – you cannot 'do' politics with a state who will kill you, jail you or injure you. Politics tended to connote a derogatory term, as something that is 'done' to you – not as something that you do – and that directly affects your livelihood in indiscriminate, largely uncontrollable ways. Thus, the majority of those I interviewed equated the term 'politics' (*al-seyassah*) with the state, and so the way they articulated the notion of politics resembled the absence of politics, akin to the established consensus (of the police order) which Rancière described as the 'non-existence of politics' (Rancière, 2010: 43). Those involved in 'politics' were, according to most of the people I spoke to, those who were already associated with Mubarak, such as the crony capitalists, businessmen and regime sympathizers – that is, the *fulool* – and therefore, they reflected the *nagaseh* (a noun) of politics and thus also considered morally and physically repugnant to those I interviewed. According to Hany Khaled, this made them illegitimate to the eyes of most Egyptians, who did not take them seriously – 'no matter what politicians say or do, they are liars' (Hany Khaled, Cairo, pers. comm., 18 August 2014).

The murder of Khaled Said

However, while most of those interviewed expressed a complete repudiation with anything to do with politics prior to the uprising and their disenchantment with political involvement, others, such as Amr Nazeer, argued that his experience with police brutality during the Khaled Said event later motivated him to expand his knowledge of the streets and to adopt less visible, underground tactics –

> After this event we thought we had to have more guerrilla tactics, we need to learn our streets more so we can mess them [the authorities] up. . . . I grew fond of guerrilla tactics and wanted to learn about guerrilla marketing, graffiti, posters, and stencil art – the ones you would spray and run. I don't know how to draw and was never interested but it started to interest me. (Amr Nazeer, Cairo, pers. comm., 9 March 2014)

Several of those I interviewed became interested in local politics as early as 2007 (from watching a video of a microbus driver being physically abused by the police) or 2008 (from watching the Mahalla strikes), but for the majority it was Khaled Said's murder that influenced their interest in local politics. Through the 'We are all Khaled Said' Facebook page[8] (created by Wael Ghonim, the former Google employee who gained notoriety during the uprising after his emotional television interview in the wake of his release from police incarceration) many found their outlet, such as Amr, who told me he was addicted to following the page and was 'so happy that whenever I would just press refresh there would be constant updates. I got so interested and would start saying what are these disgusting things that are happening, I didn't even know the police brutalities that happened before' (Amr Nazeer, Cairo, pers. comm, 9 March 2014). Even Dia, who was never interested in politics, said the 'We are all Khaled Said' Facebook page also pulled him in because it was 'reliable' (Dia Al Said, Cairo, pers. comm, 27 July 2014). KIM, the moniker of an Egyptian graffiti artist named Kareem who runs his father's small business, told me that he did not care about politics until the death of Khalid Said because it unravelled the arbitrary violence and unbridled brutality of the state:

> You are talking about a young guy sitting in a 'cyber' [internet] café and all of a sudden two informants come in to arrest him then beat him up in the stairwell of a residential apartment building and accused him of having drugs, but he had nothing on him. Then they tell you that he had *hashish* [weed] and he swallowed it – give me a break . . . it was so obvious that they were lying, really and truly lying. Don't try to lie, don't try to cover it up, and don't try to justify your lies. (KIM, Cairo, pers. comm, 18 August 2014)

Yet the question remained as to *why* Khaled Said's tragic murder became such a formative event given that there were several videos of torture in prisons and jails circulated via mobile phones and the internet years before. Hala El Sharouny argued that the reason why Khaled Said was a key transitional point was because it shattered the Egyptian middle-class's illusions that their economic and social status – and de-politicization – made them 'safe'. Khaled Said was a middle-class 28-year-old entrepreneur who was murdered right under his apartment building outside of an internet café in a middle-class area in Alexandria. This was not what the state could depict as a common thief or rapist or even a drug dealer who 'had it coming to him', a familiar narrative of the state. Therefore, for many of those I spoke to, Khaled Said's mutilated face brought to the fore the very real and ugly face of the regime to the youth, and that their brutality was not restricted to those with certain political or ideological leanings, activists or low level criminals and drug dealers, but to anyone:

> Khaled Said was from the middle class, he had a normal education, he was like us, a boy from a good family – and all of a sudden we find that they grabbed someone from the likes of him, beat him up and to top it off charged him with drug possession even after he died. This is when the revolution was starting to kick off, when people began to sense that 'this could happen to me, I just walk next to the wall [*amshee gamb el heita*] minding my own business, I don't even do anything yet this could happen to me' . . . right now any one of us is directly under threat, none of us are immune to it. You would always hear about torture and death in prisons and they come out and tell you oh he was a thief or a cheater or whatever, that they were dirty dogs . . . with the rise of social media and all that, the government was exposed and embarrassed. (Hala El Sharouny, Cairo, pers. comm., 18 August 2014)

Khaled Said represented the reality that if this could happen to him, a 'boy from a good family', it could happen to anyone, regardless of your socio-economic class or whether or not you were involved in politics. The regime's violence no longer had any logic or reason, but was brutal and sporadic – which terrified most of those I spoke to, because even if one wilfully distanced themselves from politics, they were not exempt from the state's violent tactics – no one was – which instilled a very real fear in people (see Figure 2.2–2.5).

By 2010, daily strikes and protests were a regular occurrence (Beinin, 2012; El Hamalawy, 2011), with protestors' anger aimed directly at Mubarak and his cronies, and this meant the legitimacy of his regime was rapidly eroding. By December 2011, when Tunisia overthrew Ben Ali (after widespread protests at the police brutality faced by Mohammed Bouazizi which led to his self-immolation outside a government institution), Egyptians – who have a long history of facing police brutality[9] themselves – organized protests[10] on Egypt's 'National Police Day'[11] on 25 January 2011.

Figure 2.2 The image of Khaled Said which became iconic during protests prior to the Egyptian uprising (Ahram Online, 2013).

Figure 2.3 An activist carries a picture of Khaled Said that reads 'For what wrongdoing was Khaled killed?' during a protest following a press conference for the family at the Egyptian Journalists Syndicate in Cairo, Egypt, 2010 (Photo: AP) (Ahram Online, 2013b).

Figure 2.4 Riot police surrounded supporters of Khaled Said at a protest in Alexandria, Egypt, June 2010. *Source*: Nasser Nasser/Associated Press (Preston, 2011).

Figure 2.5 A protestor holding a cartoon by Carlos Latuff, a Brazilian political cartoonist, depicting Khaled Said with the hashtag for the Egyptian revolution #Jan25, carrying a nervous Hosni Mubarak. The poster reads 'Execute the one who killed me' (my translation) (Latuff, 2012).

Artistic movements and political engagement

To trace the history of Arab art from the mid-twentieth century through the uprisings and to the present reveals a great churning of ideas, social awareness and activism that are not evident in the study of official politics. Arab art has tapped into alternative, popular histories, within boundaries that contract in times of authoritarianism and expanded during the uprisings to unprecedented levels. The creative fire of these artists has never been extinguished. Egypt's fine arts community – even during the regimes of Gamal Abdel Nasser, Anwar Sadat and Mubarak – grappled in meaningful ways with fundamental political questions, though artists' direct involvement with political struggles was minimal until the uprisings. The surge of politicized artists who occupied Tahrir from 2011 to 2013 was exceptional in Egypt's history, but also echoed the political activism and engagement of earlier generations of Egyptian artists. (Sultan Sooud Al Qassemi, 2017)

Samia Mehrez aptly notes that 'we have over-romanticized the January 2011 moment. It's not the beginning moment; it is the climactic moment. Things have been building up, not only politically but also culturally. To think that everything started then is a fallacy' (Mehrez, cited in Sanders IV, 2015). Artistic dissent during the Egyptian revolution of 2011 should never be placed in isolation but rather, seen in relation to other historical moments of dissent in Egyptian history, in which one can draw parallels between significant political moments and the accompanying creative/artistic responses deployed by Egyptian artists and intellectuals.

First, Second and Third Generation art movements

The early twentieth-century art movements in Egypt were roughly divided into the 'First Generation', 'Second Generation' and 'Third Generation' movements (Karnouk, 2005). The First Generation (as represented by the group La Chimère, which included prominent Egyptian artists such as Mahmoud Said and Mahmoud Mukhtar, among others) represented a cultural renaissance (*al nahdah*) in the early twentieth century, after centuries of foreign rule.

The First Generation was based on a more secular outlook which embraced a 'revival of classical Egyptian art' (the neo-Phaoronic style) and combined this with 'modern techniques and influences' (Mikdadi, 2004). The Second Generation was concerned with the larger political breakdown, primarily abroad (the Palestinian Arab Revolt of 1936, the First World War and the Second World War and the rise of fascism and Nazism). In response, one of the major dissident art movements – the 'Art & Liberty'[12] Movement – was established in 1939 by Egyptian surrealists George Henein, Ramsis Younan, Kamel el-Timlissany, and brothers Anwar and Fuad Kamil (Berànek, 2005: 203). However, regardless of the surrealist background of its founding members, the 'Art & Liberty Group was not a surrealist group. Rather, it was a broad-based, non-sectarian alliance of left-wing, modern minded writers, artists, and radical activists . . . in support of the FIARI [French acronym for the International Federation of Independent Revolutionary Art] platform as concocted by [Andre] Breton and [Leon] Trotsky' (LaCoss, 2010: 80).

Although the group's initial concerns were the rise of fascism and its war on alternative cultural expression, it moved on to address broader issues such as 'anti-imperialism, radical educational reform, Freudian theory and women's emancipation' (LaCoss, 2009-10: 29). The group also fought for local issues such as continuing British foreign domination, discontent with the Egyptian monarchy, the bourgeoisie and elite academicism, and the rights of labourers, workers and Egyptian women (LaCoss, 2009-10: 28). Within this context, the group released their manifesto 'Long Live Degenerate Art!', which stood in solidarity with the 'For an Independent Revolutionary Art' manifesto of Breton's group. This short manifesto called for international solidarity to fight against the cultural hegemony of authoritarian regimes that were attempting to stifle all free expression. It adopted the derogatory term 'degenerate art' which had been bestowed on it by authoritarian rulers, using it to inspire a status of veneration as the ultimate form of unhindered cultural expression, and as such resistance.

The group wanted to use art to create an open exchange of dissent through creative expression and ideas which would, essentially, work to deconstruct the very roots and causes of their oppression. In their newspaper *al-Tatawwur* ('Evolution'), a statement by one of its members, Tawfiq Hana' Allah, entitled 'A School of Discontent', essentially summed up the group's main goals as wanting to 'establish a school where we can teach people how and why they should be discontented, discontented with the chains that bind them and the society whose values are set in stone' (LaCoss, 2009-10: 30).

It was this dissent, not towards external political instability and authoritarian rule, which was now directed inwards, leading the monarchy and British rule to target them as a potential threat. According to LaCoss, 'in one police spy report filed with the Egyptian prime minister, *al-Tatawwur* was described as a publication dedicated to "spread anarchy, destroy morals and religion, and bring about the collapse of the pillars of the social and legal establishment necessary for the running of the country"' (2009-10: 30). The Egyptian Art & Liberty Group started to be viewed as a rising threat because they were more than just a group of artists writing occasional articles or painting. They also 'organized conferences, debates, film screenings, and exhibitions, including five controversial annual "Independent Art Expositions[13]" held in Cairo between 1940 and 1945' (2009-10: 28). Accompanying these expositions were manifestos which emphasized their ideological platforms, such as the 1941 'Free Art in Egypt' manifesto which called for the 'arousal of astonishment in the minds of the masses', as well as 'intractable resistance to the dominant forms of conservative neo-classical image-making, and discussions about contemporary currents of visual culture' (2009-10: 29–30).

However, due to the group's more unconventional styles and 'eclecticism [which] confused people' (Karnouk, 2005: 80), language became a dominant barrier between them and the public. They wrote their major texts primarily in French, and used language that was difficult for the general population to grasp (Berànek, 2005: 218), a population that already had a high illiteracy rate in the early twentieth century of over 94 per cent (Hollingsworth, 1986). Although they were unable to achieve a popular following and their support-base remained limited to a select group of intellectuals and activists, Luis Awaḍ (a prominent Egyptian writer and intellectual) concluded: 'Whatever we think about the originality of this art form in Egypt, it was good at dealing a death blow to academism' (Awad, 1966, cited in Berànek, 2005: 219).

In the 1940s, the 'Third Generation' artists were represented by the 'Rejectionists', a combination of several groups founded by the students of Husayn Yousef Amin (a prominent Egyptian art scholar and painter). One of the most well-known groups they formed, The Group of Contemporary Art, advocated the use of art pedagogy in promoting societal activism (Russell, 2013: 256) and was dedicated to connecting art with ordinary Egyptians by grounding art in Egyptian culture. According to Salwa Mikdadi, these groups were formed in the wake of the 'controversy over regionalism versus internationalism' (Mikdadi, 2004) spurred on by the Egyptian Art & Liberty Group, whereby the Rejectionists

> challenged previous romanticized imagery and Western academic styles by exploring the daily realities of poverty and oppression . . . the Contemporary Art Group . . . were dedicated to the quest for the Egyptian *soul [italics in original]*. Inspired by folk symbolism, popular traditions, and notions of the collective unconscious, their work is steeped in social realism. (Mikdadi, 2004)

In one of the most famous examples of dissent against the rule of King Farouk which saw poverty become more pervasive, Egyptian artist Abdel Hadi El-Gazzar, one of the most prominent members of the group, exhibited a painting which showed eight barefoot women and one girl standing side-by-side holding empty plates in front of them. It was immediately believed to be a scathing commentary on the socio-economic inequalities of the time, and led to Gazzar's (and founder Husayn Yousef Amin's) arrest.

This example shows that although their goals, styles and techniques advocated an approach that was more directly constituted within local Egyptian realities and lives, they still acted as 'successors to the Egyptian Surrealists in their opposition to the pictorial academicism and nationalist ideology of a *nahdah* [renaissance] in the arts' (Kane, 2013: 61), suggesting that although the ideological character and style of the two groups differed, their overarching goals were united through their rejection of socio-economic equalities, nationalistic propaganda, and academicism (which, they believed, restrains culture within an established mode of formal thought and expression).

After King Farouk had been deposed by the Free Army officers in the 1952 Revolution, 'artists' groups[14] were disbanded along with all political parties' (Mikdadi, 2004), and the state became the main patron of the arts. According to Karnouk, this was nothing new, as 'the question of culture sponsored from the top was not novel in Egypt' (Karnouk, 2005: 67). However, in 1952 'the rationale was different: the state as the main constituent of a revolutionary art world, took entirely upon itself the role of promoting and expressing the people's claim for freedom in creative expression' (Karnouk, 2005: 67). A group which embraced the state's goals was the Group of Modern Art, which was formed in 1947 but only gained traction in the aftermath of the 1952 revolution. What is interesting about this group is that it did not show dissent against the state, but instead embraced its revolutionary philosophy and rebelled against the Egyptian Art & Liberty Group as well as the Group of Contemporary Art. One of its most prominent members, Hamed Oweiss, outlined the group's primary goals as representative of a 'third way' of thinking about and approaching art which differed from the approach of the two groups which preceded it:

> We believed that revolutionary ideology should be reflected in art. We, the Group of Modern Art, rejected 'surrealism,' because it was essentially rebellion, or an art which did not aim at the consciousness of the people at large. For us, art expressing the Egyptian identity had to be attached to the existing social structures, like labour and the *fellahin* [peasants], but away and beyond the 'folkloric' arts favoured by the Group of Contemporary Art. (Karnouk, 2005: 1919)

In the aftermath of the 1967 Six-Day War, which ended with the crushing defeat of Egyptian forces through the almost complete destruction of its air force and the occupation of Sinai by colonial "Israel", an Islamic revival in the arts began to take hold in Egypt in the 1970s which reflected a change in the sociocultural landscape of the time (Karnouk, 2005: Ch.5). As mentioned earlier, Sadat's *infitah* policies in the 1970s caused a massive blow to the cultural field and significantly reduced cultural funding, hindered artistic activities and curbed creative expression beyond formal avenues, which meant that 'artists working outside the mainstream, exploring controversial subjects or using unconventional techniques, found themselves isolated, and many emigrated to the West, returning to Egypt almost annually to participate in exhibitions' (Mikdadi, 2004).

It was not until Mubarak's rule in 1981 – in which 'the renewed active involvement in the cultural field' was reinstated as 'compared to . . . Sadat's marginalization of the field and its actors' (Mehrez, 2008: 3) – that the emergence of Youth Salons, sponsored by the Ministry of Culture in 1989, as well as the Nitaq Festival, sponsored by the independent nonprofit Townhouse Gallery (established in 1998), began to emerge. However, after Mubarak's term as president was extended for another six years, as well as a growth in suspicions that he was grooming his son Gamal to be his successor, civil society and pro-democracy groups began to form. Within this charged atmosphere (in which Mubarak faced both local and international pressure to institute greater democratic reforms), the Writers and Artists for Change were formed in 2005 – a year which marked a 'historic mobilization of civil society organizations and groups' (Mehrez, 2008: 4). In their founding statement, read by renowned Egyptian poet Ahmad Fouad Negm, the group argued for the emancipation of the political and cultural fields, and 'reaffirm[ed] the historic role and responsibility of Egypt's writers and artists . . . as the spearhead for change, since the nineteenth century *nahda* [renaissance]' (Mehrez, 2008: 1). The group provided a powerful reaffirmation that the cultural field was directly constitutive of the political field, and that the lack of inclusion and participation in the latter meant restriction and exclusion in the former:

> For this nascent movement, political freedom *is* cultural freedom and no regime can claim to be democratic without according freedom of opinion and expression in all fields of knowledge and creative endeavour. (Mehrez, 2008: 1, italics in original)

However, the Writers for Artists and Change, which initiated several protests calling for cultural and political reform (Mehrez, 2008: 2–7), eventually dissolved due to the precarious nature of the cultural field, which found cultural producers occupying positions in which they hold an 'ambiguous relationship that is at once their patron and persecutor' (ibid: 6):

> Its gradual collapse was not much of a surprise given the continued differences in interests, ideological orientations and generational aspirations of the various cultural producers . . . their concern for the 'space of imagination' and the 'creative drive' . . . seem to gauge the question of the cultural field, yet in the statement [at the 2005 June rally] they reaffirmed their historical role and responsibility as the spearhead for change in the country: an affirmation that recasts them in a political reformist role of which they have been stripped not just by the state but by the Muslim Brotherhood who . . . have 'monopolized' the oppositional scene 'for too long'. (Mehrez, 2008: 6)

Yet regardless of the group's dissolution, artistic groups and acts of creative dissent continued, albeit sporadically. Representing an art group formed prior to the uprising was i-Catalyst (founded in 2007), which, although it was a short-lived initiative, still 'made an impact on the overall art scene in Cairo' (Jarbou, 2010) and represented the early beginnings of a more creative and informal use of art that was found on the margins of the cultural field by indirectly questioning the dominant political and cultural hegemony of the state (ibid). Another group, Graphics Against the System (GAS) (founded by artist and activist Mohamed Gaber), was a 'visual agitation project aimed at producing artworks and designs that agitate people and create political and social awareness' (ibid). Gaber was nearly arrested for creating a work with a clenched fist with the words 'Be with art' written underneath (Charbel, 2010). A conversation with the police officer who planned to arrest him is indicative of the entrenched notion that art is regulated by the state and belongs within the formal, and not public, realm:

> The officer told us, 'You need permits from the Ministry of Culture so that you can display these works in galleries.' Gaber explained that 'this is street art for public display,' to which the officer responded, 'Finish this one and leave, or else you'll come with us where you can spend the night in our company'. (ibid)

Although the most widespread forms of graffiti typically tended to be 'commercial advertisements . . . marriage registrars, driving instructors, private tutors, and slogans in support of football teams [as well as] religious graffiti' (ibid), the earlier incident is indicative that creative dissent on the walls did exist, but was typically less visible due to their immediate whitewashing by Mubarak's regime. According to Ahmad Maher, an Egyptian artist who only a year before the uprising was arrested for spray painting political slogans, all graffiti is considered vandalism, although punishable measures are evidently restricted towards certain kinds of graffiti and street art, especially those calling for political reform and change:

> Graffiti can be found just about everywhere – in the form of spray painted advertisements . . . [w]hile the authorities may object to such graffiti, what they will never tolerate is graffiti with a message of opposition. All our graffiti has been painted over since our arrest. (Charbel, 2010)

Movements and incidents such as these acted as significant precedents to the 2011 uprising and to the formation of contemporary movements such as the Revolution

Artists Union (RAU) during the revolution itself, and serve as an important historical reminder that 25 January 2011 did not emerge within an isolated context by a formerly passive and subservient population, but were subsumed within decades of historic acts of political and cultural resistance against state domination and repression.

Chapter 3

THE FIRST PHASE

THE FIRST EIGHTEEN DAYS OF THE EGYPTIAN REVOLUTION (25 JANUARY 2011–11 FEBRUARY 2011)

> Tahrir square, and particularly the 18-day protest, came to stand for a hopeful process of revolutionary change, and participation in Tahrir Square became an important category through which people experienced themselves and others as participating in a revolutionary effort that expressed the collective power of the Egyptian people.
>
> Mark Peterson (2015a: 166).

Public art – or art in public spaces – in the Mubarak era was relegated to the confines of state-sanctioned public works of art or monuments, encapsulated within state institutions and national museums or set up in approved public spaces. In this manner, art was regulated by the Ministry of Culture and the Supreme Council of Culture, two entities which were derided for their monopolization, nepotism, mismanagement and control of cultural production (see Winegar, 2006). The content of public art was thus conditioned by regulations of power and authority. Art or writing outside of these confines which contained any hint of opposition to or criticism of the regime was swiftly erased (Charbel, 2010). Independent cultural institutions are well aware that government officials can indiscriminately shut them down,[1] which is why they may not accept work which may cause them to be put on the radar of government censors, which could lead to a temporary suspension of their activities, or worse, permanent closure by state officials. The word 'independent' refers to privately run/private ownership, as they are not government affiliated/owned, yet still remain under the regulation, censorship and control[2] of the state and so do not have full autonomy over what they can showcase within – and on – their walls. This direct control of public – and private – spaces created another form of indirect control through a preventative environment of self-censorship which minimized the presence and showcase of acts of (artistic) dissent.

Prior to the revolution, street 'art' consisted primarily of advertising images of a non-threatening commercial nature, along with the scribbling of occasional profanities, support for various football teams by their fans (such as the Ultras, who support Al Ahly, and the White Knights, who support Zamalek), and proclamations of love. This omission of dissent is a 'crucial indication of what [the] current ideology [would] not allow' (Fyfe, Law, 1988: 123) and is, perhaps, one of the reasons renowned journalist Robert Fisk mused that the Arab world was 'so backwards' (Fisk, 2011) – 'the street, the country as a physical entity, belongs to someone else' (Fisk, 2011). There is no real sense of ownership by the citizens, no sense of autonomy or the ability to protest or dissent without risk of being attacked, killed or imprisoned without trial by government officials, and so their presence in public spaces is limited to passive (versus active) acts, such as 'walking, driving, watching – or in other ways that the state dictates' (Bayat, 2010: 11).

Yet this regular state of affairs was temporarily suspended for a brief moment in time, beginning with the first eighteen days of the Egyptian revolution, in which there was a breach/rupture and a subsequent 'collapse of [the normative] order' (Thomassen, 2009: 19) which saw the active use of public space in ways previously unseen in Egypt's modern history. The revolution's almost immediate disruption of the status quo saw an outpouring of individual and collective acts of dissent and creativity, which was romanticized, mystified, imagined and lived in the consciousness of those who participated in and watched the widespread coverage in January and February 2011. Millions of viewers, myself included, were in absolute awe of the massive collective energy, conduct and solidarity shown by the protestors in Tahrir Square (as the de facto centre of the revolution) and throughout Egypt. Yet viewing it was different than those who physically experienced its day-to-day uncertainties, battles and struggles, and through my interviews, I began to develop a greater understanding of why those eighteen days acted as what Hanan Sabea (associate professor of anthropology at the American University in Cairo) called a critical imaginary, a 'time out of time' (Sabea, 2013) that is able to continuously travel 'both spatially and temporally' (ibid, 2013) within the narratives of those I spoke to, even several years on after the initial 25 January 2011 revolution.

Tahrir Square

One of the most significant recurring themes that came across in my interviews as to the enduring effect of Tahrir Square as a revolutionary symbol within their consciousness was the importance of the significant blurring of 'geographical, physical, and symbolic separation [which] had been central to class distinctions' (Peterson, 2015b). This led to the emergence of communities, or a 'spontaneous communitas' (Turner, 1969: 132) – an organic manifestation leading to an intense sense of solidarity and collectivity – in which gender, class and sociopolitical distinctions were effaced and replaced by a sort of society of equals.

The inspiring sight of tens of thousands of Egyptians from all walks of life – representing every social, economic and political class – descending upon Tahrir Square in downtown Cairo to join the protests called for by the April 6 movement and the 'We are all Khaled Said' Facebook page still remains a significant imaginary to this day because it became representative of a physical and symbolic space where the status quo was suspended.

Dia El Said, an Egyptian graffiti artist who lives in a gated community in a more well-to-do area of Cairo, told me he did not get involved in any protests before the revolution, and that 25 January was the first protest he ever went to. When I asked him why he decided to join this particular protest after remaining apolitical, he said that he was encouraged by the announcement of the protest on the 'We are all Khaled Said' page, and said he felt something 'different' about this protest. He said his feelings were confirmed when he went to Tahrir and witnessed for himself people of all backgrounds interacting, sharing, supporting and helping each other. He told me he could not believe it and felt that it was

The best period in Egypt. It was really a utopia. You would see a complete *shab'eeh* [a slang word for thug], who was raised in a completely different way sitting with someone from AUC [the American University in Cairo, which implies – generally – that they were more priviliged, liberal, English speaking, amd Westernized] talking together normally. Not only was there no harassment but people were actually initiating conversations with each other. Everyone had one purpose, which was to say one word – 'leave'. So anyone who was with me saying that word it meant the both of us were on the same team, and that we're friends. (Dia El Said, Cairo, pers.comm., 27 July 2014)

This was echoed by Hala El Sharouny, who described the scene of the revolution:

The first time you saw another world was in Tahrir. You were like are these actually Egyptians cleaning after themselves? And whoever had some food in their hand would give it to the person next to them. Then you would find another person distributing juice boxes to people, people in *jellabiya's* talking politics next to activitsts. Salafi's and Brotherhood members were talking to girls who were not wearing the *hijab* [headscarf] and to the girl who drinks and smoke cigarettes.[3] Inside Tahrir it was a state within a state, the best part of people came out during those 18 days because they had one goal. I will never forget it. All of these people suffered from oppression in one form or another. (Hala El Sharouny, Cairo, pers. comm., 18 August 2014)

As most of those I interviewed relayed to me, it was on the very first day of protests on 25 January that it became apparent a seismic change had occurred, and that it was the first time that collective goals and communal solidarity took precedence over individual self-interest. Keizer drew parallels to the spirituality felt within one's revolutionary experience in Tahrir among thousands of bodies consciously moving towards a mutual objective – as being akin to the ultimate spiritual experience in Islam, which is the holy pilgrimage (*Hajj*[4]), where bodies move in unison around the *Ka'abah*[5] for the purpose of worshipping Allah.

First two weeks I was camping out in Tahrir. The experience was pretty up there with a lot of other spiritual experiences I had, for example being in Mecca around a badgillion [*sic*] people and moving in harmony in one movement, one rhythm, that is something. In terms of the amount of people, this one tops everything else I experienced . . . I think it was the most civilized state we will ever see in this country, I think we will never go back to that. I think it boiled down to the people that were really fighting for freedom and seeking it for others and themselves . . . those were the people that were there, and if you were there in that corner of time [for those first two weeks], then you really got it and felt what a revolution was. (Keizer, Cairo, pers. comm., 29 April 2014)

Keizer was alluding to solidarity acts as stemming from an 'intense feeling of community, social equality, solidarity, and togetherness experienced by those who live together in a site in which the normal social statuses and positions have broken down' (Peterson, 2012: 6). The idea of a gathering of a collective in a revolutionary moment in time being compared to a divine experience, a utopia and a spiritual ritual was a common method of describing the affective experience of bodies gathered together in unison in a spirit of community and cooperation during the eighteen days in Tahrir. As Turner argued, whereas structure 'tends to be pragmatic and this-worldly' (1969: 133), communitas (during the liminal moment of anti-structure) 'breaks in through the interstices of structure . . . [i]t is almost everywhere held to be sacred or "holy", possibly because it transgresses or dissolves the norms that governed structured and institutionalized relationships and is accompanied by experiences of unprecedented potency' (1969: 128). This is the exact sentiment that was repeatedly described to me – as a form of forlorn nostalgia – by those who were in Tahrir. This was an otherwordly, holy and sacred – 'you had to be there to truly comprehend' – experience.

Mira Shihadeh was one of those who witnessed, and then subsequently participated in, one of the uprising's key events on 28 January 2011 dubbed the 'Friday of Rage' from a friend's apartment building which overlooks the Qasr El Nil bridge, which connects Tahrir Square in downtown to the Opera House in Gezirah. She also explained the uprising as a divine experience:

I only went down on the 28th of January. . . . There was no mobile phones or internet, they cut it off for 5 or 6 days I think, and that made me go down on the 28th I knew something was happening . . . this is what made people go down, including me. . . . I went down several times at the time, there was this atmosphere of peace and uncertainty. And people were there waiting and resting from their tear gas, and there was a quiet eerie feeling in Tahrir square, not knowing if the army was going to come in again and not knowing what the army would do if they do come in again. You do know you are on the side of truth, and we are together and there is unity – there was something very divine about that, and very alive, and very 'kill me now I have done my part.' There was that feeling. The civilized conduct between people, and women, and there was a genuine sincere fight. It was like God was on our side, I really believe that. There was something amazing. (Mira Shihadeh, pers. comm., 30 April 2014)

For most of those I spoke to, the first eighteen days of the revolution were so powerful in their displays of solidarity and community that they still felt its life-changing effect on them, even years later. For example, while initially indifferent to politics, El Zeft, an anonymous Egyptian revolutionary artist, explained that the events of 25 January completely transformed him and permanently made him interested in political issues. He described his experience in Tahrir Square as 'living elsewhere in a parallel universe. It was a shock' (El Zeft, Cairo, pers. comm., 27 April 2014). He kept repeating the word 'normal' to describe behaviour traditionally deemed abnormal and unacceptable in Egyptian society, such as girls smoking cigarettes and sleeping outside in public places, and dressing as they like without threat of harassment,[6] which is a serious – and daily – threat to women in Egypt. As he recalled,

> I was in Tahrir from the first day. . . . I felt I was living elsewhere in a parallel universe. It was a shock . . . girls slept in Tahrir it was normal and they smoked cigarettes and dressed however they wanted. . . . it was normal. Everyone was sitting together, it was pure anarchy, people were living in a way I will never forget in all my life. We were living and we had food and tents and no one bothered anyone else. A mixture of levels of people together, there was no contempt no one looked at the other with a superior look (El Zeft, Cairo, pers. comm., 27 April 2014)

Hala El Sharouny reminisced about how people cleaned streets together, KIM, an anonymous Egyptian street artist, spoke of a sense of self-sacrifice that he had never witnessed, and Ganzeer spoke of a renewed sense of national identity he felt as he witnessed new forms of civility on the streets, acts that Salwa Ismail described as a method of the Egyptian public reclaiming their national dignity from the state (2011) and Jessica Winegar described as the formation of a national family (2011). Others said the experience of the revolution, its very existence, served as a reminder that if one could overturn normative conditions of the structural order, then one could also overcome their own individual, internal limitations. Mohammad Khaled, an illustrator, artist and filmmaker, also known as the 'Winged Elephant', described one of the ways the revolution affected him on a personal level:

> I wasn't confident of myself as an artist, before the revolution I was a story boarder, I draw a storyboard, and when I do something very nice and once in a while people see it and there are comments. But when the revolution happened, there were no limits. Everything inside me changed – me, as a person, no longer had any boundaries in anything I do, and I believed more in what I want to do – if I want to be a filmmaker, why shouldn't I be a film maker? (Mohammed Khaled, Cairo, pers. comm., 29 April 2014)

Most of those whom I spoke to attributed this change in themselves to seeing the change in the re-ordering of subject positions in Tahrir which made them realize that what was self-evident or real during Mubarak's regime was a fabrication. It was in this very sense that the liminal moment of the revolution initiated the 'everything is possible' sentiment that came with the disruption and blurring of ideological, political and social lines and the emergence of a heightened sense of community (*communitas*) as well as an individual agency – the two were intertwined throughout descriptions of experiences of the revolution.

I found that many of those I spoke to said it was difficult for them to articulate the affective and emotive experience one felt during the initial days of the revolution, but that for the most part, they all agreed that they had an immediate sense of kinship and mutual trust established by a greater good which made any form of difference (gender, religion, social class, economic status, age etc.) irrelevant and non-existent. What was considered as 'normal' everyday life under three decades of Mubarak's rule ceased to exist for that particular moment in time – the normal configurations of the everyday no longer existed, as this 'certainly described the situation in Tahrir, in which youth replaced elders as organizers, protests multiplied both in locations and numbers, state security forces were rendered powerless, and headless collectives emerged to manage civil society and domestic security' (Peterson, 2015b: 67–8). And so the initial eighteen days of the revolution with its communal spirit, unity, equality, the breakdown of distinctions and civilized behaviour, which, even several years after the revolution, proved to be as enduring and powerful a critical imaginary as it was during the initial eighteen days of the revolution. As Peterson aptly notes, the liminal moment of those eighteen days, in which there was '[t]his experience of intense social solidarity, creative energy, and commonality of purpose that transcended social divisions is absolutely essential to the significance of Tahrir Square as a revolutionary symbol' (Peterson, 2015b: 67). Tahrir – a physical and symbolic space – contained within it a sense of collective purpose, where protestors 'at that time they felt they were something, and that they were a part of something big happening . . . you felt you were part of a big change, you were changing your country you were doing something' (Hend Kheera, Cairo, pers. comm., 26 April 2014).

The state of being what Turner called 'betwixt and between', where sociopolitical categorizations became irrelevant, led to the intense 'sentiment of "humankindness", a sense of the generic social bond between all members of society' (Turner, 1969: 116), in which egalitarian behaviour – in the sociopolitical and cultural sphere – became a critical imaginary of the Egyptian revolution which greatly affected those I interviewed. The communal cooperation during the liminal moment and the blurring of distinctions reinforced the memory of Tahrir as the iconic symbol of the revolution, which continues to serve as an affective location of their revolutionary experience which transcends both time and space. During the first eighteen days of the Egyptian revolution, creative practices were organic, improvised and, most importantly, informed by practical considerations. Interactivity was a key underlying theme in understandings of art and would greatly affect the ways in which art was understood in the initial eighteen days of the revolution, whereby artists and the public alike were involved in the spontaneous creation and visual aesthetic of the revolution.

Yet it was more than that. As Peterson notes, liminality is not just about grand transitions or wonderfully creative, spontaneous acts – it also necessarily 'involved a breakdown of social norms at microsocial levels' (Peterson, 2015b: 68). That breakdown during the eighteen days of Tahrir involved a

> diminishment of the practices of bodily separation that are typically a means of producing class distinctions in Egypt, as doctors, tradesmen, students, housewives, engineers, shopkeepers, street vendors and many, many unemployed rubbed shoulders in the crowded Cairo centre (Hafez, 2012). Age distinctions were muted. . . . Sectarian unity was also exhibited, with Christians forming a cordon of their bodies around their praying Muslim comrades, and Muslims vowing to protect Christians in turn . . . ordinary Egyptians formed security and neighbourhood watch groups and took on the responsibilities of policing not only Tahrir but communities throughout Cairo (El-Mahy, 2012). Similarly, voluntary work crews managed the flow of rubbish during the occupation of the Square . . . [c]leaning up the trash was a literal enactment of the people taking care of the centre of Cairo because they had reclaimed it, but it was also symbolic of the growing sense that they were taking out the political trash that had polluted their country for so long, and caring for one another as fellow citizens in a national family (Winegar, 2011). (Peterson, 2015b: 68–9)

These acts could not be underestimated in their role in creating a critical imaginary which still affected those I interviewed, for the simple reason that it was entirely different from how things were before. This breakdown at a microsocial level during liminal times

> gain their salience from their difference from the norms that had been in place before. Prior to the gathering in Tahrir Square, geographical, physical and symbolic separations had been central to class distinctions in Egypt (Peterson, 2011a). Deference to elders and submission to their leadership has long been a deeply held part of family and community life (Badran, 1995). Periodic Muslim–Christian conflict, particularly over places of worship, was a feature of life, one exploited by the Mubarak regime as part of its rationale for necessary authoritarianism. And cleaning the Square is an act that can only be understood in the context of decades of indifference to dirt, litter and pollution by both civilians and the state. (Winegar, 2011) (Peterson, 2015b: 69)

The experience of Tahrir led to the creation of these civic-minded subjectivities because it produced a new way of seeing – and being – in the world, which was critical to its endurance as a revolutionary symbol, even years after the initial rupture of the eighteen days of the Egyptian revolution.

Iconic days

Although the first day of the revolution was significant in setting the stage for the rupture in the normative order, it was the 'Friday of Rage', as the events of

28 January 2011 were called, that became one of the most iconic days of the eighteen days of the revolution. This day saw protestors praying in unison during Friday prayers at the famous *Qasr El Nil* bridge (which connects Tahrir Square in downtown to the Opera House in Gezirah) being attacked by water cannons and tear gas by police (see Figures 3.1 and 3.2). This incident formed a powerful aesthetic of resistance, solidarity and continuity in their struggle in the face of unhindered government aggression, in a critical battle which lasted several hours. It was during that moment that the bridge became the space in which the 'oneness' of community bonds was incredibly displayed during a liminal time. The Friday of Rage was a turning point in the early days of the revolution – besides the powerful images of the Qasr El Nil battle on the bridge between protestors and police, the government also imposed a curfew and shut down the internet and disrupted telecommunication services in an effort to quell the protests. Another iconic moment during this time was the burning of Mubarak's National Democratic Party's (NDP) headquarters, a symbolic act further indicating that a barrier of fear had been broken between the regime and the people, which would serve as a strong momentum for the continuation of the revolution.

In his seminal work on liminality, Turner argued that liminal moments – in their inherent ambiguity – always contain an element (and the potential) of destruction. Yet destruction and danger do not necessarily indicate a negative turning point during a transformative moment. In the particular context of the Egyptian revolution, the destruction of the signs and symbols of a much-hated regime (which

Figure 3.1 Protestors praying during Friday prayers on the Qasr El Nil Bridge on 28 January 2011 – the 'Friday of Rage' – while being attacked by the police's water cannons. *Source*: EAWorldView, 2011.

Figure 3.2 Stand-offs between protestors and police on 28 January (The Friday of Rage) on Qasr El Nil Bridge, which show police firing tear gas and water cannons in an effort to push revolutionaries back. *Source*: Ahram Online, 2012.

represented the structural, normative order of the past 30 years) such as police trucks, police stations and the NDP's headquarters represented, to many of those I interviewed, a rational destruction of the dangerous and demeaning system which preserved the repressive structure of a regime which kept the Egyptian population in a state of perpetual *ihana* (humiliation). Turner also argued that spontaneous *communitas* had an inexplicably subjective affective component in that there is something '"magical" about it' (1969: 139) which contains 'the feeling of endless power' (1969: 139). This is represented by such moments of collective solidarity such as that shown in Figure 3.1, where the image of protestors continuing to pray together in light of police attacks highlights the extraordinary individual and collective power of the revolutionaries and their resilience in maintaining their ground, illustrating the strength of the convictions of their belief that it is just and right to defy Mubarak's three-decade-long oppressive regime. Violence and resistance go hand in hand – as social and cultural anthropologist Samuli Schielke aptly notes, 'we cannot separate beautiful resistance from terrible bloodshed, just as we cannot isolate the flourishing of cultural life from the spread of violent street crime in and after 2011. They belong to one and the same process' (Schielke, 2017: 205). This is reflected in Mohammad Khaled's experience of Tahrir,

> The hope we took from the revolution from 18 days of happiness . . . people died but for the first time you felt that the value of your life was very small compared to you wanting people to live a better life. . . .It was a dream, a real dream. Words arrived to you and made you believe – the moment of the word *irja'a* [come back], when we were standing and the police would come in with

hoses and ammunition and tear gas and all that, we would all run away, but there would be about fifteen or twenty people that stayed standing and would shout come back come back, and we would come back. Just the fact that 15 people from the hundreds standing would say come back, we would just listen and come back. There was no social differences no physical differences, I accepted you and you accepted me. (Mohammed Khaled, Cairo, pers. comm., 29 April 2014)

The notion of destruction during the first phase was seen not only as logical but also very much necessary. This was not wanton, irrational destruction; this was a targeted destruction of particular symbols of state power as a sign of the public's outright rejection of that power. This was put forward by Ammar Abo Bakr who told me: 'My refusal of state security institutions is because they are the ones who . . . steal and they are the thieves and then they come and reprimand the people. That is *baltageyeh* (thuggery). So I believe our refusal of these institutions is rational, because this is not acceptable' (Ammar Abo Bakr, Cairo, pers. comm., 30 April 2014). To many of those I spoke to, the Egyptian revolution aimed to destroy the status quo and that anyone who assisted in (socially, politically, culturally and economically) the maintenance and support of the status quo must be destroyed along with it. The structural corruption of Mubarak's regime was characterized as being dangerous, irrational and abnormal, and the revolution was an attempt to signify the way things should be – a civilized, rational, state of affairs. As such, the interviews I conducted indicated that for the most part, their roles and understanding of their work had been redefined within this new temporal register, or liminal time – in that the destruction of corrupt political elements *necessitated* the destruction of corrupt cultural elements. Ammar Abo Bakr makes this point clear:

I am participating in a revolution and a revolution is itself illegal and an act against the law. Terms and terminology that you want to apply in a society that is different from yours and that is in a *revolutionary* [he strongly emphasized this word] state, which means it is breaking all rules and laws and conventions – part of this is the gallery with the artist who sits in the atelier who is sad that the art market has stopped. This artist is a bastard, because he is completely isolated from his society and the goal of his art is to sell his work to the group of aristocrats and the capitalists who are all dirty *fulool* [regime sympathizers], and since the *fulool* left Egypt during the revolution and don't want to spend money on art, so he has to hate the revolution, though he may act like he loves the revolution since he is an artist. Yet he isn't an artist and isn't part of the revolution, he just wants to take advantage of capitalism, and the revolution wants to destroy capitalism and the revolution hopes to go to these people who own all this real estate and villas and take it from them. Whoever wants to call it brutal, chaotic, destructive, so be it, because the revolution wants to destroy the foundations [of the existing system]. (Ammar Abo Bakr, Cairo, pers. comm., 30 April 2014)

Destruction of Mubarak's structural, normative order as a rational strategy of the revolution (in order to make way for new ideas, a new structure, a new order) was a common theme conveyed by many I spoke to, including artist Mohamed Alaa, who said that just as the revolution sought to destroy the unjust status quo through physical and material means, art must also symbolically destroy old ideas, and parallel this notion of destruction of normative forms of artistic expressions in order to make way for the accommodation of new norms, in that

> art helps changes understandings of a lot of things, to destroy, and that is the idea behind the art project of destruction that I am working on, to break and destroy a lot of things, destroy taboos, traditions, a lot of things that we do without thinking, things that we do just because we were born into it, and the ideas of *haram* [permissible] and *halal* [forbidden] which enter into everything in differing degrees. . . . So this is the idea of destruction, that we need to destroy a lot of things, but the question is do we destroy things until they collapse or destroy up to a point and leave some things intact that we can live with? Art does this. Change changes. (Mohamed Alaa, Cairo, pers. comm., 13 August 2014)

Politics is neges

Revolution tends to be associated with political acts, and arguably it was during the critical revolutionary moments in those eighteen days that a suspension of the normative notions of 'politics' became possible. Yet, despite this, many did not see the eighteen days of the revolution as 'doing politics' in the formal sense because, as those I interviewed made clear, their understanding of the term was something that was located within the purview of the state, and so the revolutionaries distanced themselves from politics, because, as Saiko Maino said, they believed it was seen as 'something *neges* [impure, foul]' (Saiko Maino, Cairo, pers. comm., 26 August 2014). Using the word *neges* has a higher significance and level of emphasis than saying, for example, that politics is *wasekh* (dirty), as the Arabic word *neges* is used to imply something that is impure, and in Islam only by performing ablution (*wu'du*) can one 'cleanse' themselves in order to purify one's self – it is thus used to denote both a moral and physical impurity. Attaching the term 'politics' to *neges* implies to what degree the term is considered repugnant and something untouchable on both an internal and external level and therefore should be avoided for fear of one also becoming impure. When one discusses revolution as a form of 'doing' politics, it is important to understand that politics is not a blanket term that can be applied to every situation equally, nor in this particular case was it something that the revolutionaries wanted to 'do', but something they wanted to subvert (in the way it was understood as being solely within the corrupt purview of the state) and redefine altogether.

For many of those I spoke to, their experience within the revolution was not understood as 'doing' politics but as simply 'resistance in the most basic, instinctive sense' (Ryzova, 2011b) against a regime which systematically humiliated them. It was not only indiscriminate police brutality which was a source of humiliation, it was also the poor public education and health care they received, the inept and corrupt rule of a regime of crony capitalists which kept millions living under the poverty line who resorted to living on the streets or in makeshift slums, it was a lack of basic decent infrastructure, it was stifling censorship, bureaucracy and government ineptitude and corruption. Humiliation was entrenched and pervasive within all levels of society.

The writings on the walls during the eighteen days of the Egyptian revolution

The majority of those I interviewed said they were completely immersed in the revolutionary experience during the initial eighteen days of the revolution, and, as such, did not have time to produce revolutionary art during those early days, where street battles and clashes between government security forces became pervasive. Revolutionary art at the time took a backseat to the more pressing needs of the revolution.

> During the 18 days of the revolution . . . nor two months after . . . did I do any graffiti no stencils I didn't even record any videos. My cousin would ask why I didn't record anything at this time, but I was so hooked up with the operations during those 18 days I didn't have time to document it, I was living it. It was overwhelming, and I never thought for a second to record it or do a stencil. (Amr Nazeer, Cairo, pers. comm., 9 March 2014)

When the revolution began, graffiti, or the scribbling on walls and tanks, was a crucial method of information and communication for many, when all other technological forms were completely cut off (see Figure 3.3), and played a vital role in getting messages and updates across to the public as a sort of 'journal for the revolution', according to Layla Amr, who was still in middle school at the time (Layla Amr, Cairo, pers. comm., 1 May 2014). Ammar Abo Bakr labelled the walls during this time as a 'newspaper' and Saiko said that when all telecommunications were cut, the stencils he made with his friends (which, he said, played a very important role during the eighteen days revolution for its ability to be sprayed on quickly to avoid the police) acted like 'markers of the revolution' (Saiko Maino, Cairo, pers. comm., 26 August 2014), by continuously reporting what was going on or informing people where to head to for the next round of protests (ibid., 26 August 2014). As Ammar Abo Bakr noted,

> When graffiti was written all over army tanks saying 'Down with Mubarak' . . . it was a sign for the people at home as if telling them the army approved, because the army would have never allowed people to write this on their tanks if they did not approve. From what I understood in those 18 days this was a major sign that encouraged people to go down. Everyone focused on this sentence without tying it to graffiti or to writing, and artists did not write it, it was just regular

people who had markers in their pockets or random spray cans or any tool they could use to be able to write. They would lend each other money to buy things they could write with on tanks. This was pure popular action and had nothing to do with artists. In my opinion most artists at this time were acting the same way, for me during the 18 days I didn't draw anything, I was like the public I just wrote information on the walls, this was more important because it was a revolutionary tactic and we were in the midst of a revolution, how could I draw while I am in the midst of a revolution during those 18 days? I want the collective, as they move, to read crucial information on the walls. (Ammar Abo Bakr, Cairo, pers. comm., 30 April 2014)

The liminal moment made it possible for those who went out to protest to actively use the space they were in – either to communicate, create, motivate or articulate some sort of demands, in a very real effort to materialize their presence both physically and symbolically. During the early days of the revolution, when it was unclear whether Mubarak would indeed step down, it was not considered trendy or artistic to write on walls; rather, it was an organic, natural and necessary act for people from different backgrounds to communicate with drawings or words, either revolutionary slogans, messages warning revolutionaries to be careful or articulating demands from the public. Perhaps one of the reasons why one was awestruck by the graffiti and writings of the eighteen days was because it was part of a larger, improvised performance of revolution which captured the imagination in its sheer ingenuity. As Armbrust argues, Tahrir was a 'symbolically prominent performance space' which was also 'famously improvisational' (Armbrust, 2015: 88) through sociopolitical and cultural acts, which made

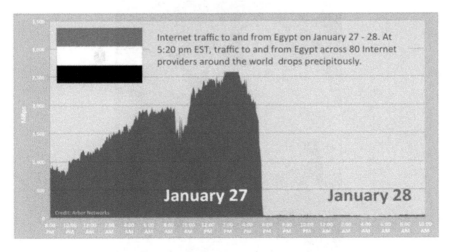

Figure 3.3 Graph which shows the sudden drop in internet connectivity on 28 January 2011 – the 'Friday of Rage'. *Source*: Labovitz, 2011.

[c]ountless observers marvel at the clever signs made, astonishingly, by novice activists with no previous history of protesting; at the creative use of history in invoking political resistance movements of earlier eras such as the student movement of the early 1970s, the 1919 Revolution against British imperialism, or cultural icons of the Nasser era; poetic slogans; 'tweets from Tahrir'; or in some moments, the flexible tactics used to organize battles against regime forces. (Armbrust, 2015: 88)

It was this improvisation, by people from various socio-economic backgrounds, which arguably 'made the 25 January Revolution so compelling to the world' (Armbrust, 2015: 88). During those eighteen days, the ingenuity of using the walls to communicate (when most forms of communication were effectively cut off) and openly delegitimize Mubarak and his regime by expressing ones disdain and dissent on the walls, on the streets, on tanks, on government buildings, as Figures 3.4–3.7 show, was not only embraced by those I spoke to, many of which became the famous revolutionary artists of the Egyptian revolution, but also embraced by non-artists, by ordinary people in the streets. This organic, popular reaction to the transformative moment of the revolution and the need to function, archive, communicate, warn, express dissent or motivate fulfilled a crucial need in that particular moment in time and produced a revolutionary narrative embodied by the improvised voices of those involved in the 'thick' of the revolutionary moment. As El Teneen said, simply the fact that one could now 'do' something that has

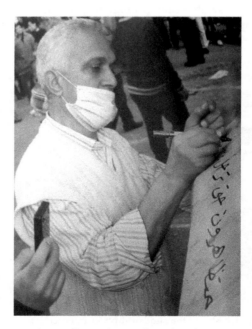

Figure 3.4 A protestor writes on 'Protesting until you leave' on an army tank.

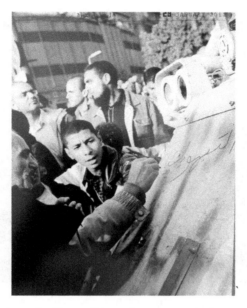

Figure 3.5 A protestor writes 'Be careful, guys', on an army tank.

Figure 3.6 A protestor writes 'Leave, Leave, Mubarak'.

Figure 3.7 Protestors riding an army tank with the words 'Down with Mubarak', on Mohamed Mahmoud Street *Source*: Walls of Freedom (2013: 26–9).

never been done before – such as openly writing or drawing one's disdain for the regime on public spaces and places – was itself an empowering and transformative act. For El Zeft, it epitomized the rupture in the structural order and that itself was revolutionary art at its finest because it was a completely new way of doing things, a transgression of the fiercely guarded public space of Mubarak's regime by everyone and anyone – 'the people who wrote "Hosni Mubarak should fall" on the tanks, this is pure art – pure art. I wish I did it (see Figure 3.8)' (El Zeft, Cairo, pers. comm., 27 April 2014).

This understanding of art as a mode of antagonistic intervention embedded within the revolutionary process was embraced by several of those I spoke to. Mohamed Alaa said that he could not separate political action from cultural action and so he wanted to take the opportunity in the early days of the revolution to use art to create deliberate connections with the people gathered in Tahrir Square. He recounted to me how he placed a blank 50-metre parchment (see Figures 3.9 and 3.10) on the ground during the early days of the revolution and entitled it 'Work on the Streets' (Mohamed Alaa, Cairo, pers. comm., 18 August 2014). In this project various people – men, women, children, conservatives, liberals – could draw and express their hopes and dreams for the future. The act initiated dialogue but it also revealed deep-seated societal tensions and created conflicts, such as when a man became angry and tore the paper as someone left their shoe imprint (mistakenly) over the name of Allah. The idea of art was about being co-present with the public and therefore about being connected – either positively or negatively (in that the art is not necessarily intended to garner approval) – and stimulating engagement

Figure 3.8 A stranger offered to carry Hany Khaled on his shoulders so he could spray 'Down with Hosny Mubarak' on a wall during the Egyptian revolution. *Source*: Hany Khaled.

Figure 3.9 Egyptians in Tahrir during the revolution, writing their hopes and dreams on Mohamed Alaa's 50-metre parchment *Source*: Mohamed Alaa.

with other artists and between members of a community. Mohammed Khaled spoke to me about a similar experience, whereby he drew on the floor in Tahrir Square which initiated a dialogue between him and other protestors which encouraged him to continue doing it, and that the conflict – between himself, the art and the public in which some people removed his graffiti – made him feel that 'this is the nicest thing about it, you truly are in a real struggle with the

Figure 3.10 Egyptians in Tahrir during the revolution, writing their hopes and dreams on Mohamed Alaa's 50-metre parchment *Source*: Mattei di Vincenzo, 2011.

street. You put something that is going to be read and seen, and people who hate it will remove it – this motivated me even more' (Mohammed Khaled, Cairo, pers. comm., 29 April 2014). The ambiguity, struggle and uncertainty of the revolutionary moment was never characterized as a negative liminal moment in time, rather, it was characterized as liberating for its endless possibilities and potential.

Revolutionary Artists Union

Although those I interviewed, for the most part, were not involved in creating art during the initial days of the revolution, an iconic group called the Egyptian Revolutionary Artists Union (RAU), or *Rabitat fannani al-thawra*', was formed in which artists and non-artists alike gathered to draw, converse and articulate their demands of the revolution and hang their art on the walls for all to see, inviting anyone to join in one of the most democratic and cultural manifestations of the Egyptian revolution. The RAU, an organic, grassroots movement initially formed by twenty-one[7] artists, poets, filmmakers and musicians during the eighteen days of the revolution, had the aim of bringing together and channelling the raw, creative and artistic potential and talent of ordinary citizens during the revolution, with their makeshift 'headquarters' and open space exhibition located near the corner of Talaat Harb and Tahrir Square, by the Kentucky Fried Chicken (see Figures 3.11 and 3.12). Revolutionaries dubbed the artwork from this location

Figure 3.11 The RAU's 'headquarters' and gallery by the KFC, Tahrir Square *Source*: TahrirNews, 2011.

Figure 3.12 RAU's headquarters during the revolution, where people drew, conversed and witnessed the organic manifestations of cultural production during the Egyptian revolution. *Source*: Alisdaire Hickson, Flickr, 2011.

as 'The KFC Gallery'. The anti-structural nature of the liminal crisis instigated an openness, inclusiveness and inherently participatory form of behaviour and impromptu acts leading to the organic formation of movements such as the RAU, which embodied the combined political and artistic liminal moment of communitas and openness to the 'play of thought, feeling, and will' (Turner, 1969: vii) of the early revolutionary moment. The importance of the ability to openly create art which rejects and resists the normative order in such a significant location – by ordinary people and artists alike – symbolizes the anti-structure of the liminal moment of those eighteen days, because this type of public, defiant and creative act of dissent was unheard of during Mubarak's rule.

Formed during the Day of Rage on 28 January, the RAU's intent was to keep a 'cultural revolution' ongoing, as their belief was that in order for the political revolution to succeed, the mentality of the people needs to be changed through cultural expression using artistic mediums to spread awareness on the demands of the revolution. However, their activities were not just limited to the first phase of the revolution within those eighteen days in Tahrir Square. They later spread their activities outside of Tahrir to hold conferences and exhibitions in Cairo Atelier, Prince Taz Palace, Giza Cultural Palace and Egypt Center Gallery during the span of 2011 (Adel, 2012). The RAU also did not just focus on cultural centres, they also spread their revolutionary cultural message in unconventional places such as the Sadat Metro Station in downtown Cairo, where they organized a 'subway gallery' to exhibit photographs, paintings and caricatures from the early days of the revolution (Adel, 2011), and 'held workshops at Dar Aytam Sondos for young orphans and children with special needs' (Adel, 2011). Guided by the belief that a shift in the political landscape necessitated a shift in the cultural landscape brought to light countless creative and unconventional exhibitions by the RAU and others[8] between 2011 and 2013

However, it seems that the movement has lost momentum in the aftermath of the final phase of the revolution (which was the case for most artists, as will be discussed in Chapter 6), as their official site on Facebook shows that their last post was in August 2015, with no activity apparent since that time.

The initial eighteen days of the revolution fit neatly into Turner's concept of liminality, and was, according to many I spoke to, representative of 'an alternative experience of ambiguity, a time when unity and possibilities for real, meaningful change seemed genuinely within reach' (Peterson, 2015b: 69). The first phase of the Egyptian revolution represented, according to those I spoke to, a period of transformation – a breakdown of old thoughts, norms and behaviours, which embodied the 'anything can happen' potential of the liminal moment, characterized by ambiguity yet also hope because at the time 'anything' (and everything) did happen, in a sense (through creative, organic political and cultural acts of expression). Yet the subsequent phases of the revolution are not as clear-cut, as after Mubarak's ouster, there were those who wanted to pack up and leave Tahrir and restore order, while others wanted to stay and insisted that the revolution was only just beginning and that their key demands had not been met. This would later serve as a key source of tension between those who saw revolutionary art as a visual return to chaos and disruption. The second phase of the revolution saw art remain as part of the revolutionary aesthetic and process, as it marked key events during significant moments of military rule, which I discuss in the following chapter.

Chapter 4

THE SECOND PHASE OF THE REVOLUTION

SUPREME COUNCIL OF ARMED FORCES (SCAF) RULE (FEBRUARY 2011–JUNE 2012)

The second phase of the revolution was characterized by mixed emotions – there was a sense of pride and accomplishment in Mubarak's resignation, however, many felt cautious and anxious when protestors left Tahrir and the military announced it would 'safeguard' the revolution. The anti-structure and communitas of the initial eighteen days seemed to give way to a return to the status quo as SCAF tried to quickly contain the revolution and its supporters. This critical phase saw the revolutionaries enter a 'situation and space' (Peterson, 2015a: 172) Turner called the arena, which is 'the situation in which new symbolic structures and cultural configurations are established and organized into a new social order. As the name suggests, the arena is a site of struggle between groups promoting different models of sociocultural structure. This describes the situation in Egypt after Mubarak's resignation' (Peterson, 2015a: 172).

For those who were wary of SCAF's takeover, it seemed to mark the beginning of the end of the revolution as political and social divisions began to take place, political alliances formed and sides taken. The main question at this time was, 'what next?'. After the initial euphoria of the eighteen days, there was no clear next step in the revolution's progression; 'while the transition from Mubarak necessarily plunged Egypt into a liminal state, experienced first as communitas, nobody knew what to do next. There was no "something else"' (Armbrust, 2017: 227).

Yet even within an environment of uncertainty and struggle after SCAF took control of the country, and perhaps because of it – the aftermath of the eighteen days inspired the continued growth of a counter-cultural scene which initially emerged from the sense of ownership and control of public space gained during the first phase of the revolution. This ushered in – as Elliot Colla suggested – a 'DIY spirit on the street' (Shenker, 2011), whereby people felt that

> they can look after themselves following a revolution. They police their own blocks, they pick up their own trash, and they can paint on walls. They don't need

permission from anyone. It's a fundamental shift. Before, the initial assumption regarding anyone doing anything on the street was always 'who let you do that?' Now the initial assumption is 'I can do that'. (Shenker, 2011)

This attitude was reflective not only within the sociopolitical sphere but also in the cultural sphere, whereby artist and activist Ganzeer argued that regardless of the potential backlash by the authorities for the open cultural scene, an '[artistic] door has been opened and you can't close it' (Ganzeer, Cairo, Skype Interview, 22 November 2013).

The importance of the street as a liminal space

This period of time ushered in an ambitious and creative new era of revolutionary art – one that evolved from more practical considerations which involved quick communication with stencils and hasty, scribbled messages declaring the illegitimacy of Mubarak's regime and the demands of the people on the walls, streets, and army tanks (which marked the urgency of the revolutionary moment and the organic need for expression and communication during those eighteen days) to large, intricate murals, posters, elaborate stencils and stickers (most of which was made available to download on the internet, such as Ganzeer's iconic 'Mask of Freedom'[1] – see Figure 4.1). The primary target was SCAF, which was extraordinary given the military's 'unquestioned prestige' (Armbrust, 2015: 101) as the central Egyptian institution (and the 'nation's pride', as is commonly reflected in narratives and images of the army). This prestige was swiftly attacked by revolutionaries shortly after Mubarak's ouster, when, on 9 March 2011, 'the SCAF began its first attempt to declare the revolution over by arresting activists who remained in Tahrir Square despite orders to leave' (Armbrust, 2015: 101) and the subsequent 'virginity tests' of at least seven women on 10 March 2011.

Not only did revolutionary art evolve from writings on the wall and rudimentary drawings but it also flourished, intensified and became more collaborative – and varied – in content. From martyr murals, scathing criticisms of the army (where *yasqut hukm al-'askar*, or down with military rule, was frequently seen all over the walls, accompanied by chants during protests), attacks against Mubarak and supporters/remnants of the regime (*fulool*), were all efforts to remind the public of the importance of maintaining the momentum of the 25th January revolution. The intensification of revolutionary art was largely a response to the struggle against military rule in an effort to reconstitute the liminal moment of the initial eighteen days, and characterized most of the second period of the revolution. This would only increase with the escalation of conflict and the militarization of downtown Cairo and Tahrir Square in the winter of 2011 and 2012, which will be discussed in this chapter in greater detail.

Figure 4.1 The Caption on the Poster Reads – 'New! The Mask of Freedom! Salutations from the Supreme Council of the Armed Forces to sons of the beloved nation. Now available for an unlimited period of time.' *Source*: Ganzeer, 2011.

Quelling the revolution and a return to 'Order'

During this transitional period – and in the aftermath of the initial eighteen days of the Egyptian revolution – the authorities swiftly tried to subdue the revolutionaries and regain 'control', instil 'order' and curb any potential 'disruptive influences' (Shenker, 2011). This characterized the struggle of the second phase of the revolution, which would be marked by the magnification of violence and tension between the revolutionaries and the military, as they felt that Mubarak's regime continued under a different guise.

This narrative was articulated in such graffiti as that shown in Figure 4.2, the infamous image of the half-Tantawi/half-Mubarak face. The site of this artwork – on the corner of Mohamed Mahmoud Street and Tahrir Square – is of particular relevance as it is in the midst of two iconic locations of the Egyptian revolution. Tahrir Square being *the* epicentre of the revolution, and Mohamed Mahmoud, nicknamed 'the street of the eyes of freedom' (the site where many revolutionaries lost their eyes to snipers), was a place where many intense street battles between security forces and revolutionaries took place. This particular area is a significant liminal space where the revolution was experienced and lived, and thus a central location of revolutionary art primarily in regards to its position at the centre of key

Figure 4.2 Revolutionary art on the corner of Mohamed Mahmoud Street, showing Mubarak and former field marshal Tantawi's face as one and the same face in March 2011, indicating that the structural order of Mubarak's regime simply continued in a new – military – guise. Above is written 'the Revolution Continues', and below is written '*illi kal'af ma matsh*' or 'whoever delegates does not die' (*kal'af* is a word play on the word *khal'af* from the well-known Arabic proverb, *illi khal'af ma matsh*, or, 'whoever has children does not die', a common proverb in the Arab world) in reference to the continuation of Mubarak's regime (even though he was ousted) under Tantawi's helm. *Source*: Huffington Post, 2014.

revolutionary events, where lives were lost, martyrs mourned and commemorated (see Figures 4.3–4.5), and battles between the government and protestors raged on. Abaza argues that the centrality of this now-iconic street corner represents a 'site of an unfolding continuous dramaturgical performance that visually narrates the history of the revolution' (Abaza, 2013).

This specific corner also represented the state of being 'betwixt and between' and the ambiguous, conflictual nature of the liminal moment of the revolution, as the revolutionary art evolved during different moments in time, which reflected the uncertainty of the revolution's continuity after SCAF took power. Abaza had argued, at the time she published an article on the second anniversary of the Egyptian revolution (January 2013), that as long as the revolution was as of yet 'inconclusive', and that 'as long as Egypt's wielders of power continue to undermine calls for revolutionary change in the country, the walls of Mohamed Mahmoud Street, and many others, will continue to offer an arena for the lively expression of political dissent and resistance. The dramaturgical performance that Mohamed Mahmoud Street is witnessing today will continue to unfold' (Abaza, 2013b). The conflict, ambiguity and danger of the liminal moment produced creative forms

Figure 4.3 Revolutionary art on the street corner of Mohamed Mahmoud Street/Tahrir Square depicting the martyrs of the revolution and an image which says 'Murderous army'. *Source*: Photo by Mona Abaza, Captured 29 August 2012.

Figure 4.4 Revolutionary art on the street corner of Mohamed Mahmoud Street/Tahrir Square, the caption inside the white speech balloon says 'Bread, Freedom, Social Justice' (the slogan of the Egyptian revolution), next to the image of martyrs of the revolution. The red heading says 'Glory to the Martyrs [of the Revolution]'. *Source*: Photo by Mona Abaza, Captured 26 September 2012.

Figure 4.5 Martyrs commemorated on the street corner of Mohamed Mahmoud Street/ Tahrir Square. *Source*: Photo by Mona Abaza, Captured 30 November 2012.

of expression which, even years after the initial eighteen days of the Egyptian revolution, serve as enduring – and powerful – artistic representations reflecting the deep-seated emotions, hopes, struggles and uncertainty of the revolutionaries during a particular moment in Egypt's political and cultural history.

In regard to the importance of location to the creation of art during the second phase of the revolution, many of those I spoke to reaffirmed Abaza's emphasis on the importance of art being located within the actual sites of revolutionary events, such as that particular corner of Mohamed Mahmoud Street/Tahrir Square, and that revolutionary art only made sense when it was created and displayed within these locations to the revolutionary moment, and so should strictly remain within these sites as they serve a particular purpose during a specific moment in time as being part of the revolutionary discourse, through their narrative, commemorative and reflective function. However, it was not just about creating art in symbolic places and spaces which were in the thick of the revolutionary moment, it also became about artists' continued presence in those spaces. In the early days of the revolution, during the first phase, stencils and writings which communicated, for example, new protest locations or warning revolutionaries of the presence of the police were made in haste out of sensible considerations of avoiding Mubarak's security forces. The initial success of their collective efforts leading to Mubarak's ouster saw people reaffirm their sense of ownership of space which meant that they understood that their very presence became necessary in establishing a revolutionary repertoire between their art and the space they were creating it in. Why should they paint hastily and hide, when – after an intense struggle with government forces and the success of their immediate demand that Mubarak was no longer in power – they won their right to claim ownership and active presence in public spaces. Almost everyone I interviewed expressed a similar sentiment, in that they felt it became necessary to firmly establish their hard-won presence in public space while they create revolutionary art which disrupts the 'order' (i.e. the status quo) that SCAF was so intent on restoring at that moment. To them, the revolution was not over, and street battles on the ground to resist political efforts to marginalize them by evicting them from key revolutionary sites such as Mohamed Mahmoud Street meant that it was all the more critical for artists to remain visible and active in public space, and to establish their presence by artistically countering SCAF's efforts at quelling the revolutionaries efforts.

Ammar Abo Bakr said it simply 'made sense' (Ammar Abo Bakr, Cairo, pers. comm., 30 April 2014) as to why he chose to remain in Mohamed Mahmoud Street – during that liminal moment when they were in a moment of trying to keep the revolution's momentum and resist SCAF. When there is a breach in the structural order, the street (a previous unnatural location for art during the status quo) became not only the natural but also the necessary location in which to create revolutionary art. Ammar told me that he would create art based on the revolutionary situation occurring at that moment, in that particular place – thus emphasizing the importance of both time and space coinciding within particular revolutionary moments. Ammar argued that not only was the location central but also that drawing revolutionary art as the events itself unfolded was even more crucial and powerful than drawing in its aftermath, as the art of the moment – in the actual moment – has greater credibility, impact and power for being a visual narrative situated within the present.

> It is impossible for me to miss a situation if for example a protest of 5,000 or 10,000 passes by me in Mohamed Mahmoud and I draw the martyrs as I see them, and I don't take advantage of participating in this opportunity which contains this massive collective energy. I was so lucky and was the first person on the wall and the first one to stay and sit on the wall, not just draw and run – now drawing and running is it's own graffiti style and is its own revolutionary tactic as a form of protest. However it depends on the place. Being in a place like Mohamed Mahmoud and being in an area which we [protestors, artists, activists] were essentially occupying anyways [in downtown Cairo], and the Ministry of Interior was barred from entering it, so why would I run? I am occupying this space, it is mine. The Ministry of Interior put barricades all around their building and cut themselves off from the street and isolated themselves. For me it was a genius opportunity given the situation to stay standing in this place to draw, to talk to the people and have conversations, and to counter false media narratives with art. (Ammar Abo Bakr, Cairo, pers. comm., 30 April 2014)

El Zeft was also careful to choose where he created art as he said 'location is connected to an idea' when it comes to revolutionary art in public spaces

(El Zeft, Cairo, pers. comm., 27 April 2014). A key example is his Nefertiti mask which he said he drew intentionally on Mohamed Mahmoud Street – a street he called very 'masculine' – in an effort to remind the public that women played a significant role in the revolution, and continue to play a significant role in sociopolitical issues, even if they are not as visible as men in the media's coverage. The timing and location of El Zeft's Nefertiti mask (Figure 5.14) were intentional, as he told me that he drew it at a time when the Muslim Brotherhood were undermining women's role in the social and political sphere. El Zeft's other iconic work, the smiley face on the barricade wall (see Figure 4.26), was also intentionally chosen, he said, because he drew it in a place where fierce clashes were occurring with protestors occupying that space and that it was an intentional – and sardonic – attempt to mock security forces that even if they were beating them and killing them, the revolutionaries were still smiling and continuing their fight for the revolution regardless. Had this ironic juxtaposition been in any other space or time outside of the revolution's events, it would not have had the impact it had at that intense moment. The juxtaposition of a smiley face situated on a barricaded wall in the middle of bloody street battles between revolutionaries and security forces is a primary example of the sheer power a simple visual like a smiley face has within such a crucial political moment in Egypt's history.

El Zeft also told me that his very cheerful 'Rainbow' painting on Mansour Street (see Figure 4.25), was intentionally located on the site of violent street clashes in order to provide a message of hope that the revolution will continue, and that although 'we (the revolutionaries) paid the price for tomorrow we are going to take it, and that no matter what happens we are going to live happily later, because we paid the price' (El Zeft, Cairo, pers. comm., 27 April 2014). El Zeft's portrayal of happiness and hope on the streets which were the site of death, destruction and bloody clashes is a stark reminder of the ambiguity – and danger – of the liminal moment, which sees contrasting images and behaviour as the norm.

El Teneen also argued that location was crucial and that one had to adapt revolutionary art to the space it occupies, which also includes important elements to consider such as language, which, to many of those I interviewed, had to be accessible to those witnessing the art.

> Anything that is done in the streets, any artistic or non-artistic act, it matters where it is done. So when we went down to the street which we believed was ours, you had to pick a good location – just like when you tidy your own house, you carefully choose how to rearrange it according to how you want. Everything has its own audience, it doesn't have to say anything directly but can contain a specific idea, which fits in a specific location. So if I draw something in Bulaq (a working class district near Downtown Cairo and the River Nile), for example, I won't write something in English. Everything has to fit its context. I want to do this and I want people to see it, it acts as a marker. (El Teneen, Cairo, pers. comm., 30 April 2014)

Although there were those I interviewed who focused on creating art outside of places and spaces of revolutionary events, I will focus in particular on the significant political moments which occurred and the iconic artistic moments which emerged from them, as these remain part of the enduring and powerful visual aesthetic narrative of the revolution which evolved as events unfolded.

Martyr Murals, Mad Graffiti Weekend and the Tank vs. Biker (spring 2011)

In one of the earliest examples marking the beginning of the demise of the revolutionary process and the contentious political battle over the symbolic and physical control of public space between revolutionary artists versus the authorities – a struggle which would remain throughout the revolution – was Ganzeer's ambitious 'Martyr Murals' portrait of Islam Raafat[2] in Maidan Falaki in Cairo which was repainted over by the authorities. The 'Martyr Murals' was a collaborative project initiated by Ganzeer, along with his friends and volunteers, in March 2011 to document and commemorate all the martyrs of Egypt's 2011 revolution. According to Ganzeer, not only did he have many volunteers who contacted him via social media, he also had people on the street organically join and assist in the project, something which, he said, was new, and indicative of the liminal moment whereby organic collaborative art projects in public spaces became the norm during the height of the Egyptian revolution. Ganzeer had intended to do a separate mural for every martyr, however, as he mentioned to me – and as is documented in his website – it 'proved to be difficult, as the death toll continued to rise and the revolution was evidently far from over' (Ganzeer, 2017). Only three murals were completed (see Figures 4.6–4.8), Islam Raafat, Seif

Figure 4.6 The mural of martyr Islam Raafat, which was painted over by government authorities in the spring of 2011. *Source:* Ganzeer, 2017.

Figure 4.7a and 4.7b The other two martyr murals of Ganzeer's collaborative 'Martyr Murals' project. On the left, the mural of martyr Saif Allah Mustafa, and on the right, Tareq Abdel Latif. Ganzeer also managed to create a fourth mural of the martyr Omar Mohsen (not pictured here). *Source*: Ganzeer, 2017.

Figure 4.8 The original 'Tank vs. Bike' Mural in Zamalek. *Source*: Suzeeinthecity, 2012a.

Allah Mostafa in front of the High Court and Tarek Abdel Latif in Zamalek next to the Gezirah Sporting Club.

The effacement of martyr iconography was seen as a direct – and hostile – act towards suppressing their remembrance in order to erase traces of what the authorities called the 'chaos' of the revolution in public space, in an effort to return to the so-called 'stability' of the status quo. This came across in the remarks by Ganzeer for whom the erasure of the mural of Islam Raafat was a sign that the system was attempting to return under SCAF, and that artists should continue to disrupt the return of the status quo by now directing their creative efforts towards criticizing – and delegitimizing – the military's rule. As he recalled,

> There was this martyr mural portrait in Failaki square, which was the second one I did [of Islam Raafat], there weren't that many martyr murals yet, it hadn't become a huge phenomenon yet, that one lasted about a month, and that was the first one to be erased, first martyr portrait to be erased . . . there was like kind of this reaction by people on the Twitterverse like who did this whatever, and they got very angry [saying] you have to do something you have to go repaint it again whatever. So from that angle you get rid of Mubarak and then the military comes in and says alright we're safeguarding the revolution, and during this time we are painting martyr murals to commemorate them, during which someone . . . comes and paints over it. (Ganzeer, Cairo, pers. comm., 26 April 2014)

It was this specific act that triggered Ganzeer to organize the two-day 'Mad Graffiti Weekend', the first collective graffiti campaign of its kind in May 2011, which he announced over several social media platforms. Ganzeer called on all individuals – artists and non-artists alike – to come together to collaborate on dissident revolutionary art in public spaces. This was the first concrete initiative which had brought many graffiti artists, as well as members of the public, together to collaborate on revolutionary art in a centralized effort to cement the status of this art as a cultural movement, not a passing trend. This would mark the beginning of more concerted efforts, in the aftermath of the eighteen days of the revolution, to bring artists and ordinary people together in an act of creative – and very public – defiance against the military's rule efforts to stamp out all traces of the February 2011 revolution. The momentum of the liminal moment was regaining traction after the first phase of the revolution, as organic and collaborative acts of creativity by not only artists but also the public was increasing in its effort. As Ganzeer said,

> the first Mad Graffiti Weekend was the first consolidated effort between several revolutionary artists along with volunteers and bloggers, it was the biggest at the time. . . . So we repainted that martyr [Ismail Raafat] and we also did the Tank vs. Biker one in Zamalek, and then also simultaneously we did an anti-military piece and an anti-Tantawi[3] piece, and a 'no to military trials' piece over the portrait of someone who was arrested in the middle of a protest and got sentenced in a military trial. So that was the first effort of many revolutionary artists working on one kind of topic at the same time. . . . it was also the first time to kind of collaborate with bloggers and photographers and the media to all cover this event at the same time, it was met positively and very widely covered and blogged about and well documented. (Ganzeer, Cairo, pers. comm., 26 April 2014)

Figure 4.9 'Tank vs. Bike': After the Maspero killings in October 2011. *Source*: Caledoniyya, 2012.

The Tank vs. Biker mural was arguably one of the most iconic pieces created during this initiative in May 2011 as a collaborative effort by Ganzeer and his friends, volunteers and other revolutionary artists (see Figure 4.9). Initially, the image was of a tank aimed at a boy carrying '*aish baladi* (local bread, a staple food of most Egyptians) on his head – a harsh criticism of the army as actually being a repressive force against the revolution and the common Egyptian, an image which also reverses the narrative during the eighteen days of the revolution – when the military took to the streets on 28 January 2011 – that 'The Army and the People are One Hand' (scribbled by people on the walls, and which protestors chanted in Tahrir). The melancholy panda on the right, created by the anonymous revolutionary artist Sad Panda, passively watches the confrontation as a sort of resigned witness to the scene before him which symbolized the violence and clashes which marked the post-eighteen days 'utopian' revolutionary period.

However, although the military was increasingly becoming unpopular in the aftermath of the eighteen days of the revolution, particularly when military trials were held for individuals accused of working against the state, it was the Maspero (in reference to its location outside of the Maspero building in Cairo, the headquarters of Egyptian state television and radio) killings in October 2011 that cemented – for many of those I spoke to – the brutality of military rule, and was essentially the 'subtext of which was to bury any attempts to forge cross-confessional pro-revolutionary alliances in an avalanche of sectarianism' (Armbrust, 2017: 222). In what was known as 'Maspero's Black Sunday', twenty-seven people were killed by the army when unarmed, peaceful protestors marched against the destruction of St. George's church. One of those killed was Mina Daniel, a 20-year-old Coptic Christian activist whose face was memorialized on Mohamed Mahmoud Street graffiti. Mina Daniel, like Islam Raafat, was a 'representative martyr' (Armbrust, 2015: 83) – in which he symbolized the martyrs of the tragic event at Maspero, gave it a name, a biography and a face to relate to. For many, Maspero would mark the beginning of intense and bloody battles between the authorities and revolutionaries in the winter of 2011 and 2012, which was supplemented by the intensification – and flourishing – of revolutionary art. This was the beginning of the unravelling of the revolutionary process which cemented the need to solidify their physical efforts on the streets and become increasingly critical of the army in their art. As Mohammed Khaled noted,

> I started [taking revolutionary art seriously] after the Maspero incident, not in the very beginning. . . . Maspero to me was the real beginning, because my brother Ali was injured and almost died. He was in Maspero photographing and was shot by live bullets. We spent that time in the hospital, and my hatred began to increase. It became personal. (Mohammed Khaled, Cairo, pers. comm., 29 April 2014)

Mohammed and a group of friends (who would later become known as the Mona Lisa Brigades – an Egyptian revolutionary art collective formed during the revolution which primarily focused on political issues but then shifted its focus on social issues concerning women and children)[4] directly referenced the Maspero attack with an image of unarmed Coptic protestors being run over by the tank, swallowed in a sea of blood (see Figure 4.10). This was then defaced in January 2012 by a group named the 'Badr Brigades', who altered the piece to a pro-military narrative by replacing the masks the protestors were holding with Egyptian flags, removing the dead bodies and the blood under the tank and spray painting (in Arabic) the formerly fraternal slogan during the eighteen days of the revolution that 'the Army and the People are One Hand' (see Figure 4.11a and b). In response, Mohammed Khaled and the newly formed Mona Lisa Brigades returned to the mural and painted over the people holding the Egyptian flag a monster-like image of former field marshal Tantawi, viciously eating a female protestor (see Figure 4.11a) – which was later censored over with black paint. The mural would then undergo several transformations and additions, with artist Bahia Shehab[5] adding the 'blue bra' stencils (see Figure 4.11b) and her simple, repetitive and powerful 'no' stencil as a sign of protest in reference to the veiled 'girl in the blue bra' (see Figure 4.12), who was dragged and beaten by the army during large anti-military protests in December 2011. The mural was completely effaced by a group of volunteers called the 'Zamalek Guardians' in June 2013 (Hamdy, Karl, 2013: 129), which occurred roughly around the same time as the mural was completely erased, perhaps indicating that the status quo effectively returned and that the unabated, uncensored and public dialogue of the revolutionary period had effectively ended. This will be discussed in greater detail in Chapter 6.

Figure 4.10 The Badr Brigades alterations of Mohammed Khaled's additions, in which they removed the protestors being crushed in a pool of blood under the tank, with people holding the Egyptian flags. Above are the words (spray-painted in red), 'The Army and the People are One Hand'. *Source*: Gröndahl, 2012: 28.

The evolution of revolutionary art – such as that represented by the Tank vs. Bike mural – was celebrated as being a living, breathing being and not a stagnant piece of art simply to be viewed and observed, but rather an aesthetic revolution, a form of archive, dialogue and debate, which essentially represented a liminal narrative, in the sense that it was not intended to offer a final meaning; rather, it was a narrative which continuously reconstructed itself with overlaying narratives by different players to include multiple and opposing voices of the revolution (see Figures 4.13 and 4.14). This was one of the most important contributions of revolutionary art according to those I interviewed – not to remain untouched in perpetuity, but to parallel the conflict and multiple discourses on the streets in which they were displayed. Mohammed Khaled captured the essence of this sentiment when he said: 'That wall always had a struggle – we draw, people mess it up, and we draw again, and they mess it up again, and so on and so forth – it was an intense conversation, there was always a struggle between us and the regime for domination of these spaces. It

Figure 4.11a A 'monster-like' Tantawi eating a female protestor next to stencils of a woman holding a gun and the Mona Lisa Brigade stencil. *Source*: Gröndahl, 2012: 28.

Figure 4.11b Several other additions were later added to the mural, such as the 'blue bra' stencils and the word 'no' in Arabic, before the mural was completely removed in June 2013. *Source*: Gröndahl, 2012: 29.

was very comedic, and interactive between you and something mysterious, which is the government' (Mohammed Khaled, Cairo, pers. comm., 29 April 2014).

The street was the central location for political and cultural acts, in tandem. The site of cooperation, conflict and struggle, and where people made meaning of the Egyptian revolution and their experience in it. In the liminal moment, it

Figure 4.12 The infamous image of the 'girl in the blue bra', which shows Egyptian soldiers attacking and dragging a veiled female protestor in December 2011. This image was largely seen by revolutionaries as indicative of the army's blatant abuse of power and force. *Source*: Stringer/Reuters/Landov, in Amaria, 2011.

was the (now) ordinary (versus unordinary during Mubarak's era) space in which all forms of expression were performed. In writing about the public space in the Egyptian revolution, Peterson argued that the street was the central space within which contested narratives 'construct[ed] moments of meaning in the contingent, unfolding experience of the ongoing revolution' (2015b: 65) by the revolutionaries and army/regime loyalists. It was the street itself, according to those I spoke to, that was the source of art's political nature because of its feature as a space of civic as well as cultural performances and engagement.

The street was the most natural venue for revolutionary art because the street was the site of not only revolutionary expression but also revolutionary action. Those I interviewed were constantly present on the street making art during the Egyptian revolution, yet at the same time actively participating in stand-offs with the government, sharing experiences and communicating ideas. Thus, art at this time can not be disassociated with revolutionary acts/events, which is why most of those I interviewed would insist that even if they just said the word '*fann*' (art), it was a given that they meant '*fann el thawra*' (revolutionary art), as there was no artistic discourse outside the revolution at that moment. These two terms became indistinguishable at the time – all art was revolutionary art, from a smiley face on a barricaded wall to an elaborate mural on Mohamed Mahmoud Street.

Furthermore, the conflict and struggle through the effacement and erasure of revolutionary art were not viewed in a negative light – according to several of those I interviewed, in order to create a new order you had to destroy the (symbols) of the old order, and so conflict and struggle are crucial components

Figure 4.13 Representative of revolutionary art and graffiti during all three phases of the Egyptian revolution was the existence of multiple voices on the same wall. This was representative in a photo I took of a wall in downtown Cairo in May 2014, prior to Sisi's elections, near one of the remaining wall barricades built around the Ministry of Interior. On the top, the phrase written in black says 'Morsi is the President of the Republic', to emphasize that his supporters still view him as Egypt's legitimate president even after his ouster by the military. Beneath it is the phrase the 'Nahda (Renaissance) Program', in reference to the Brotherhood's 'political platform full of unrealistic developmental projects' (Armbrust, 2017: 230). Directly beneath it, a response to the 'Nahda Program' graffiti, is another graffiti written in black which says '*Nahda' 'Ar*', which translates into a 'Shameful (or disgraceful) Renaissance', for what critics say is Morsi's failed economic policy. On the bottom, in red, is the Ultras' famous anti-police graffiti (which existed even prior to the revolution), which is A.C.A.B. – 'All Cops are Bastards'. On the right, in red, is the iconic name 'Gika', in reference to the young martyr Mohamed Gaber Salah. And finally, on the far left is a stencil of Sisi with an eyepatch. Underneath his image it says *a'tara*, which means, 'do you see?' in reference to professional snipers of the central security forces targeting the eyes of revolutionaries. In the lead-up to the elections, art which criticized Sisi was plentiful, as many believed that his soaring popularity guaranteed him the upcoming election, despite the fact that under his authority, several atrocities were committed, not least of which were the virginity tests of March 2011 (this will be discussed in greater detail in later chapters). This wall is intended to highlight the fact that they were not homogenous sites of unified opinion, but were the sites of multiple voices and dialogue, which were usually in conflict with each other. *Source*: Photo by Author. Taken in 2013.

Figure 4.14 Revolutionary art and graffiti on Mohamed Mahmoud Street. The existence of this diverse dialogue in public spaces – which reflected both conflict and cooperation – was, to many of those I interviewed, one of the most celebrated elements of the Egyptian revolution. One of the most interesting phrases can be seen in the centre, above the eagles, where it says '*Al Magd La'l Mushaghibeen*', which means, 'Glory to the Troublemakers'. SCAF would regularly refer to the revolutionaries as troublemakers causing chaos in an effort to undermine them and contain the revolution, so this phrase is in mocking reference to their 'troublemaker' label by the authorities, for their efforts to continue the revolutionary struggle. *Source*: Photo by Author. Taken in 2013.

to creating a heterogeneous public space and an active public sphere. Multiple narratives should exist, and may be in conflict with each other versus – as in the normative order during Mubarak's regime – the overwhelming presence of one dominant narrative which was sanctioned in the public sphere – the government narrative.

> It is very liberating to see the counter opinion defiantly existing in public space on the street when all of the other modes of expression are being highly regulated by the government. I mean people could even talk about it all the time, but it's just talk [on the internet vs. cementing opinions in public space]. It is liberating and also I think it is so important for it to exist, the counter opinion that a lot of people have to find a venue of expression. (Ganzeer, Cairo, pers. comm., 26 April 2014)

Therefore, the second phase of the revolution was largely defined by competing groups to control the narrative. The protestors wanted to continue to push forth their revolutionary narrative to continue the struggle, the Muslim Brotherhood attempted to regain power with their newfound credibility with their participation in the first phase of the revolution, and SCAF tried to quell any and all 'destabilizing' revolutionary discourse. And so, although 'the eighteen days [the first phase] in Tahrir Square neatly fit Victor Turner's concepts of liminality, communitas and antistructure, the revolution failed to exhibit the inexorable "decline and fall into structure and law" that Turner's model predicts (Turner, 1969: 132)' (Peterson, 2015b: 65). What ended up happening was that

> the Egyptian public sphere turned into what Turner calls an arena, in which the many political and social visions of a new, post-Mubarak Egypt are contested and struggled over, and various political institutions – from the remnants of the old regime to the narrowly elected president and his Muslim Brotherhood associates to the revolutionary youth to the Supreme Council of the Armed Forces (SCAF) – struggle to create a new hegemonic narrative to define Egypt. (Peterson, 2015b: 65)

El Zeft emphasized that most artists at the time understood that art should play a subversive role in the 'return to the statuos quo' narrative of SCAF, as art itself is conflictual and part of the revolutionary struggle, even if its existence in the public sphere means the erasure or criticism of that art, as it is indicative that at least a dialogue is able to exist, versus a homogeneous, controlled public sphere of the normative order which subdued dialogue. The art of the revolution was intended to create active participants versus passive observers, which many described as being characteristic of art (and politics) during the Mubarak era – conflict and controversy-free, where only those within the cultural scene would come and passively view – and consume – art works –

> for me when I do something and then someone writes something I become very happy, because I am creating conflict and people cared enough with what I did to the degree that they didn't like it so they wipe it off or they write no on it or they write a different message. It is awareness, it is awareness, and in the end, conflict. You want to create conflict not impose your own ideas, that was never right, that would be a dictatorship in the end. (El Zeft, Cairo, pers. comm., 27 April 2014)

The conflictual nature of revolutionary art during the liminal moment was celebrated, even with the counter-opinions of the authorities sprayed in response to revolutionary art, as it represented a turning point in public discourse where the street turned into a place of debate, conflict, cooperation and struggle all at the same time. This effectively led to a breach in the structural order, and most of my respondents said that it had seemed, at the time, that they regained the same feeling of the eighteen days of the first phase, that 'anything was possible'. Yet this was gradually going to start to change, as security forces became significantly more violent and repressive, former allies left the revolutionaries (i.e. the Muslim Brotherhood), and more lives were lost in street battles against the security forces.

Violent winter of 2011–12

The battles of Mohamed Mahmoud Street/Tahrir Square

The winter of 2011 would mark the beginning of a very bloody period of the revolutionary process. Perhaps no incident was most representative of the intense conflict of the 'Second Revolution' (or the second wave/the second life of the revolution, as many of those I spoke to labelled it) during the military transition period than the Mohamed Mahmoud Battles which started in November 2011, and would mark the beginning of a bloody 2011–12 winter which would lead to the second Mohamed Mahmoud Street battle in February 2012. Much like the first phase of the revolution during the eighteen days, the first Mohamed Mahmoud battle would be the second wave of revolutionary struggle through a renewed battle for *karama* ('dignity') and against *ihana* ('humiliation') – however this time, it was a symbolic and physical fight as a response to the blockaded Ministry of Interior (*dakhiliyya*) building. As Ryzova notes, it is 'not of *karama* as a universal human honour'; it is rather *karama* understood as

> a historically and socially constituted honour that has a lot to do with how honour and masculinity were constructed locally. They were not fighting for any high-minded outcome such as democracy; in fact, most possibly they do not think anything 'good' would come out of the fight. But the fight gave them back their dignity, even if temporarily. *Karama* for them means their bodies not being subject to torture, not being mistreated at checkpoints and police stations, and having the small cash in their pockets extracted by each officer they pass so that they don't get thrown in the police station overnight – until they can produce more cash. They don't necessarily believe that any force (any political outcome that might come as result of this fight) would help them to recover their dignity. They fight to beat the *dakhiliyya*, to have beaten the *dakhiliyya*. (Ryzova, 2011)

Mohamed Mahmoud's strategic location, just off of Tahrir Square and leading to the Ministry of Interior, saw it become the prime battleground and emerging memorial space over the course of the revolution (Abaza, 2012a; 2012b; 2013b; 2013c), as well as what Mona Abaza calls the 'revolution's barometer' through the art which continuously emerged and evolved in response to the events in the street (Abaza, 2012b). As Jankowicz notes, 'Many places in Cairo are home to revolutionary graffiti art; many others have become synonymous with revolutionary conflict. What makes Mohamed Mahmoud street unique is that it has become both' (Jankowicz, 2016).

First Mohamed Mahmoud Street battle

The first Mohamed Mahmoud Street battle on 19 November 2011 saw central security forces violently disperse a sit-in organized by the families of those injured or killed during the eighteen days of the revolution in January and February 2011 who called for the transfer from SCAF rule to civilian rule, and stated that they will boycott parliamentary elections scheduled to begin at the end of November 2011. This move by the authorities, Armbrust argues, was 'sparked by tensions in the wake of the Supreme Council for the Armed Forces (SCAF's) machinations to guarantee itself freedom from civilian oversight in whatever political order was to emerge' (Armbrust, 2017: 222), and would instigate one of the most brutal battles on Mohamed Mahmoud Street by those angered by the attack on the families, during which more than fifty people were killed. This street battle saw former allies of the revolutionaries, the Muslim Brotherhood, condemn the protestors as they allied with SCAF. Within a social drama (such as a revolution), after the initial breach phase (the 25 January 2011 first phase of the Egyptian revolution) of the normative order, the crisis stage brings in a period of anti-structure, where sides are taken and coalitions formed. This period of time saw the reconstitution of the experience of anti-structure and communitas of the liminal moment of the initial eighteen days of the revolution when social distinctions were irrelevant and Egyptians from different walks of life came together in solidarity against the brutal pushback of the security forces. As Ryzova writes,

> Increasingly distinctions between the young men on the front line (Islamist youth, ultras, and *wilad sis*[6]) are blurred. All of them share a history of engagement with the regime and its harshly imposed order and an articulation of codes of honour. . . . One saw a social mix rarely seen in Egypt (though it was famously present in the First Revolution): middle-class men and women, some of them activists but most of them not; young and old, in suits, *kefiyehs* and jeans, alongside the *galabiyas* and long beards of the salafis; bareheaded women as well as *munaqqabat* (fully veiled women). On the front line, by contrast (and naturally so given the nature of the battle), the demographic was predominantly (though not exclusively) young male and socially marginal. As in some of the key engagements of the First Revolution, major credit for holding the frontline goes to Egypt's football ultras. They know how to manoeuvre collectively, how to engage the police, and how to and play 'hide, seek and hit' with the security forces. Crucially, they have a long-standing 'open account' with the security forces, meaning that they had suffered at the security forces' hands, and wanted payback. (Ryzova, 2011a)

The first Battle of Mohamed Mahmoud was marked by an increase in violent tactics used by riot police against protestors, in which the extensive use of tear gas, rubber bullets, grenades, 'eye snipers' and live ammunition was used to suppress the protestors. 'Eye snipers' were labelled as such because several protestors were shot directly in the eye by professional snipers, in a move believed to be an intentional targeting by the authorities to maim and kill protestors.[7] A disturbing video which circulated on YouTube shows a central security force officer targeting a protestor's eyes with rubber bullets, with his colleagues congratulating him. The officer in the video, Mahmoud Sobhi el-Shinawi, was later arrested for three years after turning himself in after 'Wanted' stencils were sprayed in downtown

Figure 4.15 A stencil of the 'eye sniper' on the wall of the Mugama building which lies on the south side of Tahrir Square, which says (above) 'Wanted: Look with the People', (below) 'First Lieutenant, Mahmoud Sobhi El-Shinawi, an Officer of the Central Security Forces accused of targeting the eyes of tens of revolutionary heroes in Tahrir'. *Source*: Hickson, A., 2011.

Cairo calling for his arrest after the video was made public (see Figure 4.15). According to Ahmed Aboul Hassan, an Egyptian political editor, this particular stencil 'nourished revolutionary identity, growing it from infancy to adulthood, culminating in a fully formed entity that tracks down killers and taunts them on the walls near their neighborhoods and workplaces' (Aboul Hassan, cited in Hamdy, Karl, 2013: 134). Revolutionary art was continuously evolving, evading generalization and responding – and reacting – to revolutionary events as it constituted itself aesthetically, physically and symbolically within the liminal experience of revolutionaries.

The most publicized victim of the eye snipers was Ahmed Harara (see Figure 4.16a and b), who was profiled in *Time* magazine as one of thirty-six iconic activists all around the world who participated in protests in 2011 (Hauslohner, 2011). Ahmed Harara lost both eyes during two decisive battles of the Egyptian revolution – Friday's 'Day of Rage' on 28 January 2011 and the first Battle of Mohamed Mahmoud on 19 November 2011.

Harara, a former dentist who lost his job when he lost his eyesight, became a 'living martyr' (Agence-France Press, 2011) of the revolution, and his image – and the use of eye patches – was used as a symbol of resistance, respect and endurance, as well as a show of solidarity against SCAF rule. Graffiti and art of revolutionaries and martyrs wearing eye patches were drawn all over Cairo and incorporated within protest signs (see, for example, Figure 4.18 and 4.19).

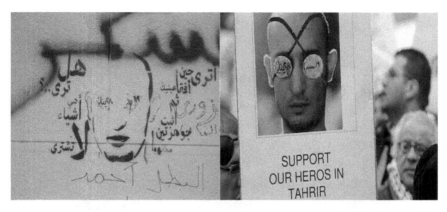

Figure 4.16a and 4.16b Ahmed Harara, who became known as the 'blind hero of the revolution', became an iconic figure in the revolution, having lost both of his eyes in two of the revolution's decisive battles – written in Arabic on his right eye is 28 January [2011] and on his left eye 19 November [2011]. *Source*: Suzeeinthecity, 2011 (the image in this book); Rashwan, 2011 (the image in this book).

Figure 4.17a and 4.17b The lion statue on Qasr El Nil bridge with an eye patch, and graffiti of the lion statue with an eye patch. *Source*: Hart, D., 2012; Tomlin, J., 2011 (image 4.16b).

The eye patch was even drawn on famous statues, such as the iconic stone lion on Qasr El Nil bridge (see Figure 4.17a and b), the site of one of the most intense stand-offs of the revolution – the Friday 'Day of Rage', on 28 January 2011. The image of the eye patch became not only a symbol of resistance and solidarity but also a symbolic sacrifice over what revolutionaries have lost – and are willing to lose – in their fight against oppressive security forces and military rule. It also was a sign that police brutality – one of the most significant underlying factors which spurred the 25th January revolution – was just as barbaric as ever under the rule of the military junta, the 'faithful ally of the *ancien régime*' (Abaza, 2013c: 122), and that the structural, normative

Figure 4.18 Ammar Abo Bakr's eye patch mural of injured protestors who lost their eyes during the November 2011 Battle of Mohamed Mahmoud Street, on the wall of the AUC Main Campus on Mohamed Mahmoud Street. *Source*: Suzeeinthecity, 2011.

Figure 4.19 Protestors outside Qasr El-Aini hospital, wearing the eye patch as a symbol of solidarity with those who lost their eyes since the January 2011 revolution, particularly after the brutal Mohamed Mahmoud battle in November 2011. *Source*: Ismail, 2011.

order of Mubarak's regime still existed in full force. As one journalist noted, '[t]he Eye Sniper may have been jailed, [b]ut the police culture that enabled his actions has barely changed' (Kingsley, 2013).

This particular event indicated that the liminal period was far from over and that the revolution's fight was only just beginning. SCAF's intent was to swiftly put a decisive end to the revolutionary process through physical (blockading the streets, arresting, killing and injuring protestors) and symbolic (by targeting and arresting artists, discrediting the revolutionaries through state media coverage and whitewashing graffiti) means.

Figure 4.20 A mural showing Mina Daniel and Sheikh Emad Effat together ('representative martyrs of the revolution'), signifying Muslim and Christian unity as they spread their hands over the faces of the other martyrs. *Source*: Suzeeinthecity, 2012b.

The Mohamed Mahmoud battle in November 2011 was followed by renewed, bloody clashes during the peaceful Occupy Cabinet sit-in which started on 26 November 2011, to protest the appointment of Kamal El-Ganzouri as the new prime minister (responsible for forming a new Cabinet) for his previous deeply held ties to Mubarak's former regime. The sit-in lasted three weeks during parliamentary elections,[8] until 16 December when military police and revolutionaries clashed after one of the protestors was detained and beaten the night before. During the clashes on 16 December, Sheikh Emad Effat, the iconic 'Sheikh of the Revolution' – a senior cleric at Egypt's famous Al Azhar Mosque and the director of *fatwas*[9] at Dar Al-Ifta (Hamdy, Karl, 2013: 113) – who was well-known by revolutionaries for his frontline participation in the 25th January revolution and his criticism of military rule – was shot and killed and subsequently memorialized in iconic graffiti, which depict him and Mina Daniel side-by-side, in a symbol of religious unity through the sacred status of martyrdom (see Figure 4.20).

The next day, 17 December 2011, saw military police raid Tahrir Square and beating, dragging and detaining protestors – one of the most iconic images of this merciless attack was the shocking 'blue bra' girl image mentioned earlier chapter, in which a veiled woman was beaten on the street, her blue bra revealed when the security forces dragged her by her clothes. This day saw clashes with revolutionaries, journalists and even innocent bystanders, while the Institute of Egypt[10] burned down amidst the fighting (effectively destroying significant archives of Egypt's rich history), as live ammunition was frequently used.

Amidst the clashes, then-prime minister Kamal El-Ganzouri – whose initial appointment was the main cause for the sit-ins – ironically called the protestors members of the 'counter-revolution' in an effort to discredit them in the eyes of the public. During this time, state media narratives continued their oft-repeated claims that the clashes were influenced by a 'foreign conspiracy' and that the protestors' primary goals were to aid and abet this conspiracy by attempting to cause chaos and disrupt daily life (Hamdy, Karl, 2013: 114, 116). To many of those I spoke to, this was the standard discourse of the authoritarian regime which used the narrative of 'order' to reconstitute the status quo and discredit the liminal experience of the revolution as being one of destruction, instability, and chaos, in order to delegitimize the revolutionaries cause and generate fear among the public that these protests were not, in fact, about basic rights for Egyptians, but was a malevolent foreign conspiracy at play. It was the revolutionaries' portrayal by state media and the authorities' public statements as thugs, foreign agents and troublemakers, which – according to many I interviewed – led to a major public loss in the support of the revolution's fight, and would lead to the emergence of (and this was always said in a sarcastic tone by those I interviewed) *almuwateneen el shurafa'a* – 'honourable citizens' – who would also attempt to take it upon themselves to undermine the revolutionaries activity and discourse.

Besides the prolific media discourses that attempted to discredit and contest the validity of revolutionary actions and isolate protestors from the support of the Egyptian public, material attempts to isolate them also took place in urban (public) spaces. In a move which indicated the authorities' desire to cement control, another concrete wall was built in Qasr El-Aini Street[11] to block the way to the Cabinet from Tahrir, and the Ministry of Interior was further barricaded with the erection of two more walls in Yousef El-Guindy Street and Sheikh Rehan Street. This, according to Abaza, made 'life practically impossible for many' (Abaza, 2013c), and led to greater public contempt towards the revolutionaries for what seemed to be an added disruption and undesirable obstacle to their everyday mobility. Furthermore, this military zoning of downtown Cairo marginalized revolutionaries from key protest points and restricted their movements, thus significantly impeding their ability to effectively mobilize. Through the zoning of downtown Cairo, the military wanted to expunge the Egyptian revolutions 'public culture of protest' (Abaza, 2012c: 125), which included a 'novel understanding of public spaces as spaces of contestation, of communication and debate, as spaces of the "spectacle"' (Abaza, 2012c: 126, Mehrez, 2012). Abaza argues that, in an ironic twist, the authorities wanted to reappropriate urban space by applying

> the lesson it learned from the 'frozen moment' of the 18 days of January, which paralysed the entire city – and was thus highly effective in bringing about the downfall of the regime. It has been counteracting the revolutionaries by 'zoning' and confining the protesters, segregating them in limited spaces of war. The junta imagines that what will bring the skirmishes to an end is the erection of multiple cement walls and the blocking of entire parallel streets with stone walls and military vehicles. (Abaza, 2012c: 127–8)

The militarization of downtown Cairo

In a further move to subvert the public culture of protest and reassert dominant control over urban space, during the course of the winter of 2011 and the spring of 2012, the authorities erected eight stone walls throughout key points in downtown Cairo (see Figure 4.21 for a complete illustration of the walls/blockades set up by the military during this time, effectively segregating downtown Cairo). By February 2012, 'there were eight walls around the area of Mohammed Mahmud, Noubar and Mansur Sheikh Rehan Streets, not counting the barbed-wire zones in front of the Ministry of Interior, check-points, the tanks blocking access and large green police vehicles filled with hundreds of security soldiers' (Abaza, 2013c: 126; Trew, Abdalla, Feteha, 2012). Abaza argues that the main goals of the zoning of downtown Cairo were twofold. The first was to place the 'blame on the revolutionaries for paralysing the downtown area' (Abaza, 2012c: 127) to further discredit them in the eyes of the public and represent them as forces of undesirable chaos. The second was to contain and 'conf[ine] the space of conflict' to restrict 'the street fights' and 'contain rebellion' (Abaza, 2012c: 127–8), in an effort to divide the city into a 'normalized' space versus the 'war zone' space (Abaza, 2012c: 128). This tactic of 'confining the protesters [and] segregating them in limited spaces of war' (Abaza, 2012c: 127) is one of the ways in which the military authorities attempted to implement violent redressive measures to ensure an end to the liminal phase to return to the much-desired 'order' of the status quo and to go back to politics as normal. In a clear message by SCAF that the politics of the ruling authority is the only politics allowed to exist, the zoning of downtown Cairo was a signal by the ruling authority that it intended to regain its ability to effectively control public space and expunge any unwanted, dissident elements swiftly. This led to increased clashes as there was a ferocious attempt – by both the revolutionaries

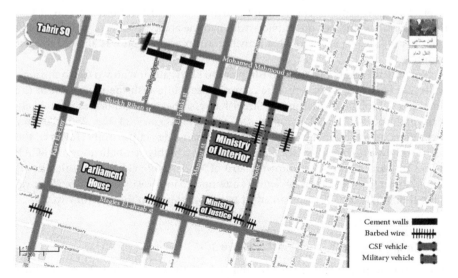

Figure 4.21 The militarization of downtown Cairo. *Source*: Trew, Abdalla, Feteha, 2012.

Figure 4.22 Whitewashing the AUC wall of revolutionary art. *Source*: Abaza, 2012a.

and SCAF – to establish control of the street. For the revolutionaries, the street had become a space of play, struggle, communitas and creativity. For the authorities, the street was the site where redressive measures (through violent tactics) needed to be implemented in order to ensure a full return to the structural order, where it was the authorities – and not the public – who had the ability to control and define the contours of urban space, and what activity/form of expression was allowed to exist within it.

Not only was there this initiative in place to segregate downtown Cairo through walls and barricades, but a prolific campaign to whitewash the murals off of the now-iconic Mohamed Mahmoud Street had also begun. Authorities completely repainted the AUC wall prior to the first anniversary of the 25th January revolution, an effort which did not last more than a day at the time. However, the act of whitewashing graffiti (see Figure 4.22) was a highly symbolic move by SCAF to 'clean' – and purge – downtown Cairo of 'undesirable elements [which have] served to demonstrate the new regime's attempts to impose its own order' (Ryzova, quoted in Jankowicz, 2016) in an effort to restore things to the way they were.

Mad Graffiti Week (November 2011–March 2012)

These tumultuous events led to two major initiatives in an effort to reconstitute the anti-structure of the revolution and counter SCAF's redressive measures to bring about a return to the much-hated status quo. The first is the 'Mad Graffiti Week', a response to the army's brutal tactics and continued hold on power, and the second was the 'No Walls' campaign, a response to the increasing militarization of downtown Cairo from November 2011 to March 2012. Mad Graffiti Week (held on 13–25 January 2012, which coincided with the revolution's first anniversary) was an open call by Ganzeer initiated on 20 December 2011, in which he appealed upon artists everywhere to

> help save lives. The Egyptian Military Council has unleashed a brutal crackdown on peaceful protests by the Egyptian people, calling for the resignation of the military council and a cancellation of the sham [parliamentary] elections that they've been running under their supervision. Soldiers have shown us no mercy, hitting fallen women with their batons, stomping on skulls with their boots, and shooting unarmed civilians dead. . . . Our only hope right now is to destroy the military council using the weapon of art. From January 13 to 25, the streets of Egypt will see an explosion of anti-military revolutionary art. If you are a revolutionary artist elsewhere in the world, please do what you can in your city to help us. (Hamdy, Karl, 2013: 120)

This revolutionary art initiative significantly differed from Mad Graffiti Weekend, which was centralized primarily in Cairo and whose aim was to create a few large murals by several artists and volunteers. In its openness at a transnational level (where people in North America, Europe and Africa participated in their cities), Mad Graffiti Week saw a surge in anti-military art and the documentation and archival of this art, through Facebook groups (the most prominent being 'Mad Graffiti Week', 'Mad Graffiti Week Alexandria' and 'Graffiti the streets of Egypt', among others), Twitter accounts and Flickr pages. A participatory, decentralized and collective initiative, this was not a project revolving around the revolutionary artist 'darlings' but was intended for everyone to do as they like. During this time, stencil booklets were available for download, making it easy for anyone who was not familiar with art or graffiti to be able to print and use them to spray paint in their cities or towns. As Ganzeer said,

> I think Mad Graffiti Week was actually the first time an explosion a little bit [happened]. I want to say like revolutionary art but just people summoning up the courage to just go out on the street and scrawl something on the wall, even not just Cairo but shady little towns that are out in the middle of nowhere [in Egypt]. There were a couple reports of some kids getting arrested[12] for spraying slogans on police stations, stuff like that, in small towns. All this happened in Mad Graffiti week. And also there was this thing that we did, myself and other people, we just started sharing lots of designs online, that other people would take and use and cut and stencil and whatever and use it their own ways, so yeah I wouldn't say there was a big art movement from the art crowd . . . just from regular people. (Ganzeer, Cairo, Skype Interview, 22 November 2013)

According to El Teneen, an event such as 'Mad Graffiti Week' was significant in establishing local and transnational connections between the physical and virtual world – through participatory, collaborative and archival efforts – and that this was one of the main – and most significant – legacies of the revolution,

> I joined in Mad Graffiti week, mostly doing stencils and giving it to people to use it. . . . If I take a picture now and put it on Facebook, a link has been created since the revolution that has remained, whereby any picture of graffiti or any doodles on the walls, it would fly everywhere. The connection between the wall as a public sphere and social media outlets is strong. They have different domains and people deal with them differently, writing on the wall for example and writing on Facebook and Twitter by a public figure that has thousands of followers is different, you will take what he says differently than when some random guy writes on the wall in the streets. Writing on the wall is more democratic because it is more accessible and because most of the time you don't know who it is who did it. (El Teneen, Cairo, pers. comm., 30 April 2014)

Mad Graffiti Week further cemented calls by revolutionaries, the public and artists alike that military rule needed to end, and to reassert their right to public space and to take back the streets, as indicative of some of its most iconic stencils seen in Figures 4.23 and 4.24.

Subsequently, the 'No Walls' campaign in March 2012 was a collective initiative formed as a response to the segregation imposed by the zoning of downtown Cairo

Figure 4.23 One of the most prominent stencils of Mad Graffiti Week was a Guy Fawkes mask, written underneath it says, 'Thoughts against Bullets', as well as a fist raised in defiance, under which it says, 'The streets are ours, go down on 25 January [2012, for the one year anniversary of the revolution].' *Source*: Charbel, 2012.

Figure 4.24 Stencils which read 'the revolution continues' – one of the most repeated slogans seen on revolutionary art during the first anniversary of the 25th January revolution. *Source*: Suzeeinthecity, 2012a.

through concrete walls and steel barricades placed in certain strategic points. The mission of the creative 'No Walls' campaign was to aesthetically 'open' and retake the streets using art, in order to symbolically subvert the walls' very physical and obstructive existence. Artists and non-artists (volunteers) from the public worked together to defy the authorities' attempt at marginalizing their physical movements and disrupting citizens' ordinary lives in an attempt to maintain the liminal moment of the revolution by continuously subverting the physical (and symbolic) barriers characterized by the establishment of the ruling authorities dominant power and control. As El Zeft told me in one of our conversations, the revolutionaries saw the barricades in downtown Cairo as a form of physical occupation that ultimately failed in its attempt to dissuade them from mobilization,

> I felt exactly like I was drawing on the Apartheid Wall in Palestine [a common sentiment used by those drawing on the walls at this time], exactly, you feel like they occupied this place and they made a wall around it saying 'this is ours and this is yours'. The point for me [of drawing on these walls] was that this wall does not exist. At the time . . . I remember the tone at the time was that the revolution was defeated and that we lost and that there was no more hope. So I went at night and the soldiers were still standing behind the wall, so I drew a rainbow, happy

scenes, and a little girl sitting with a dog [Figure 4.25], it was a hopeful image, to say that no matter what you do no matter how long you stay and no matter how long the wall stays, tomorrow is going to be nice as long as we are alive and as long as we are resisting we will stay, we won't stop. Then we got together and we agreed that we would draw on all the walls – they were about seven [at the time], as if these walls don't exist. One of my drawings was in Mansour Street, and everyone was helping each other, there was nothing [artwork] that was specifically [attribute] for one person. It was really nice. People would come and would want to help, it feels great. (El Zeft, Cairo, pers. comm., 27 April 2014)

El Zeft's other iconic drawing was on the wall blockading Qasr El-Aini Street, which, to him, was a sardonic, sarcastic and mocking gesture against the authorities (Figure 4.26 and 4.27), in which he said his message was a simple one – 'There were people in clashes [at the time] and I put a smiley face looking at the square. Like "do whatever we want we still love what we do and we will keep doing it even if you kill all of us, fuck you"' (El Zeft, Cairo, pers. comm., 27 April 2014). Other collaborative works used the technique of *trompe l'oeil*[13] (see Figure 4.28) where artists and volunteers together cleverly painted landscapes of what looked like the 'normal' continuation of the street – an ironic twist on a wall which was anything but normal with an obstructive barricade that effectively disrupted the movement of everyday life – in order to efface its presence as 'non-existent' to

Figure 4.25 El Zeft's Rainbow Drawing, which he collaborated on with several friends, on one of the walls blockading Mansour Street in downtown Cairo. The left side is entitled 'Tomorrow', which shows a brighter future, while the left size is entitled 'Yesterday', and commemorates the martyrs of the Port Said Massacre. *Source*: Suzeeinthecity, 2012d.

Figure 4.26 El Zeft's 'smiley face', which he made in collaboration with revolutionary artists Amr Nazeer and Layla Magued, on the wall blockading Qasr El-Aini Street. *Source*: Abou Bakr, 2013.

Figure 4.27 A protestor holding up a picture of the 'smiley face'; underneath it is written in Arabic, 'Smile (or laugh) . . . no matter the obstacles (or barriers, in reference to the wall) and hardships'. *Source*: El Zeft, Facebook post, 2013 (photo by Mohamed Abd El-Hamid).

Figure 4.28 A clever *trompe l'oeil* on the wall blockading Sheikh Rihan Street in downtown Cairo. *Source*: Suzeeinthecity, 2012d.

revolutionaries and their continued efforts to fight for the causes of the revolution. It was also used as a form of satire, to mock what those I interviewed saw as the authorities' pitiful and desperate attempts to stop their revolutionary activity by closing their physical space. The clever use of this technique was to transcend the material obstruction by the authorities to 'impose' restrictions on revolutionary activity by symbolically 'opening up' the street as an imaginary space (Abaza, 2012c: 128), as a powerful testament to the continuation of revolutionaries efforts to creatively subdue the authorities attempts at silencing them and removing what they viewed as their 'disruptive' presence from public space to get things back to 'the way they were'.

It is in such subversive acts that illustrate that at that time public space would no longer be easily relinquished, yet is constantly being re-appropriated in novel ways in order to reconstitute the liminality of the revolution, indicating that the battle of contestation over public space is a symbolic one as much as a physical one. Attempting to reassert the ability to be actively present in public space – one of the most significant achievements of the liminal moment of the Egyptian revolution – through the use of art on the actual physical symbols of obstructions (walls/barricades) is a powerful attempt to discredit the return of the status quo and a clever way to delegitimize its tactics.

The first Mohamed Mahmoud Battle of the Occupy Cabinet clashes in November 2011, and the ensuing violence in Tahrir in December 2011, were decisive moments in the Egyptian revolution's history. Not only did it effectively illustrate SCAF's efforts to sideline the revolutionaries from taking any part in the political decision-making process and discredit them as 'foreign agents' and 'troublemakers', but it showed complete disregard for their demands and a continuation of the police and security forces brutality that characterized

Mubarak's regime. This illustrated, to all of those I interviewed, that the authorities wanted a swift return to the status quo, by any and all repressive means necessary to achieve that goal.

The Port Said Massacre and the Ultras

This conflict was renewed in February 2012 after the Port Said Massacre and the ensuing second Mohamed Mahmoud Street battles. The Port Said Massacre occurred on 1 February 2012, after the home team (Al Masry) won against Cairo's Al Ahly team. It was reported that Al Masry supporters attacked Ultras Ahlawy fans with knives, sticks and clubs, although those I interviewed said they were undercover *baltageyeh* (paid thugs) of the authorities posing as football fans in order to extract revenge against the Ultras Ahlawy for their support and participation in the Egyptian revolution, as they were a significant mobilizing force[14] in the fight against security forces. Many of those I spoke to said the evidence indicated that the attack was pre-planned[15] and organized, and that the exits of the stadium had all effectively been blockaded, obstructing Ultras Ahlawy fans from escaping.

The Ultras, an Egyptian football fan club and movement, deserve a special mention as they present a significant force in Egyptian society since they became a fully established organization in 2007 (Jerzak, 2013: 242). The Ultras have a long history of conflict with the Egyptian authorities (see Rommel, C., 2015), and are known for their extreme devotion to their football clubs. Whether they are Ultras Ahlawy (or UA-07 as can be frequently seen stencilled on the walls), the largest Ultras group which support the El Ahly football club, or Ultras White Knights who support the Zamalek football club, they are a highly organized collective movement – even before the Egyptian revolution of January 2011, they were infamous for anti-police graffiti and skirmishes with the authorities.

> The Ultras used to draw before the revolution. . . . the history of the Ultras with the regime is a book on its own. . . . they have their own cat-mice chase with the authorities, especially with the police – they draw for example pictures of their friends that were arrested, what happened in a certain soccer match, how the authorities have treated them. A.C.A.B. – this was one of the main things that Ultras write [even before the revolution], all cops are bastards. (Radwa Fouda, Cairo, pers. comm., 13 August 2014)

The second Mohamed Mahmoud Street battle and the importance of Martyr Murals

The Port Said Massacre of the Ultras, one of the revolution's most vital – and organized members – and the subsequent second Battle of Mohamed Mahmoud Street on 2 February 2012, produced a surge of murals on Mohamed Mahmoud Street to commemorate the martyrs of the tragic event. Hanaa El Degham, an

Egyptian artist who lives and works between Cairo and Berlin, said she happened to be in Cairo in February 2012 during the Port Said Massacre, and that she (as well as other volunteers from the street) spontaneously collaborated with Mohammed Khaled, Ammar Abo Bakr and Alaa Awad, another Egyptian artist and lecturer in Luxor's Faculty of Fine Arts. As El Degham said,

> Going to the street was what had to happen at that moment because the situation decrees that we have to all be together outside and discuss and draw. We found this is the best way to reach people, to show them the truth, and for me to find out the truth from them. Because newspapers and the media made it difficult to know what the truth was. . . . Drawing on the streets attracts people. Standing in the street makes people take notice of what is going on, they want to know what we are doing and what our message is. It doesn't need a specific language to know what we are doing . . . When you are in the street and talking to the people, ideas come to you. (Hanaa El Degham, Berlin, Skype interview, 29 November 2013)

Spontaneous events such as these whereby artists and non-artists alike performed creative acts of dissent, commemoration and protest were a defining factor of the liminal experience of the Egyptian revolution. The Port Said Massacre unified artists and non-artists alike to come together to draw the portraits of the seventy-four Ultras martyrs, in the largest yet communal effort, which clearly indicated that this was not just a 'vibrant form of revolutionary art' (Abaza, 2013c) but, as Abaza argues, 'extends also to the interactive and 'performative' encounters of various publics with the walls that visually narrate the dramatic events that happened in the street' (Abaza, 2013c). As Figure 4.29 shows, people would create impromptu commemorative signs to the martyrs, using leaves and sticks, whereas others would regularly place flowers and candles under martyrs' portraits, creating sites where people could gather, mourn and pay their respects. The Port Said Massacre was a key revolutionary event which would lead to the resurgence of communitas, and brought the public within the performative impact of revolutionary art in greater force,

> After the February 2012 Port Said massacre of the fans of the Ahli Ultras, even more publics came to interact with the space of the street after the appearance of many new martyr portraits on the walls. The street was transformed into a memorial space, a shrine (a *mazaar*) to be visited and where flowers could be deposited. (Abaza, 2013c)

Soraya Morayef, one of the most well-known bloggers to document Egyptian revolutionary art, described the interaction between the public and artists in the immediate aftermath of the Port Said Massacre, observed that artists were not - for the most part - passive creators who paint and leave, but were actively creating art while mourning, resisting, and interacting alongside the public. She describes her account of this time:

Figure 4.29 A man arranges leaves to spell out 'Glory to the Martyrs' on Mohamed Mahmoud Street, as Alaa, Ammar and Hanaa as well as volunteers continue to work on the murals in February 2012. *Source*: Aboul Hassan in Hamdy, Karl, 2013: 135.

For three consecutive nights on Mohamed Mahmoud, Ammar and his friends worked tirelessly, ignoring jeers by passersbys [*sic*] and taking breaks to engage in heated debates with Islamists or to head to the frontline to throw rocks, only to return and resume painting. They are demonstrating artists, or artistic demonstrators. One moment that I was privileged to observe was on Thursday night, where four young men – barely in their twenties – stopped in front of the mural Ammar was painting of the 19-year-old martyr Mohamed Mostafa, and stood completely transfixed [see Figure 4.30]. Then they began to cry. I asked them what was wrong, and they said 'He's our friend; we just came from his burial now.' And they stared at the mural. Ammar approached them, explained that he wanted to commemorate each and every one of their friends who'd died, and that he'd found their photos on Facebook. 'If you know any others who died, if you have any photos, please give them to me,' he pleaded. And they nodded. (Suzeeinthecity, 2012b)

These ritual activities in public spaces, where people gathered on the streets in public displays of commemoration and mourning the martyrs of the revolution, were a significant strategy not only for political mobilization but also for public performance. Abaza narrated the ways in which the act of commemorating the martyrs and the utilization of the space of Mohamed Mahmoud as a communal site of public mourning further cemented one of the primary gains of the revolution,

Figure 4.30 The friends of Mohamed Mostafa – an Ultra Ahlawy and a 19-year-old student, one of the seventy-four martyrs of the Port Said Massacre – in front of his portrait. *Source*: Suzeeinthecity, 2012b.

which was the ability to actively (versus passively) be present and active within a previously restrictive public space,

> a man named Mr Emaisha came every evening to clean Mohammed Mahmud Street and decorate the area in front of the paintings of the young Ultra martyrs with bundles of dried jasmine. Every evening Mr Emeisha brought a vase with flowers, which he left in the street. On the ground, he shaped the bundles of dried jasmine to form the word Sun (Shams). On some days, he shaped them into the words: life + freedom=Egypt. Mr Emeisha told me that to experience the feeling of freedom once makes it impossible to give it up. This is why he will continue to bring in flowers to the street whenever possible. . . . It was also during the beginning of March that one could observe in the evening young women and men stopping their cars to pay a visit to the street and leave flowers in front of the martyrs' graffiti. The trauma of the massacre of November 2011 was illustrated in the collective act of turning the street into a memorial space. (Abaza, 2012c: 134)

The repetitive use of the portraits of martyrs has been key to developing what Abaza calls a 'repertoire' of revolutionary art, which can be used to reconstitute the liminal moment of the Egyptian revolution through certain aesthetics by recounting fundamental events or tragedies to remind the public 'this is what we were fighting for'. A key example is the solemn questions written under martyr murals, such as 'have you obtained your right?' or 'have you been vindicated?', as well as sombre reminders written under these murals, embodied in the oft-seen phrase 'do not forget why I died'. As Armbrust notes, the 'martyr inconveniently asks, "who killed me?" and true revolutionaries take up the cause, also asking,

Figure 4.31 a (top), 4.31b (bottom left), 4.31c (bottom right). Martyr murals of young Egyptian Mohamed Gaber Salah, famously known as 'Gika'. Gika was killed on the first anniversary of the Mohamed Mahmoud Street clashes in November 2012, when he was shot in the head by security forces under Morsi's rule – above the image where his mother can be seen mourning him is a stencil which says 'The Day you came is the Day you Leave, 30/6' in reference to the massive protest planned on the first anniversary of Morsi's rule, where revolutionaries would call for Morsi's departure. Scenes from Gika's funeral, (drawn in Figures 4.31a, b, c by Egyptian revolutionary artist Moshir), in which thousands marched across Cairo, became so iconic that his image became one of the most important revolutionary symbols of the 25 January revolution, reproduced on walls, t-shirts, as well as protest posters. *Source*: Photo by Author. Taken in 2013.

"who killed them?" in the hope that they can beat the false patriots out of the fog' (Armbrust, 2013). However, there is also a more existential meaning to martyrdom which transcends the materiality of the need to vindicate. The imagery of martyrs 'becomes an act through which the world is constituted in particular ways: in this case, as a deeply moral cause' (Peterson, 2015b: 71) which makes it 'unthinkable that these men and women would have shed their blood for an uprising that failed' (Peterson, 2015b: 71). Many of those I spoke to, such as El Zeft, told me that even when they felt frustrated at the setbacks during the uprising (such as during SCAF's transitional rule or Morsi's presidency), the martyrs became a deeply emotional – and personal – reminder that they should continue the revolutionary struggle, because it was their duty not to have the martyrs' ultimate sacrifice – their lives – be in vain. He recalled this to me in a conversation we had, when he told

Figure 4.32a On the right-hand side, above the green-shaded martyr mural of 12-year-old martyr Omar Salah, is the repeated phrase 'Glory to the Martyrs' on Mohamed Mahmoud Street. *Source*: Photo by Author. Taken in 2013.

Figure 4.32b A martyr mural of 12-year-old martyr Omar Salah, a sweet potato seller, who was shot 'accidentally' by an Egyptian army conscript in February 2012. On the left it says, 'The Child Martyr, Omar Salah', and on the right it says, 'Through what fault was he killed?', and above is the signature of the Revolutionary Artists Union. *Source*: Photo by Author.

Figure 4.33 A portrait of a martyr of the Egyptian revolution. Written underneath is a sombre reminder to others to continue the revolutionary struggle – 'Don't you dare forget why I died!' *Source*: Photo by Author.

Figure 4.34 One of the most frequently seen revolutionary art is that of the mothers of martyrs grieving. *Source*: Photo by Author.

me his frustrations at fellow revolutionaries who would complain that it seemed their efforts were a waste of time, and would subsequently tell them 'if you feel like you are wasting your time, well what about the people who died and wasted their lives? When you say you are wasting your time, well what about the people who wasted their lives?' (El Zeft, Cairo, pers. comm., 27 April 2014). Amidst hesitation, it was the powerful image of the martyr, as a sacred symbol of the ultimate price people paid for the revolution, which, at the time, made it unthinkable not to continue to uphold the momentum of the struggle until the goals of the Egyptian revolution had been achieved, and the martyr's life finally vindicated. In his article, 'The Ambivalence of Martyrs and the Counter-revolution' on the different uses of martyr's images during the Egyptian revolution, Armbrust observed, 'In the early days of the Revolution, martyrdom was an actively performed rhetorical position – a kind of irresistible force in the eyes of those who took it up as a weapon in their continuing struggle' (Armbrust, 2013a). This made their aesthetic presence in revolutionary art a key element in regaining the liminality of the primary phase of the revolution (see, for examples, Figures 4.31–4.34).

Reinventing Egyptian cultural symbols within revolutionary art

The connection between artists (who are also revolutionaries, as mentioned previously), protestors and the public is an indication of the significance of the street as the primary site where a physical and cultural communitas emerges and re-emerges and solidifies itself with the revolutionary process. It is also a place where the language of dissent and revolution can be used to reconnect with the historical and cultural past. As Mona Abaza notes, it was not only the aesthetic appeal which led to the popularity of the Mohamed Mahmoud Street murals in February 2012, but also that they 'exemplify a fascinating fusion between a variety of cultural artistic traditions that portray Egypt's rich history, namely Pharaonic, popular Islamic and contemporary traditions. They all reinvent, adapt to and adopt universal schools of painting, adding a fascinating 'Egyptian twist' to express – sometimes humorously – the spirit of rebellion and resistance' (Abaza, 2012c). This tactic was intended as a method of reinventing new ways of reconnecting people to their cultural past, as a way to 'show people how much civilization and culture we have but we seem to have forgotten it because we stopped seeing it' (Hanaa El Degham, Berlin, Skype interview, 29 November 2013).

When I discussed with Alaa Awad, a lecturer at Luxor's Department of Fine Arts, regarding the significance of his murals having an Egyptian narrative (see, e.g. Figures 4.35–4.37), he argued that an understanding of culture is an existential one in the sense that it is a basic structural element of society, not an aesthetic one, akin to Turner's emphasis on the centrality of culture as being an 'existential bending back upon ourselves' (Turner, 1969: vii). For many of those I spoke to, Egyptian culture under Mubarak's regime was desecrated, and the only culture which truly existed was a capitalist one. Many felt that revolutionary art needed to find new and innovative ways to incorporate Egyptian cultural elements in the

Figure 4.35 *Haraaer*, which are 'free fighters, non-slave women in ancient Egypt' (Abaza, 2012c) drawn by Alaa Awad heading into battle carrying batons. Above is the *buraq*, an iconic figure of Egyptian (and Islamic) aesthetic culture that Ammar Abo Bakr wanted to include in the murals as part of Egypt's visual memory. *Source*: Abaza, 2012a.

context of a revolutionary struggle in an effort to meaningfully reconnect with public space and reconstitute societal awareness – and newly discovered pride in the aftermath of 25 January 2011 – in their cultural background. This is what Alaa said to underscore the point:

> Culture is a basic part of the structure of the community. As I mentioned earlier, culture is to be able to overcome disasters and catastrophes, because . . . these are temporary phenomenon. Culture is not painting and drawing; it protects. Culture is beliefs and principles; the principles of the community that were rooted during thousands of years. Culture's strength comes from its continuity. It continued for thousands of years despite the occupation of Egypt from 2000 years; hundreds of years of occupation by the Romans and before that the Ptolemaic rule, among others. (Alaa Awad, Cairo, pers. comm., 28 August 2014)

Alaa, Ammar and Hanaa, all seemed to retreat from adopting a conception of art as an ahistorical, universal idea towards an understanding of art as necessarily being located in narratives constituted within local socio-historical and cultural contexts. As Alaa noted, arts' true power stems from its ability to adopt the context and language of society: 'I am in Egypt, so I address the society through its culture and its political, cultural, and social situation. I have to express the society. Art that does not voice the whole society, politically and economically, does not exist. The artist cannot be separated from the world that they live in' (Alaa Awad, Cairo, pers. comm., 28 August 2014).

What is interesting about Alaa Awad's work (such as those depicted in Images 4.35–4.37) is that even though he was using traditional symbols as 'forms of dissent

Figure 4.36 The Funeral mural by Alaa Awad, which is 'a scene depicting ancient Egyptian women accompanying a sarcophagus symbolizing the death of the football Ahli Ultras youngsters who were massacred on 2 February 2012 in the stadium of Port Said. Demotic writing (i.e. ancient Egyptian script) appeared a few metres away. According to Alaa Awad, up to the present ancient Egyptian mourning traditions persist and can still be witnessed in Upper Egypt. Mourning women enact customs identical to Pharaonic ones, such as tearing their clothes, hysterically shaking their bodies, weeping and smearing bodies and faces with mud to let sorrow out. The muses at the top of the mural receive the ascending soul of the martyr. The tiger is the symbol of anger for the 75 young martyrs who died in Port Said. The women carry the black lotus flowers as a sign of great sorrow'. This was drawn in the aftermath of the Port Said Massacre. *Source*: Abaza, 2013c: 131–2.

and resistance' (Morayef, 2015: 197), he was not simply reflecting on the past but rewriting it (Morayef, 2015: 204). According to Soraya Morayef – he took traditional symbols and decontextualized them in order to 'subvert[] the established [and traditional] art form and empowered anti regime protests' (Morayef, 2015: 204) by taking, '[f]amiliar images that surrounded Egyptians – on advertising billboards, one-pound notes, restaurant menus and schoolbook covers – and placed them in a different, contemporary context, surrounded by broken glass and shrapnel-filled walls that made the murals look so out place, they demanded we stop, stare and think about their relevance' (Morayef, 2015: 197).

The idea that revolutionary art materialized itself within symbols and forms of Egyptian culture in order to restore the forgotten (and rich) cultural heritage and history of Egyptians and reach the consciousness of the society was also a strategy adopted by Ammar, who added that the revolution emphasized the importance of connections between people and their everyday space through revolutionary acts. Therefore, he argues that one of the ways in which revolutionary art played a role in forging an active (versus passive use of space as Asef Bayat, professor of Sociology, mentioned) connection between people and their space was by adopting the aesthetic and cultural language of the everyday, and so he,

Figure 4.37 The Cat and Mouse mural by Alaa Awad, which, according to Alaa in our interview, is intended to show that 'things are reversed' (Alaa Awad, Cairo, pers. comm., 28 August 2014) – an aesthetic representation of the reversal of the structural order, with the cat (the government) fanning the mouse (the people) *Source*: Suzeeinthecity, 2015.

Adopt[s] a vulgar art, an expression with no boundaries, the art I adopt is this art, from the motifs on the *koshari* food stalls and the art that the shoe shine man does on his shoe shine box, I adopt this art that comes from a country which has been devastated over the years. It is impossible that you are going to reach the entire society if you don't reach his link, that is if you don't understand his tastes, you should be following his taste to see the material and the colours the regular Egyptian uses in his day to day life and how he uses it, such as what he uses to decorate tombstones. (Ammar Abo Bakr, Cairo, pers. comm., 30 April 2014)

Countering conspiracy claims

The murals of Mohamed Mahmoud Street in particular (and revolutionary art in general), not only represent a collaborative, cultural and creative effort that brought together members of the public, artists and protestors alike (and they usually all fall under at least two of those categories) to actively be present in public space, connect with one another and commemorate the martyrs but it was also used to counter the claims by authorities that revolutionaries were thugs and foreign agents. Immediately after the eighteen days of the revolution, SCAF and the state media

moved quickly to contain the revolution by endorsing it, at the same time limiting the term to refer only to the eighteen days in Tahrir Square, By reducing the 25 January revolution to the events at Tahrir that ended on 11 February, the SCAF was able to limit the meaning of the revolution to the fall of Mubarak, rather than interpreting it to denote the larger national reform called for by many vocal participants in Tahrir Square. This also allowed the SCAF, in many speeches, proclamations and media statements, to portray all subsequent protest activity as either hooliganism or itself counter-revolutionary activity. (Peterson, 2015b: 73)

This tactic was one of the main motivations of revolutionary art to subvert, what many of those I interviewed called a 'false narrative', and so the iconic murals produced during that time represented the importance of an Egyptian narrative as a marker of identity, by including a repertoire of recognizable cultural symbols commonly found in the aesthetic landscape of Egyptian culture that is both familiar and accessible to the wider public.

> The media was very dirty in their coverage, they publicized this street as being dangerous and that it was filled with *baltageyeh*. People kept accusing us – the revolutionaries – of being traitors and taking money from abroad, Israel, America, Serbia, all that stupid talk. So for me [to address these accusations] I cared a lot about my graffiti being very Egyptian, so you'll find next to my drawing of a martyr the traditional depiction of the Islamic star that's drawn on people's houses, and the *Buraq Al Nabawi Al Sherief*[16] that's drawn on houses. So even if people don't connect these images together, they have a visual memory, I rely on the visual memory of our society. (Ammar Abo Bakr, Cairo, pers. comm., 30 April 2014)

The murals, and the consistent presence of revolutionaries within public space during this time, transformed the significance of the street – into a living, breathing, being of sorts. The function of the street evolved in accordance with the need of the moment, from being an impromptu memorial space to a public site for performance. This is a testament to the material – and symbolic – ways in which revolutionaries were able to redefine the very space they occupied.

The artistic legacy of the second phase of the revolution

The bloody events in the winter of 2011 and 2012 during the second phase of the revolution significantly altered the revolutionary art scene in two primary ways – first, several people informed me that this was a time was when revolutionary art 'really' gained momentum and strength after the success of Mubarak's ouster. Revolutionary art altered from the hasty, scribbled writings and 'spray and run' stencil tactics, which served their own strategic purpose during the initial eighteen days of the revolution which acted as a sign – a marker urging people to join in the collective refusal of Mubarak's regime, a critical form of protest and communication in the midst of a telecommunications blackout – to a physical occupation of the street and public places with their presence, by creating elaborate murals which responded to – and were located within – the events of the ensuing street battles on Mohamed Mahmoud Street. The second phase saw artists and non-artists alike be more physically – and permanently – present in the street, paralleling their lived reality as they participate in the revolution while simultaneously collaborating on more intricate and detailed imagery. As artist Tefa observed,

> people did not actually draw in the beginning of the revolution, drawing really began on the walls during the Mohamed Mahmoud street battles. Before that it was just stencils. We were thinking we are still afraid of the military but we would go down and do stencils so we couldn't get caught, because it is quick. . . . Mohamed Mahmoud [battles] is when people started to go down and actually take their time and draw. People from the Fine Arts would sit with each other and would talk about how they wanted to go down and draw, so people like Ammar Abu Bakr went down and drew murals in Mohamed Mahmoud, and I went with Moshir and did stencils. (Tefa, Cairo, pers. comm., 28 April 2014)

Tefa's comments suggest that artists had to respond to revolutionary events in real time, in an act which involved a type of archiving, as well as historicizing, narrating and criticizing, the events around them as they were situated within those events – and not its aftermath. It was through the creation of revolutionary art – that art became a source of power and agency, and not solely an aesthetic endeavour,

> Art doesn't have to be beautiful, for me what defines art is that something moves you from the inside. While a war is going on and people are falling you will find a person writing 'you are sons of dogs', this is history. The bodies and bullets will be removed and everyone will leave but in the end this is history, not what they write in their books or what we write, what is written on the walls, the people who were fighting they are the ones who did it. This is art. This is history. (El Zeft, Cairo, pers. comm., 27 April 2014)

The battles of Mohamed Mahmoud Street were revolutionary events through which efforts to re-establish the normative order were taken in the physical and symbolic sphere. The creation of revolutionary art cannot be addressed in isolation from the revolutionary events it is situated from, or within the community or the collective from which it is produced. As many of those I interviewed emphasized consistently in our interviews, it became necessary to occupy public space and establish physical presence with their art in public to delegitimize the state's narrative that the revolutionaries are foreign agents seeking to plunge Egypt into chaos and disarray and resist efforts by SCAF in what became the inevitable return of the status quo. This will be addressed in the third – and final – phase of the revolution, discussed in the next chapter, which would see a maturation of revolutionary art, much more direct, scathing and imbued with political satire, in their efforts to portray Mohamed Morsi's presidency as a (disastrous) return to the status quo and an extension of Mubarak's rule.

Chapter 5

THE THIRD PHASE OF THE REVOLUTION

MORSI'S PRESIDENCY (JUNE 2012–JULY 2013)

Mohamed Morsi (the former fifth president of Egypt) and the Muslim Brotherhood's unpopular rule was marked by an intensification of revolutionary art, as they became prime targets (just as Mubarak and SCAF before them) for their failure to deliver on their campaign promises. Most of those I spoke to said that the widespread sentiment in the street was that Morsi's Brotherhood rule, from its early days, was viewed as a continuation of the crony capitalism characteristic of Mubarak's regime (see Figure 5.1a), under an Islamic guise.

May 2012 elections

Graffiti targeting Morsi began during the lead-up to his election in June 2012, such as the iconic art produced in Mad Graffiti Week in January 2012 – the marionette graffiti which came out of the collaborative efforts of several artists (such as Far3on and KIM, among others). This marionette depicted SCAF controlling the candidates of the presidential elections. Initially, they were faceless, however, towards the last phase of the elections it came down to two candidates (after the elimination of other candidates such as Hamdeen Sabahi, Khaled Ali, Abdul Moneim Abul Futouh and Amr Moussa). These candidates were Morsi and Ahmad Shafiq-a former prime minister under Mubarak's regime, who was also found to be responsible for the 'Battle of the Camel'.[1] This made them the target of what Abaza calls the 'professional whiteners of walls' (Abaza, 2012c: 125), who would regularly erase their drawing. KIM told me that when the candidates were faceless, it was not as controversial than the second time they edited the drawing with the two candidates faces (Morsi and Shafiq). For KIM, this is when he believes that it took on a more outright political message that all the candidates – even though they present themselves as occupying different ideological platforms, they were initially the same person as were both controlled by the SCAF puppet master (see Figures 5.1b and c, and also Figure 5.2). As he noted,

There was a funeral service for the army, and this was the second time we did it. . . . The second time also what ousted the picture was that Shafiq and Morsi's face were drawn in the puppets and they were quickly erased – Morsi's face was erased three times. The first two times it was erased within an hour. We finished and then after an hour we found the face crossed out. Our friend that drew his face redrew it and it got erased within an hour. (KIM, Cairo, pers. comm., 18 August 2014)

Figure 5.1a Protestors carry an image of Morsi and Mubarak's face converged as one, with the name 'Mohamed Morsi Mubarak' written underneath.*Source*: Jones, 2013.

Figure 5.1b The Puppet Master 'SCAF' controls the faceless candidates of the Presidential elections in May 2012. *Source*: Qantara, 2012 (Reuters/Amr Abdallah Dalsh).

Figure 5.1c Phase 2 of the 'Puppet Master' – SCAF, controlling the two final candidates of the presidential elections – Morsi's face has been covered in black paint in this image while Shafiq's image remains. The rest of the candidates are shown as skeletons. *Source*: Abaza, 2012c.

Figure 5.2 Phase 2 of the mural of the half-Tantawi/half-Mubarak face, which included the half-faces of then-presidential candidates Amr Moussa and Ahmad Shafiq, all seen as being a continuation of the structural order through their former close ties to Mubarak's regime. According to those I spoke to, they were all essentially the same face. *Source*: Abaza, 2012c.

Mona Abaza emphasized that the 'depressing choice between two authoritarianisms: the Islamists and/or the army represented by Shafiq' (Abaza, 2012c: 124) had confirmed 'the fact that the nation has been witnessing a farcical masquerade, with the SCAF creating a semblance of elections and the setting up of a parliament with a majority of Islamists who have previously made a pact with the army' (Abaza, 2012c: 124). Hend Kheera, a fashion designer and structural engineer, also expressed her disappointment at how the elections ushered in Morsi's rule.

> I didn't vote, when they announced the results and that Morsi won, we cheered and were happy because the other side [Ahmad Shafiq] didn't win. After a moment we looked at each in the coffee shop and we were walking celebrating as we were leaving the coffee shop and then when we arrived to Mohamed Mahmoud Street we started crying. Why should we be happy? We went to an even worst direction. Then we had a lot of depressing moments after every one of Morsi's speech, it was a difficult time. (Hend Kheera, Cairo, pers. comm., 26 April 2014)

Most of those I spoke to said they felt that the elections were an orchestrated act, and so revolutionary art such as that made by Ammar, where he wrote the words (over his own martyr mural) 'Forget the past and stick with the elections' (see Figure 5.3), was intended to be 'a bitingly ironic statement that attacks the entire procedure of elections and those who believe that elections could be the solution to circumventing the might of the military junta. Abu

Figure 5.3 Ammar Abo Bakr painted over the martyr murals in late May 2012, where he intentionally 'graffitied' over with the words 'Forget what is past and support the elections'. Although many people thought it was being vandalized, in a video posted on Facebook, Ammar said he was the one who actually graffitied over the martyr murals because 'I think you don't need to see the martyrs' faces anymore, because you didn't follow the way of the revolution. An election under military rule has nothing to do with what the martyrs were fighting for.' *Source*: Abo Bakr, 2015.

Bakr's words convey the idea that elections are merely a bluff to divert citizens from the martyrs and the 12,000 people incarcerated under military rule' (Abaza, 2012c: 138).

Those I conversed with at the time all described feeling underwhelmed by the elections and the choice between Shafiq, a remnant of the Mubarak regime, and Morsi, a member of the Muslim Brotherhood, who had lost the credibility they gained with the revolutionaries when they formed a temporary alliance with the military under SCAF's transitional rule. Among those I spoke to, the ones who voted for Morsi (they choose not to be named) did so because they did not want a former Mubarak crony to win. They said they later regretted this decision and wished they did not vote at all since their choices were initially one and the same and that the status quo was continuing under the guise of 'democratic elections', in a way to define the end of the revolution. The repertoire of revolutionary art leading up to Morsi's election was primarily focused on emphasizing that the normative order was continuing under a different guise and that nothing would change with the elections.

Morsi's presidency

These sentiments would set the tone for the third phase of the revolution, which saw Mohammed Morsi elected as the first president since Mubarak's three-decade rule.

Morsi immediately reneged on every campaign promise he had made during his initial alliance with 'a segment of the revolutionary forces named the National Front. The Front campaigned for the Brotherhood's then-candidate in return for pledges he made. Their role was decisive given the slim victory he obtained – hardly 51% of the votes. Today, almost all of them have turned against the president' (Khorshid, 2013). This is the main reason why most revolutionary art painted Morsi out to be a liar because he never fulfilled his campaign promises such as forming a national salvation government, and turned his back on the National Front (Khorshid, 2013).

Several of those I spoke to said that Morsi began to transform into what they called a Brotherhood version of Mubarak, as he implemented measures which went against the revolution he once supported, such as forming 'temporary alliances with the interior ministry accused of killing protestors; with the military responsible for the deaths of protestors in the months that followed Mubarak's ousting; and with the businessmen accused of corruption under Mubarak' (Khorshid, 2013). Furthermore, instead of 'restructuring the interior ministry, Morsi praised it, saying that the police was "at the heart" of the revolution. And instead of holding the army responsible for the deaths of protesters under military rule, Morsi said they "protected the revolution"' (Khorshid, 2013).

Morsi's use of the revolution to justify – and suit – his political goals, was a continuation of the recycled SCAF narrative that they would 'protect the revolution' in an ironic effort to actually contain it.

Morsi, like SCAF before him, appropriated the 25 January revolution to legitimize his authority and protect his presidency. In light of the nationwide protests calling for Morsi to step down on 30 June 2012, Morsi asked, 'How can we protect our revolution from being stolen? I'll tell you: the revolution of the 25th of January and its goals, protecting its legitimacy – the price for this is my life because I want to protect your lives' (The Telegraph, 2013). In the aftermath of the 25 January revolution, where 'distinctions of class, religion, gender, education, political loyalties and religion coloured the ongoing and unpredictable post-Mubarak political process' (Peterson, 2015b: 67), the use of the revolution (and Tahrir Square, in particular) was a common practice appropriated by different political parties to 'generate[] political capital' (Peterson, 2015b: 67) as it reminds people of a time 'where such divisions did not matter' and that everyone participate in 'a unified Egyptian nation above and beyond the state' (Peterson, 2015b: 67).

In light of Morsi's unpopular rule – where, according to one journalist, '[s]tep by step, Morsi turned his back to the revolution' (Khorshid, 2013) – revolutionary art intensified in an effort to deconstruct what they saw was Morsi's failed campaign promises. According to Mona Abaza, the backlash against Morsi was fierce, and the art on the walls did not fail to address every one of his shortcomings.

> *Al-ikhwaan khirfaan* (The brotherhood are sheep) was one main slogan that has multiplied all over the walls [referring to them as followers void of critical thought], which was often accompanied with plenty of tamed white sheep. *Dustuurhum ghair dusturna* (Their Constitution is not our constitution), *Dustuur al-ikhawan Baatel* (The Muslim Brotherhoood's constitution is invalid). Morsi has been portrayed in graffiti as a hand puppet [see Figures 5.4 and 5.5], as a thug, as a liar [see Figures 5.6 and 5.7] displaying his chest (alluding to his performance during his first speech after becoming president when he bared his chest to the crowd at Tahrir Square to show that he is one of the people and does not require a bullet-proof vest), or as the queen of clubs card being manipulated by a bigger evil looking joker. (Abaza, 2013c)

The continuous evolution of revolutionary art on the street corner of Mohamed Mahmoud Street/Tahrir Square once again addressed the Brotherhood's unpopular rule (e.g. Figure 5.8), and Figure 5.9 was taken by Mona Abaza in September 2012, after the walls on the corner of Mohamed Mahmoud Street and Tahrir Square were once again erased by 'professional whiteners'. This time, there was an addition of a portrait of Muslim Brotherhood General

Figure 5.4 Morsi depicted as a hand puppet. Portrayals of him as such were common, representative of notions that he was controlled by the Murshid (the supreme leader) of the Brotherhood, Mohammed Badie. Next to him is the symbol of the Egyptian republic, the Eagle with a beard, representing the 'Brotherhoodization' of the Egyptian state. *Source*: Photo by Author.

Figure 5.5 Morsi sitting on the lap of the Supreme Leader (Murshid) of the Brotherhood as a puppet, with the Murshid being the ventriloquist. Popular sentiments on the streets was that Morsi was simply the face behind the organization, and had no real power. He only said what he was told to say by the Murshid. Above it says 'I am the decision maker'. Many of those I spoke to believed that Morsi was a puppet to larger powers, such as in one conversation with Sad Panda, where he told me that 'Morsi isn't the problem, he is the most one who was taken advantage in all this, because he really didn't have anything to do with this. When the Murshid doesn't tell him what to say he doesn't know what to say' (Sad Panda, Cairo, pers. comm., 28 April 2014). *Source*: Photo by Author.

Figure 5.6 An image of a 'Super Morsi', with the Muslim Brotherhood logo altered to read, 'if it happens, he will deny (or lie) about it'. *Source*: Suzeeinthecity, 2013.

Figure 5.7 Graffiti which says 'You are Liars', which is against 'religious extremists and the Muslim Brotherhood's attempts to censor art' (Suzeeinthecity, 2013). *Source*: Photo by Author.

Figure 5.8 More art mocking the Brotherhood and their rhetoric. This one says 'we will implement *shari'a* law even if we break it'. *Source*: Photo by Author.

Figure 5.9 'The half-Mubarak-half-Tantawi portrait was repainted in a smaller size, with the addition of a portrait of Muslim Brotherhood General Guide Mohamed Badie. Below it is an image of a painter using his brush fresh with dripping paint as a weapon in confronting a policeman's stick.' *Source*: Abaza, 2013b.

Guide (*murshid*) Mohamed Badie, as well as an image of a painter using his brush as a weapon in confronting a policeman's stick (Abaza, 2013b). A poem at the bottom reads:

> You, a regime scared of a brush and a pen
> You were unjust and crushed those who suffered injustice
> If you were honest, you would have not been fearful of painting
> The best you can do is conduct a war on walls, and exert your power over lines and colors
> Inside, you are a coward who can never build what was destroyed (Abaza, 2013b)

This art is in reference to the 'war' declared by the 'professional whiteners' on the 'growing dissenting underground culture' (Abaza, 2012c: 125) of the Egyptian revolution, and that their art would continue regardless of the authorities' attempt to whitewash the walls into the homogeneity so representative of the status quo.

The re-emergence of the status quo

In November 2012, on the first anniversary of the Mohamed Mahmoud Street battle, clashes once again occurred and many, such as the iconic revolutionary Gika, died. Ammar Abo Bakr repainted the martyr murals (see Figure 5.10); however, his intention this time was not to commemorate the martyrs, but to serve as a stark reminder (through graphic images) that violence would continue and that nothing would change under the Brotherhood rule.

Figure 5.10 November 2012 Martyr Mural on Mohamed Mahmoud Street. On the left, it says 'the reality is uglier'. *Source*: Abo Bakr, 2015.

On November 2012, on the first anniversary of the fights against the security forces in Mohamed Mahmoud Street, I came back to paint a martyrs' gallery again. But this time, I painted them with really gruesome faces – exactly as they looked after they died. I wanted to give the people a sign that there would be more bloodshed. (Abo Bakr, 2015)

It should be noted that the majority of those I interviewed were not as comfortable discussing this period as much as they did the first and second phases of the revolution. In hindsight, this was perhaps because my fieldwork, and hence my interviews, began at the end of November 2013 (in the aftermath of the second anniversary of the Mohamed Mahmoud Street clashes), when the state media narrative against the Muslim Brotherhood was prolific and when any show of sympathy with or any conversation around the Brotherhood was considered suspicious and potentially dangerous. Most of those I spoke to did not speak much about the art they did, nor about their activities during this time. It was, as such, clear to me that without exception, all of those I spoke to did not agree with Morsi's rule while those who voted for him said they did not vote for him with conviction because they felt 'forced to vote for him because of the choice between bad and worse' (Amr Nazeer, Cairo, pers. comm., 9 March 2014).

Many were hesitant to speak about particular pieces they produced during this time – for those who did produce any revolutionary art – as they were more focused during our interviews on explaining their resentment towards Morsi's presidency, which was – for almost all of those I spoke to – expressed as the same resentment they had towards the former military rule under Tantawi and Mubarak. In their words, they were all simply an extension of the same, corrupt structural order under different ideological guises and different faces –

the content of my graffiti has not changed . . . my first target was Mubarak, then Tantawi, then Morsi . . . the principle is the same . . . you do not support any of these people. When I was cursing the army the public was against us when we were against Morsi . . . So we are in a perpetual state of being everyone's enemy because we stick to our principles. (Amr Nazeer, Cairo, pers. comm., 9 March 2014)

Mohammad Khaled also explained to me that for him, his revolutionary art stayed the same (although he did not want to speak in detail about specific pieces since we were speaking in public), only the target kept shifting because he was essentially attacking the same status quo: 'I did revolutionary art on the army. Of course during Morsi's time I did stuff on the Brotherhood because I believe they are on the same degree of filth and dirt. To me, they are both one and the same . . . they are at the bottom of filth. They both commercialize on people's dreams' (Mohammed Khaled, Cairo, pers. comm., 29 April 2014).

This was a sentiment echoed by the majority of those I spoke to – that the structural order was simply repeating itself over and over again in what seemed to be an endless, and deadly, cycle. Although this was not put on any walls but was available on social media platforms, Mira Shihadeh told me that she created a piece (see Figure 5.11) that reflected a popular opinion among those I interviewed that the *fulool* and Brotherhood are essentially one and the same, all part of the 'system', which Ammar describes as a 'system is repression, and everything is a sickness' (Abo Bakr, 2015).

> There is another piece I did that is out there [initially she put it on Twitter] but that I did not put on a wall – it says 'the revolution continues in the past and the present'. It is these three figures, I really believe this is about the three figures, the Army, the Brotherhood, and the *fulool* – they are really one and each other, they need each other. (Mira Shihadeh, pers. comm., 30 April 2014)

Pieces such as that made by Mira Shihadeh earlier, as well as the half-Mubarak face which evolved under SCAF and the Brotherhood illustrate, that 'graffiti artists have drawn- and continued to draw – the strong analogy between Mubarak, the SCAF and the Muslim Brotherhood for being one and the same continuing mode of rule. The artists wanted to convey one main point: nothing has changed [see Figure 5.12]' (Abaza, 2013b).

Figure 5.11 Mira Shihadeh's 'Circle of Evil', which depicts the shadowy figures of a member of the military, a member of the Muslim Brotherhood, and a member of the *fulool* as continuously re-enforcing the normative order. *Source*: Sultan Al Qassemi, 2015.

Figure 5.12 An image of a police officer with the words 'The [Ministry] of Interior is still exactly the same', indicating that the culture of police brutality which instigated the Egyptian revolution of 2011 still exists in full force under Morsi's presidency. According to one journalist, Morsi's biggest downfall was that '[i]nstead of restructuring the interior ministry, Morsi praised it, saying that the police was "at the heart" of the revolution' (Khorshid, 2013). *Source*: Photo by Author.

Challenging the notion of the political, rethinking politics

During my interviews, there was no consensus on understandings of street art to the political. For some, the 'political' was a judgement of taste, in that they stated that their art had to be directly aligned to the political goals of the ongoing revolution, whereas for others, the term 'political' as a description of their art was inconsequential. Although not articulated as political, many aligned the importance of street art to not only discussion but also debate, and necessarily argued that conflict was necessary.

For most of those I spoke to, the political was neither a 'radical' rupture in the way scholar Jacques Rancière conceived it, nor was it a space of conflict. Rather, the very notion of something 'being' political was simply the normative condition of existing with others, and being with others (akin to the way scholar Ariella Azoulay describes her notion of the political as not something existing on the margins which occurs when certain preconditions are present) who articulate similar demands as you and exist within the same space, affected by the same social, political and cultural processes. Yet others, such as Sad Panda, completely disavowed politics and the political altogether, which he essentially saw as one and the same (Sad Panda, Cairo, pers. comm., 28 April 2014).

Hanaa El Degham told me that after working in the street and creating art in the midst of a constant dialogue with other members of society, her view on art significantly altered and that she realized her previous concern for what she saw were more 'societal' issues could not be separated from the political, even though she does not articulate art in terms of political/non-political; instead she sees the political as the normative condition of art as being situated within social relations and discourses:

> Art ends up being political because in the end we are all people living in the same place and want the same thing. We don't like our lives and want to change the policies of the country and the unjust regime. In the revolution we focused on these everyday items that should be available. For example, when you criticize that the basic everyday needs of people that they need to eat isn't available, and it should be available, it is a basic right for people to have it, they should live in their country with dignity, he is able to eat and to be educated – basic rights. So even if I do not criticize someone directly or it is overtly political, I am still criticizing the whole system. So I don't think whether it is political or not, I say what I want to say, whatever way people see it, it all depends on their background on how they think. (Hanaa El Degham, Berlin, Skype interview, 29 November 2013)

Hala El Sharouny also told me that she does not differentiate between political and non-political art because the context will always affect the personal direction of one's art, in that,

> Whether you wanted to or not politics is living inside you, in a sense that socially I am affected politically because politics affects you socially. So even though I may not speak about politics directly but the anger inside you comes out especially when you express yourself through art. I don't paint flowers or boats or the ocean or sun or a beautiful girl sleeping on her side I paint emotional reactions because art for me is a form of therapy, if I didn't draw I would have went crazy a long time ago. I draw when I am upset not when I am happy . . . so my problems are reflected in my art, which are usually social, but in the end you always feel there is a political part affecting you, even if it is not visible in your art. (Hala El Sharouny, Cairo, pers. comm., 18 August 2014)

Conceptualizations of art – in terms of whether they felt that they were coming from a political perspective – were irrelevant to most that I spoke to because they believed this interpretation went beyond the work and beyond the artists' intentions. They found this label unhelpful and irrelevant, because art being located in the street, created within and through societal relations, in this 'being-together of humans' (Azoulay, 2010: 248), enacted the political without having reduced the art to a 'political judgment of taste' deeming it a political work (Azoulay, 2010: 248).

In this sense, then, the political is not necessarily only a disordering of the visible order of the police, nor is it only the space of ever-present conflict antagonism, nor was the political necessarily reduced to 'rare moments of epiphany when it seems to emerge in all its glory' (Azoulay, 2012: 37). Azoulay argues that constantly rendering the political as a practice 'centring on problematisation, resistance or contestation' (Azoulay, 2012: 108) does not allow us to take other practices into account, such as Ammar's experience of the *mulid*. Ammar told me that the *mulid* was one of the most political manifestations he has ever experienced, akin to his participation in the uprising (Ammar Abo Bakr, Cairo, pers. comm., 30 April 2014). Thus, understanding the ways in which notions of the political can also displace notions of the ways in which we can enact the political beyond conflict and aesthetic re-ordering, but also to include symbolic and spiritual contestations over space allows us to understand the importance of the political as 'inherent in every encounter between human beings' (Azoulay, 2012: 101) and can include less 'obvious' political ruptures.

Although this may be an over-conflation of notions of the political which may lead to the 'everything is political' notion Rancière is against, it is helpful in this sense to think about the political outside of the margins of a certain configuration of experiences or issues of disarticulations of the hegemonic structure and instead of being located between people. Azoulay emphasizes that 'politics' can be found in 'other domains' outside of the state or in the presence of certain configurations which renders the political visible (Azoulay, 2012: 108), a notion that came across in Ammar Abo Bakr's[2] recollection of his experience of the *mulid*, or 'Saints Festivals', which are common across Egypt. The *mulid* finds hundreds of thousands of people coming together to celebrate the birth of the Prophet Muhammad (specifically called the *mulid Al-Nabi*); however, in Egypt it also includes the birthday of those regarded as saints by Sufis, such as Imam Al-Hussein, the Prophet's grandson, or Sayeda Zaynab, the Prophet's granddaughter. The idea that the *mulid* is comparable to the revolution is in the transformative power of both in their ability to gather large groups of equal – under the principle of equality – to foster a collective with unified goals, and so Ammar says he

disagree[s] with people who do not see the strength or power of the collective – look at the revolution. The meaning of revolution in its most essential meaning is groups of people going down in the street – it has no other meaning. How can you be with the revolution and reject the collective? Don't speak of the revolution then if you can't speak of the collective. The acceptance of the other is one of the main conditions of the collective. The romantic and beautiful [he speaks sarcastically] state during those 18 days of everyone accepting everyone during the revolution of which everyone speaks of is what we mean when we say the acceptance of the other in the collective. Go to a *mulid* as you are now [pointing at me] and you will see how they will accept you as you are, they will not ask you if you are Muslim and Christian. Go to the *mulid* in this spirit of acceptance of the other. (Ammar Abo Bakr, Cairo, pers. comm., 30 April 2014)

Ammar's intimate experience participating, documenting and observing the *mulid* is indicative of the ways in which aesthetic experience is central to how we come to know and feel the world and how we gain knowledge about the world. Perhaps during crucial junctures which demand a reflection of internal social processes we try to understand art – and the conditions of its emergence – as attributable not only to the politics of resistance or the production of artefacts (i.e. 'revolutionary') or even to examine the power dynamics of their appearance, we have to understand that the aesthetic lies in the heart of experience, in which we come to perceive, feel and know the world, much in the same way philosophers such as American philosopher John Dewey articulated an understanding of art as constitutive of everyday experience.

For example, Ammar's knowledge and connection with the collective in the *mulid* transcends an experience confined to a certain time and space – it affected the very way he understands public mobilization and the ways in which one can come to occupy space. Thus, our engagement in the world was expressed by many of those I interviewed as a creative engagement, one which is never actually complete or final. Experiences are constantly transferred into other realms of experience, and this can enrich our understanding of the political not only as a rupture of the consensus with the hegemonic order as conceived by Rancière but also by a rupture within understanding the political as the way in which we understand ourselves and relate to others.

Raymond Williams has consistently argued that culture is a signifying practice, a place where we share and contest meanings of ourselves and the worlds we live in (Williams, 1981) – yet based on the interviews it seemed that art and the political also constituted a space for meaning-making. Not politics in the sense of the ordering preserved by the police – but a more 'authentic' politics which Rancière speaks of, which is staged by 'supplementary subjects' – whose political and creative acts alike disrupt the space of consensus (Rancière, 2001).

And so while several of those I spoke to complained that they halted their activities in the street during Morsi's election from their disillusionment, Ammar Abo Bakr said Morsi's presidency as well as Brotherhood rule was not an impediment to his cultural and creative activity because it was an underestimation of the Egyptian people to assume that their identity was tied to any one political or ideological basis. As he said,

> artists would keep whining that they could not be creative during Muslim Brotherhood rule, that they could not draw in the streets. This is evidence that these artists don't know or understand or are connected to the people, that they don't know the behavior of society – that they underestimate their society. The media kept ranting that the Brotherhood would halt the Egyptian Opera, that they would close the door on Egyptian film and cinema that all creative cultural production would stop and that they would divide everything into *halal* [permissible] and *haram* [forbidden]. I do not like the Muslim Brotherhood, we do know that the Muslim Brotherhood and some Islamists in general are backwards all the way to their roots, however for those who know Egypt well and have been around in Egypt and been exposed to and integrated in Egyptian society will understand differently. (Ammar Abo Bakr, Cairo, pers. comm., 30 April 2014)

The point Ammar was emphasizing was that the concepts of communitas and anti-structure experienced during the liminal time of the revolution were familiar notions to Egyptians because of their experience and participation in another liminal time, the annual *mulids*. Ammar's continued involvement (both before and after the uprising) in documenting and participating in the *mulid* made him 'drawn to the collective because of this background with following the *mulid*. I have a collective form of thought, a collective way of thinking' (Ammar Abo Bakr, Cairo, pers. comm., 30 April 2014), and he said this occupation of public space – where they simply carved a space for themselves and performed spiritual rituals crucial to understandings of who they are – convinced him that Egyptians could impose their presence regardless of any governing authority, if they did it out of conviction and for a higher cause.

Azoulay argues that constantly rendering the political as a practice 'centering on problematization, resistance or contestation' (Azoulay, 2012: 108) does not allow us to take other practices into account, such as Ammar's understanding of the *mulid* and the revolution as existential experiences (Ammar Abo Bakr, Cairo, pers. comm., 30 April 2014). Thus, the political can also include symbolic and spiritual contestations over space, allowing us to understand the importance of the political as 'inherent in every encounter between human beings' (Azoulay, 2012: 101) and thus can include less 'obvious' political ruptures.

Re-emergence of violence against women

Although several people I interviewed, such as Ammar, continued working on revolutionary art focusing on the Brotherhood and Morsi and calling for the public to arrest him, he said he stopped in December 2012 in order not to 'give the Army or the *fulool* any more ammunition', and so focused more on issues of culture and identity (Ammar Abo Bakr, Cairo, pers. comm., 30 April 2014). There were many artists I spoke to who felt this way, which translated into a shift of the primary subject of their ire in their artistic activities. For Mira Shihadeh, it was the attacks against women in Tahrir, particularly on the second anniversary of the revolution, that prompted her to create art (see Figures 5.13a and b). As she said,

Figure 5.13a and 5.13b The 'Circle of Hell' by Mira Shihadeh and El Zeft, on the wall barricading Mansour Street where the image of El Zeft's rainbow mural used to be. *Source*: Photo by Author.

I told El Zeft lets go down and do something, and I read about the sexual harassment. . . . I am trying to talk about organized harassment, it is not just random . . . I was trying to address the organization of it during protests. The men in the image are saying things like, 'I am tired so what else should I do', 'Don't be scared we are trying to help you' but he is also harassing her, 'Look what she is wearing', 'But she isn't my sister' because there is always the comment to these people like 'what if this was your sister?' People need to see this kind of image in front of their eyes to realize how horrific it is. (Mira Shihadeh, pers. comm., 30 April 2014)

The issue of sexual harassment during this time was horrific not only because it became so prolific but because it was – as Mira Shihadeh mentioned – not spontaneous. This period of time started to exhibit anti-structure *without* the communitas of the first two phases of the revolution, where there was a breakdown within the social sphere which restored the divisions of Mubarak's regime and saw sexual harassment return in full force. These assaults took on a different form – they were more of a targeted and concerted attack against women in public places where, only two years prior, the communitas of the revolution saw men and women mingle together equally and protect one another during clashes with the central security forces. It was this anger, this return to the anti-structure of the normative order in the absence of the

Figure 5.14 El Zeft pays tribute to the significant role Egyptian women played in the revolution. *Source*: El Zeft, Facebook post, 2012.

communitas which propelled the revolution, which made El Zeft announce his iconic 'Nefertiti' mask in September 2012 in a Facebook post (see Figure 5.14) which he had stencilled on Mohamed Mahmoud Street. El Zeft told me he was greatly affected by the widespread reports of incidents of sexual harassment and assaults in Tahrir Square and downtown Cairo during Brotherhood rule, and the undermining of women in speeches by Muslim Brotherhood members which would further degrade the status of women in Egyptian society. He said that it felt as though, all of a sudden, the chaos of the normative order under Mubarak returned when people started to forget that women played a crucial role in the revolution.

Everything bad was happening suddenly, harassment increased. It snapped suddenly. I don't understand. It was brutal, 20 people raping someone in Tahrir. At the time the Islamists were saying things about women like marrying girls when they are 9 and I don't know what they were saying, the image of the woman was becoming distorted a lot. But the nature of the battle that had transpired in Mohamed Mahmoud in the past made it, in a way, a very masculine street. So I wanted to say that they [women] had a role exactly like ours, that they existed, they were with us. I wanted to tell people we are all together, that she has a role, that she is equal. In a lot of the clashes we would find the women were with us not just spraying water, they actually [physically] joined us in the clashes. What I was thinking is that Nefertiti was known as the strong queen and she supported her husband against everyone. She is the most known Egyptian woman in history. And I used the gas mask as a global symbol for the revolution. (El Zeft, Cairo, pers. comm., 27 April 2014)

El Zeft's aesthetic visualization of strong Egyptian women was an attempt to highlight one of the most significant achievements of the liminal moment of the revolution, which was the visibility, participation and importance of women as one of the revolution's most celebrated achievements, even if it was temporary. The image of the woman, for El Zeft, is an attempt to counter the more masculine image of the Egyptian revolution and reaffirms the importance of location in the creation of revolutionary art. As El Zeft told me, he chose to put Nefertiti in Mohamed Mahmoud Street because it was a 'masculine street', and his image of a strong Egyptian woman in a gas mask was intended to remind and solidify the importance of women in the Egyptian revolution as being equally significant as men's, even if their image is not as prominent or publicized. This image would later be appropriated for sexual harassment campaigns and protests not only in Egypt but also in places such as Germany, where Amnesty International organized protests against the widespread cases of sexual harassment in Egypt during Morsi's rule (see Figure 5.15).

Walls of Freedom: Street Art of the Egyptian Revolution
shared Amnesty International Deutschland's photo.
22 May 2013 · 🌐

The amazing El Zeft 's Nefertiti mask once again in an Amnesty protest against Sexual Harassment in Egypt. This is the power of art at its best!

ÄGYPTEN: SEXUELLE GEWALT GEGEN FRAUEN STOPPEN!

AMNESTY
INTERNATIONAL

Amnesty International Deutschland ✅
22 May 2013 · 🌐

Figure 5.15 Protestors in Germany against sexual harassment in Egypt. *Source*: Walls of Freedom, Facebook post, 2013.

The beginning of Morsi's end

Morsi's unpopular rule was met with continuous protests, and according to Ahdaf Soueif, renowned Egyptian author and commentator, '[Morsi] failed to honour every one of the promises he made in order to be elected. He basically behaved as though he had somehow legitimately inherited the old Mubarak regime with a veneer of piety' (Soueif, cited in Abdel Kouddous, 2013). In response to overwhelming public anger at Morsi's performance as president, in April 2013 a grassroots movement entitled *Tamarod* ('rebellion') was founded by members of the Egyptian Movement for Change (also known by its slogan *Kefaya*, or 'Enough') and set as its main goal the collection of signatures in order to call for early presidential elections.

On 29 June 2013, *Tamarod* (see Figures 5.16–5.18) announced that 22 million signatures (their original aim was 15 million) had been collected and on 30 June 2013, millions of Egyptians called on Morsi to step down. The next day the military gave the president a 48-hour ultimatum to solve the current crisis otherwise, as Sisi stated in a television address: 'If the people's demands are not met, the military, which is forced to act according to its role and duty, will have to disclose its own future plan' (Bradley, Abdellatif, 2013). Muslim Brotherhood members and Morsi's supporters gathered in Rab'a Square in solidarity with

Figure 5.16 The word *Tamarod* ('rebel') is written, and underneath it says 'The Beginning of the End' (of Morsi's rule), in reference to 30 June when massive protests were planned calling on Morsi to step down. *Source*: Photo by Author.

Figure 5.17 In red it says 'Tamarod' (rebel), and below it says 'On you and the Brotherhood'. The background is Morsi's face. *Source*: Photo by Author.

Morsi, until the army forcibly removed them, killing hundreds, in what was known as the Rab'a massacre of 13 August 2013. This day decisively marked, for many of those I spoke to, the end of the revolutionary process, whereas for

Figure 5.18 Morsi's face in the background with an 'X' drawn on it. It says on the upper right corner '30' in reference to Tamarod's call for action on 30 June 2013, the day when nationwide protests were planned, to call on Morsi to step down. Next to Morsi's face it says 'Red Disaster'. *Source*: Photo by Author.

others, it indicated a severe setback. On 3 July 2013, the military intervened and removed Morsi as president, overruled the constitution and installed an interim government until the next presidential elections, which Sisi won by a landslide in June 2014.

Chapter 6

THE END OF THE REVOLUTION

Revolutionary euphoria had significantly waned by the end of 2013. This was the post-Rab'a moment, when the military re-assumed its authoritative position of power – resuming, full circle, to life under SCAF rule once again. Unlike other moments of the revolutionary process, this phase was different than the first SCAF transitional rule from February 2011 to June 2012. The first phase of SCAF's initial rule was marked by an openness to revolutionary art and revolutionary artists critical of the army and its conduct. During this period, campaigns such *Kazeboon* ('liars') emerged in December 2011 (following the Mohamed Mahmoud Street battles), which were intended to counter state media narrative through public screenings of footage of the army's brutality and to call for an end to SCAF rule (and later, Muslim Brotherhood rule). Other significant, and public signs of dissent against SCAF rule such as the Occupy Cabinet sit-ins and Tahrir Square clashes of December 2011 amidst parliamentary elections also saw scathing revolutionary art against the army and its officers.

Interestingly, however, open criticism of the army in the aftermath of Rab'a was no longer acceptable, not only by the authorities but mainly by the public themselves – the 'honourable citizens' whose resentment towards the Muslim Brotherhood through Morsi's controversial presidency saw the forced removal and killing of his supporters in Rab'a. The political trickster (as Armbrust argues) par excellence which emerged victorious from this period and led to the 'defeat of the Revolution's architects' (Armbrust, 2017: 233) was General Abdel Fattah El-Sisi, who led the assault in Rab'a.

In the aftermath of Morsi's ouster, and in the run-up to the presidential elections of May 2014 (during which I conducted the majority of my fieldwork), Sisi's popularity sky-rocketed, as he was depicted as the iron fist saviour and national hero of Egypt, as his supporters declared 'Sisi is my President' (see Figure 6.1) in songs, posters and banners. During this time, 'supporters tried very hard to make him the new [Gamal Abdel] Nasser, not the Nasser of war and defeat, but the Nasser of progress and national pride' (Armbrust, 2017: 235), in an attempt to cement his status as parallel to that of the iconic Nasser, the charismatic face of Arab socialism and Arab nationalism, who had massive public support.

Those whom I interviewed for my research were caught in a dangerous predicament – they did not approve of the Muslim Brotherhood and resented

Figure 6.1 On the third anniversary of the revolution (25 January 2014), a supporter outside of the El-Itihadeya Presidential Palace hugs a 'Sisi is My President' poster, a familiar slogan repeated in the run-up to the presidential elections in June 2014, indicative of the 'cult of Sisi' (Lindsey, 2013) that developed in the aftermath of Morsi's ouster. *Source*: Reuters/Amer Abdallah Dalsh.

Morsi's presidency, yet they had hoped that plans to remove him from power were led by a legal, peaceful and public initiative rather than armed confrontations and violence. They did not want the return of army rule, which they said was inevitable with Sisi's rise to stardom in the public sphere which led them all to (correctly) predict that he would win the presidential elections in June 2014. Their position – of supporting neither the Brotherhood nor supporting Sisi's rule – located them in a precarious grey zone where any expression of disdain for the military and its actions in Rab'a made them susceptible to the violence of the public (which they now feared more than the authorities).

This uneasy time – which could also be characterized as a liminal moment in terms of being 'between two (uncomfortable) states' – was not marked by intense creativity, social solidarity (communitas), or a foregrounding of agency, though it most certainly was marked by anti-structure, ambiguity and violence. The atmosphere when I began my interviews was during a time when revolutionary art was no longer being celebrated, but whitewashed by authorities and the public alike, and when revolutionary artists were being ostracized and even killed (such as the tragic case of Hisham Rizk and Issa[1]). In this tense atmosphere, and by the end of 2013 and the beginning of 2014, most of those I spoke to said they were taking an indefinite break from revolutionary art or created it sporadically, at certain times when they could not be seen for fear of attacks not by authorities but the general public.

The sentiment I felt from the people I interviewed during this period was one of cautious hope combined with a disenchantment of 'look at where we were and where we are now', in terms of their freedom to create art in the street and the intense social bond they formed fighting and creating art alongside the public, who were, for the most part, in solidarity against the authorities. Some, such as Keizer, said that although they felt 'deflated' by the divisions and sociopolitical atmosphere at the time, still had hope that the 'chaotic unpredictability which allowed the first revolution to happen' – would return and that the liminal moment would again be a reality (Keizer, Cairo, pers. comm., 26 April 2014).

For the revolutionaries, the liminal moment of the revolution represented the ultimate time they aspired to return to – where solidarity, communitas, agency and creativity flourished, even amidst the backdrop of struggle against the normative order, which, to them, represented chaos and uncertainty and destruction. However, in the aftermath of Rab'a, state media claimed that those who continued the call for a revolution were seeking to disrupt normal life in Egypt and return it to a chaotic state, and that lack of support for the army meant *de facto* support for the Brotherhood – a dangerous narrative that was replicated within Egyptian society. I witnessed an example firsthand, sitting in a coffee shop in downtown Cairo, when two young male AUC students who were speaking with each other against the military were reprimanded by one of the waiters, who called them traitors and members of the Muslim Brotherhood. They were harassed and eventually forced to leave after a light skirmish.

As I have shown in previous chapters, the initial phase of the revolution in 2011 and 2012 was marked by violence of the authorities and security forces against the public, who collectively retaliated and gathered around unified demands and goals, first against Mubarak, then the first SCAF transitional rule, and then Morsi's presidency. Yet in the aftermath of the Rab'a massacre in the summer of 2013, the violence was between Muslim Brotherhood members and the army, and between members of the public – those who supported Sisi (which represented the majority) and those who did not. This divisiveness marked a volatile period, and most of those I spoke to had halted their artistic activities in the street altogether as they said that fear returned as a central component of their lives. They also expressed feeling anger and disappointment when they used to exist in mostly civil conditions with the public while creating art during the early phases of the revolution but were now harassed, beaten, or insulted for creating revolutionary art by 'honorable citizens' who were either supporters of Sisi or Brotherhood members. They said this backlash effectively marginalized them from public space, as it was the general public that they feared more, even more than the bullets of the regime during the revolution.

> Now you are afraid more of the people than from the regime. If you insult the army in the street people will fight with you and push you around, not the regime itself. I wasn't afraid at the time at all, for example in the morning you could be at the front lines facing live bullets, and at night you were drawing on the walls. So you felt it was so silly what you were doing at night compared to what you were doing in the morning, so I didn't feel much fear. Now you don't know anything, so now you will be more are afraid from the people. (El Zeft, Cairo, pers. comm., 27 April 2014)

The uncertainty and violence of the liminal moment during the initial phase of the revolution were not portrayed negatively – the ambiguity and struggle of that moment, as well as the violence of the street battles between the authorities and the public was reflected upon as a period embedded with hope because of the sense of community and agency. The uncertainty and violence of the period after Rab'a was depicted negatively, as being a return – to an even greater degree – of the fear, displacement and humiliation of the status quo as the revolution was being dismantled by the authorities. As Sad Panda told me in this regard,

> the whole Mubarak regime was really bad, it was horrible, the whole system, and people used to live in misery. But somehow, it was stable. You understand? We're in shit, but we know it is shit, and it is there. So people, after years, they started to figure their way out around the shit. But now no, now nobody knows anything, and this shit keeps on going, it is not stable. So you can't even find your own way. And people are so stressed out now – even during Mubarak's time regardless of everything he did, there wasn't as much blood as there is now, many people died. Right now everyone has had someone that died, we have artists friends who died and they had nothing to do with anything, there are Muslim Brotherhood members who died, there are NDP members that died, there are people from the Ministry of Interior that died, people from the army that died, from every part of society, regardless of who is right and who is wrong, somehow you feel the city is so bloody. (Sad Panda, Cairo, pers. comm., 28 April 2014)

This period suggested that the liminal moment remained, but, unlike the ones preceding it, was not imbued with a sense of hope, purpose and direction but with a sense of defeat, uncertainty, loss and betrayal. That moment, and the sentiments it evoked, underscored the tense and uncertain atmosphere I found myself conducting interviews in, as the shadow of Rab'a and its aftermath remained a source of trauma and a glaring symbol of the end of the revolutionary process. As Armbrust notes, liminality 'can be seen as both the beginning and the end of revolution' (Armbrust, 2017: 221), and this period of time seemed to indicate a decisive end.

The process of revolutionary art: A real and tangible legacy of the revolution

Although this period of time in the aftermath of the Rab'a massacre saw a surge in repressive measures to establish Sisi as Egypt's next strongman in the presidential elections of May 2014, many of those I interviewed were optimistic about the sporadic existence of revolutionary art, even if it at the time it had significantly slowed down,

> The future of the street in Egypt is that artists and people know that going to the street is influential and has an effect. In the past three years, people understand more about politics and how to say no, they know more about their culture,

so there is no more fear. People will keep drawing on the street and may take different forms, and more artistic development, beyond the galleries. Our culture started with drawing on walls, it just took on a different form, and will come back stronger. People tried it and realized that it reaches faster to the people and to the world in regards to what is happening in Egypt, and there is no going back, only forward. It doesn't matter who rules Egypt, what matters most is that people are more aware and that whoever rules Egypt they can go out on the street and say no if they aren't happy with them. (Hanaa El Degham, Berlin, 29 November 2013)

Others said that revolutionary art will continue to exist because it endured as part of the revolutionary cultural aesthetic which attempts to democratize the cultural sphere. As Ammar Abo Bakr said:

I am Art should be for the people. It should be everywhere for the people. It has to be for the people, it's not an option, it's a necessity. The people have been isolated from everything beautiful in our country for 40-50 years. Can you imagine how much effort it is going to take from the artists to directly participate in returning to the people their original visual memory, which contains the form and hints of their identity?. (Ammar Abo Bakr, Cairo, pers. comm., 30 April 2014)

Ammar was disdainful of modern art because he believed it was representative of the normative order aimed at subverting Egyptians' identity in the state's aggressive push towards profits and gains. Ammar's experience in the revolution with the collective, and his involvement in countering the state's media against claims of 'foreign agents' disrupting the country by adopting a more Egyptian aesthetic mural in his revolutionary art, was an existential crisis, which informed his understanding that art can no longer be a practice created by the few for the few but is essentially located within the collective, both in its creation and consumption. This is how he put it:

I am always preoccupied with extending the cultural heritage of Egypt from the past to the contemporary, and I do not feel like so-called enlightened academic contemporary modern artists are interested in this extension when they present their artworks in galleries . . . As artists we understood our role [in the aftermath of the revolution] was not to draw portraits and rush off to sell them in galleries – you as an artist who are drawing some random man in a café smoking shisha and then sell them in galleries for 20,000 pounds – this would make an artist a con man, because his art is not reaching the modest Egyptian man in his painting. You are using him. This was the opinion of the majority of artists who went down in the streets. (Ammar Abo Bakr, Cairo, pers. comm., 30 April 2014)

However, others felt that the enduring aspect of revolutionary art was in the act of making or creating art along with the spontaneous participation of the wider public. Mohamad Alaa told me that the widespread existence and creation of art in public spaces during the revolution was a necessary indication of a different form of thought materializing which would render alternative forms of cultural expressions in unconventional spaces more common, even after the revolution. Furthermore, he noted that regardless of the revolution's apparent end, the art of the revolution continues to be relevant because it emphasized a time which highlighted the importance of accepting difference, in that the idea behind art is 'to accept the Other, the Other which looks unfamiliar' (Mohamed Alaa, Cairo, pers. comm., 13 August 2014). Keizer also said that this concept was significant because the unfamiliar always scared Egyptian society, because it represented the unknown, which was unwelcome as Egyptians 'like things that have worked, and I think that is one of the most dangerous sentences ever – it has always worked this way. And that is such a scary way of thinking, there is no progression or revolution in that' (Keizer, Cairo, pers. comm., 29 April 2014).

For El Zeft, revolutionary art was about delivering a personal message, and, as such, was about communicating feelings, akin to the way Bahia Shehab argued that art in the aftermath of the revolution was about translating emotions (2016). El Zeft repeatedly told me that during the revolution he felt that 'real' art was raw, spontaneous and occurred within the moment – he cared more about the doing than the actual image. Echoing Mohamed Alaa's sentiment, he said it was not revolutionary art that would endure, but the process of making art – in other words, what mattered was not the image itself, but the ability to create it: 'revolutionary art can't do shit' (El Zeft, Cairo, pers. comm., 27 April 2014).

In times of revolution where the media was already highly regulated, it was this unmediated, spontaneous, visible and most importantly organic form of communication that was a significant achievement of the revolution. As El Zeft commented in one of our conversations,

> I like imposing my idea on people and telling them this is what I have to say. This is it. Revolutionary art in Egypt is not just stencils or beautiful murals, its origin was the people writing on the tanks coming into Tahrir on January 28 saying 'Mubarak has to fall' with spray, this is the real revolutionary art this is the right message. It is one of the forms of resistance, in a way. (El Zeft, Cairo, pers. comm., 27 April 2014)

Both Mohammed Khalid and Ganzeer emphasized that revolutionary art was one of the most enduring material gains of the revolution. As Ganzeer said,

> a door has been opened and you can't close it, and I mean whether it is a hunger to create art or a hunger to see art in the streets the hunger is there, and I think many people have identified revolutionary art as the one only attainable tangible kind of outcome of the revolution so far, and so I don't think it will go away easily. I think it will remain and will probably evolve as it has been evolving, what it is now is probably not same as it was on January 25. The first revolutionary art that was done it was such a new thing that any small scribble would have an

impact, now of course because so much of it has been created the past few years so there is this constant need to up your game, and it is easy for the viewer to ignore art on the street, so you really have to up your game and create something more impressive more powerful, and it has to go on that path forever. That's the evolution you are creating, bigger better art, hopefully. (Ganzeer, Cairo, pers. comm., 26 April 2014)

Mohammed Khaled also echoed this sentiment, noting that revolutionary art was a primary gain of the revolution and that it was 'real', in the sense that the revolutionary process was materialized through the existence of revolutionary art, 'The one thing that was real and happened was that we did something that will remain [in reference to revolutionary art]. It has flourished, I thought it was just a wave and would end. Especially during the Military Council's rule, I thought that it would run its course and would end. But currently I see what people still do and it is still on the walls and on the contrary it is increasing, and a lot of people are doing it, and this gives you confidence that it will stay alive and will continue' (Mohammed Khaled, Cairo, pers. comm., 29 April 2014)

In this sense, although several of those I spoke to were deflated by what seemed to be the apparent close of the revolutionary process, many emphasized that the importance of revolutionary art was that this was a 'real' (in other words, tangible) and felt outcome of the revolution. There was a dislocation in understandings of art – that it was not a private, formal endeavour but one which could be for everyone, by everyone, to challenge the discourse of power, narrate and respond to revolutionary events. This enduring legacy of what art is and can be will remain, according to many of those I spoke, even when all the walls have been whitewashed.

The liminality of the revolution and its effect on the creation of art

It was interesting how many of those I interviewed were not concerned with how to interpret art or define it within previously set-out conceptual frameworks. It was also fascinating to hear the debate going back to discussions around the role of the state in the production of art, debates that marked the pre-revolutionary period. As Moussa writes:

> While modernist art trends have subsided in many parts of the world and given way to post-modern or contemporary genres, they remain heavily promoted in Egypt by domestic and foreign art institutions. . . . The effect of this global modern art movement's influx into Egypt has been selective marginalisation of works with critical political or social meaning – meanings that are relevant to the realities of given localities within Egypt. (Mousa, 2015)

It was this type of thinking that I came across in my interviews as most seemed to retreat from adopting a conception of art as an ahistorical, universal idea towards an understanding of art as located in narratives constituted within local socio-historical and cultural contexts. In this sense, then, revolutionary art would continue to exist even in the aftermath of the revolution because its foundation lies within the Egyptian culture and identity.

However, 'universal' versus 'local' does not necessarily mean authentic versus inauthentic, binaries that have been challenged by the revolution as cultural producers 'fuse[d] familiar and foreign, old and new' (Kraidy, 2016: 16). In fact, the disillusionment with art, as many artists told me, does not only stem from the promotion of Westernized, modern, universal art disconnected from local realities; rather, it also comes because of the Ministry of Culture's control, regulation and promotion of abstract art devoid of action, or what Radwa, an artist and the former head of the Media Unit in the Egyptian Center for Economic and Social Rights, characterized as art 'before the revolution [that] was about a state of numbness, people being tired and dragging themselves' (Radwa Fouda, Cairo, pers. comm., 13 August 2014).

Under Mubarak's regime, the normative understanding of art was to 'showcase' it to the public to make them more 'cultured' or 'raise their tastes', a common theme Winegar found among more formal artists who worked within government institutions and/or private galleries (Winegar, 2006). This depiction is embodied by the famous Egyptian singer Muhammad Abd al-Wahhab, who once was quoted as saying,

> the artist of genius, no matter what era God creates him in, is a unique creature. He believes firmly that his natural place is among the vanguard. He studies public opinion thoroughly so that he knows its desires and inclinations. This helps him to present his message of innovation as a 'pill' which the people can easily digest. He can lead the new generation – can inscribe his name in capital letters on artistic history. (cited in Armbrust, 1996: 63)

However, art produced during the revolution challenged generalized conceptualizations of artists as unique, isolated, cultured beings working within private spaces, but as artistic revolutionaries whose work in public spaces was the outcome of a collective collaboration within revolutionary events. As Radwa noted, the power of art in the street is not as a cultural form, but essentially in it being the only legitimate communicative tool and media form – she argued that even in the aftermath of the revolution, its existence acts as an important intervention within formal understandings of art because its power stems from its

> interactivity. This is the power of revolutionary art. If it is not interactive it will be just like exhibition art, nothing. It says what the artist wants but it doesn't say what people think of what the artists think, this dialectic kind of conversation going on between the art piece and the people, it shows how diverse the country is, or the society is. If that dialogue kept going, and it kind of pushes forward it will change things . . . because we do not have an equivalent media, especially the

media, we do not have a media that is interactive or intriguing. (Radwa Fouda, Cairo, pers. comm., 13 August 2014)

This connection between art and the revolution was one of process and context. Art was no longer seen as a private, elitist endeavour to be displayed in private spaces – it was seen as a continuous, organic process which should necessarily be located in public spaces and respond to revolutionary events in order to continuously reassert itself through participation and dialogue, and generate new understandings and ideas through discussion and debate.

> The idea is that you don't just go down to the street and draw and that's it. You went down because you had an idea, and when you go down you will find that people will ask you what you are doing and what is that, and you will find people disagree with you, and you will disagree back, and they will tell you something you never heard of, so there are nice conversations that occur between you and the people. Our role isn't to draw something and leave, it is to make people understand what you are drawing and their input in turn will allow you to understand things you may not have before. (Hanaa El Degham, Berlin, Skype Interview, 29 November 2013)

Most of those I spoke to noted that galleries were representative of the monopolization, regulation, and censorship of art (and culture) embedded within the political and social articulation of the state. The Ministry of Culture reinforced the normative, hegemonic order of the state by legitimizing a certain way of producing and consuming art, with consumers seen as passive viewers or economic consumers. Mostafa El Hosseiny, an artist and member of the Mona Lisa Brigades told me that galleries are only relevant to the artist and their clique, 'What do all the big artists do? He draws and presents in galleries and only his friends and family come to the gallery, and he is happy about it – it is wrong. Galleries are very fake' (Mostafa El Hosseiny, Cairo, pers. comm., 1 May 2014), whereas Mohammed Khaled said the streets represented reality:

> I feel revolutionary art is real, compared to art in the gallery. I can draw a painting and put it in a gallery. It is a nice thing. For me to put a painting in a gallery is lovely. But people will come to it and ponder it and then walk away, and if someone buys it he will buy it to put it above a couch. (Mohammed Khaled, Cairo, pers. comm., 29 April 2014)

Mohamed Alaa said that art was a byproduct of a personal, historical and social process, and conceptualized his understanding of art as being tied to a process, a form of documentation and an archive to be used beyond the particular place and time of the revolution. He added,

> I see that the process of creating an art work is more important than the finished
> art work itself. So I document the process of creating my art work, which I think
> is more important than the image that ends up on the street . . . You put the art
> work in the street to be seen and it could be erased and gone and something
> else comes up to replace it but the process remains for the future generations.
> (Mohamed Alaa, Cairo, pers. comm., 13 August 2014)

For Keizer, his disillusionment with the formal cultural field and its preoccupation
with 'defining' art played a large part in the way he approached revolutionary
art even after the revolution (and because of the revolution), in that he was
against any 'abstract art' and detachment from society, and instead, conceived
of revolutionary art as a 'visual' dialogue which should produce questions, not
answers.

> I don't believe in abstract art anymore after the revolution, I believe in hard
> pounding impactful art, it is way too late in the game to be pessimistic about
> life, maybe because we did that in the 70's. Now you have to be pro-action, in
> a way that has to move people. We have been paralyzed and become passive
> observers, it is the paralysis of the human condition . . . revolutionary art to
> me is much grander than just art or just politics and all the other fields of
> life. . . . I think it is the most powerful medium for me because of the visual
> dialogue between me or the piece of art and the person on the street, which
> makes them question the environment where they live in, and hopefully
> question reality through this art. . . . The other thing that is powerful about
> revolutionary art, unlike the news which desensitizes peoples senses and their
> whole perception of the world and what it is and reality. I define revolutionary
> art as being consciously aware of social political issues and not just abstract
> art, which is very gallery oriented in that sense. (Keizer, Cairo, pers. comm.,
> 26 April 2014)

Non-elitist conceptualizations of art

Most of those I spoke to emphasized the importance of the revolution as igniting
a debate over a different understanding of art not only in it being created in the
public and for the public but also in new understandings of its aesthetic form,
which Ammar saw as reflecting the everyday local 'visualities' seen in the most
mundane of objects, such as food stalls and shoe shine boxes. As Radwa put it, the
recognition of such diverse banal societal forms, sensibilities and discourses meant
that art – even after the revolution – can relate, or speak to, the consciousness of
people who had become accustomed to being talked down to by intellectuals and
politicians alike, 'if I come down from my ivory tower . . . you have to learn how
to get your message across in a language that people understand' (Radwa Fouda,
Cairo, pers. comm., 13 August 2014). Most of those I spoke to saw intellectuals
as co-opted by the state and therefore as detached from society while speaking

a language obscure in its terminology, excluding the majority of the population from their discourse. As Quijano-Gonzales notes: 'The overarching position of the "enlightened elites at the service of the ignorant masses", institutionalized since the Arab Nahda, is thus subject to a criticism so radical as to reveal a lack of even the slightest consideration on the part of the young Arab underground artists for this role of gatekeeper, which largely stands for the symbolic power of institutional mediators' (Quijano-Gonzales, 2013).

The Egyptian revolution unravelled the underlying tensions inherent in the elitist cultural field in Egypt, and the art which emerged during this time gained strength and legitimacy because it acknowledged and addressed this reality. Keizer, who was instrumental in promoting revolutionary art in *sha'bi* (traditional, low-income) areas during the revolution, said that it was the revolution that opened a space to foster the notion of an accessible art and that even though the revolution was defeated, elitist notions of art would continuously be challenged. This was the reason, as Ammar said, why he adopted a different style altogether that embodied local narratives and visualities that one can find in the mundane, in the everyday, in the ordinary. It was also clear that the end of the revolution did not mean the end of revolutionary art. For several people, such as El Zeft, the revolution was still ongoing (when we last spoke in August 2014).

> After the revolution implies something ended, it is still going. Three years is nothing, if you see what happened in three years, too much happened we changed a lot in three years, we broke a lot of taboos in three years. Protesting in the street was a taboo, going down and distributing pamphlets or anything to people was impossible for it to happen, drawing in the street, making pages in Facebook and insulting whoever you want, all of these taboos broke. You will always do it with caution but you still do it. People still go down and protest all the time but the media doesn't cover it because they don't want to show that the country is still a mess. (El Zeft, Cairo, pers. comm., 27 April 2014)

However, he also said he wanted to leave Egypt because he was worried about the return to the pre-revolution status. He said:

> I have too much hate towards everybody, my friends my family the country the army, hate towards anyone because I feel I am suffering . . .. All I can think is when I will take this certificate [from the army] so I can leave . . . where I don't know. I want to forget everything. When you go in the army you feel how much we [the revolutionaries] didn't do anything. You see all the people in the army and they don't care what happened at all. When you leave outside and talk to people you feel yeah they care a little but the army not at all as if nothing happened. (El Zeft, Cairo, pers. comm., 27 April 2014)

For some, the three revolutionary phases I described in the preceding chapters and their consequences had now become a symbol of undesired chaos for the general Egyptian public which prompted some of those I spoke to talk about leaving the country. As KIM put it, 'I cannot stand the situation, people are walking and you feel like they hate each other, you might say barely a word to them and they will have your neck' (KIM, Cairo, pers. comm., 18 August 2014). Others called the clampdown on revolutionary art an attack on critical thought, expression, revolutionary memory and creative dissent. As Hala El Sharouny said, 'the authorities don't want us to think with our brains . . . didn't I tell you that art can immortalize culture, it immortalizes a certain time, it immortalizes ideas . . . so they want to erase our memories' (Hala El Sharouny, Cairo, pers. comm., 18 August 2014). The political crackdown by authorities was paralleled by a cultural suppression, which, for most of those I spoke to, marked the 'end' of the revolution, and the art which emerged from it.

Key events marking the symbolic 'End' of revolutionary art

Martyr monument – November 2013

In November 2013, a monument was unveiled in Tahrir Square to commemorate those who died during the ouster of both Hosni Mubarak and Mohamed Morsi in 2013. For the revolutionaries, this was a clear indication of the authorities' attempt to co-opt the revolution and its legacy, and also served as an insult to those who died. As Ahmed Maher, one of the revolutionaries who initiated the protests in Tahrir in January 2011 said, a 'Tahrir memorial was long overdue, but it should not have been built by the same people who had created the need for a memorial in the first place. It's funny, they are the killers, and they killed our colleagues and our friends, and now they say they are very sad about what happened, and they respect us' (Kingsley, 2013). Tahrir Square, yet again, was used as the site in which,

> Specific meanings emerge in rhetorical performances, in efforts by particular political actors to invoke the symbolic power of Tahrir Square, to evoke a particular set of its potential meanings and to articulate the limits of meaning that Tahrir Square should carry for the specific context in which it is being used. At the same time, each of these utterances, once entered into public circulation, becomes part of the larger universe of meanings for which Tahrir Square can stand. The invocation of Tahrir Square is thus a communicative act through which a particular context is assigned a meaningful place in the revolution, but also an act through which the revolution itself is constituted in particular ways. (Peterson, 2015b: 75)

Mosireen, which is a collective of filmmakers and activists, released a video at the time which mocked this attempt to co-opt the meaning of the revolution by its perpetrators, which ended with the message 'Never Forget' and 'Always Remember' the atrocities committed by the police and military forces. The memorial was defaced and destroyed within 24 hours, in light of the revolutionaries' anger at the authorities' attempt to co-opt the revolution and banalize their role in it, versus the reality whereby it was the violence committed by their security forces which led to the deaths of so many revolutionaries.

The pink camouflage – November 2013

The unveiling of the monument in Tahrir coincided with the second anniversary of the Mohamed Mahmoud Street clashes in November 2013, and, according to Ammar Abo Bakr, the atmosphere was tense as

> everybody had warned us not to go to Mohamed Mahmoud Street that day, the second anniversary of clashes there. Even the activists who supported the revolution! They said the military would catch us and claim we were Muslim Brothers – because everyone who opposed the military was being labelled an Islamist by the military regime and in the media. But we felt we had to go. (Abo Bakr, 2015)

Abo Bakr said that as the memorial was destroyed, he decided to go to Mohamed Mahmoud Street and paint the entire wall in pink camouflage (see Figures 6.2–6.7), with one message written on it: 'You may kill people, strip

Figure 6.2 Part of the 'pink camouflage' mural – this image is that of the martyr Sayed Khaled, which Ammar Abo Bakr intentionally made in the image of the famous 'crying boy' print made by painter Giovanni Bragolin. *Source*: Photo by Author.

Figure 6.3 Leonardo da Vinci's 'Vitruvian man' amended to include a fish (the symbol of eye opening), as well as an injured protestor and an image of a Pharaoh with one missing eye, in reference to the eye sniper. *Source*: Photo by Author.

Figure 6.4 Military forces seen above a pile-up of the skulls of revolutionaries, with the words 'Bread, Freedom, and Social Justice' underneath the skulls. This was the legacy of the revolution, according to many I spoke to – unfulfilled promises, the return to the normative order, and martyrs. *Source*: Photo by Author.

them, arrest them, have fun after arresting them – but we won't forget. We are prepared for you. We put glue on your back that won't come off' (Abo Bakr, 2015).

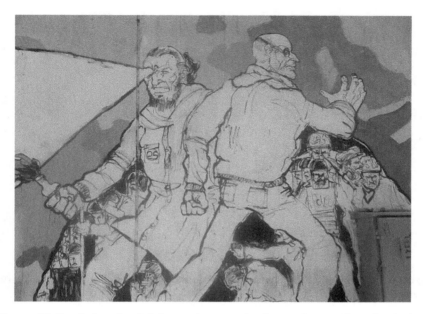

Figure 6.5 Revolutionaries fighting against security forces. *Source*: Photo by Author. *Source*: Photo by Author.

Figure 6.6 Another part of the 'pink camouflage' mural. It depicts the faces of several martyrs (such as 23-year-old journalist Mayada Ashraf who worked for the private newspaper, El-Dustour) and the mother of martyrs mourning. *Source*: Photo by Author.

Figure 6.7 Graffiti on the left in reference to the 'virginity tests' conducted by the military. *Source*: Photo by Author.

Of the pink camouflage, Ammar said that they used vulgar words on it intentionally as the

> Islamists never use vulgarity; they always try to express themselves in a very polite way. With these words we wanted to make crystal clear that we, the authors of this sentence, are not linked to the Islamists, even though we were criticizing the military. In part, we also painted this camouflage to fool the media. They had understood that the paintings on Mohamed Mahmoud Street were important, and on the second anniversary of clashes there, they had rented balconies to get a nice shot. But when they arrived at 7 am, they only found the pink camouflage: a sign they couldn't explain to the audience. On TV they said it's a piece on the blood of the martyrs. They didn't actually get it. And that's what we intended. (Abo Bakr, 2015)

The pink camouflage was also intended to show that there was a 'third way' out of the repetitive structural order cycle (from Mubarak, to SCAF, to the Muslim Brotherhood, to SCAF again) – that there existed those who were against the *ancien regime* of Mubarak, as well as the Muslim Brotherhood as well as military rule, and they wanted to illustrate that they were neither Islamists, through the use of crude language (as Islamists use more formal language), and that they were against military rule, through the revolutionary art which depicted the violence and injustices committed by military forces.

Bassem Mohsen portrait – December 2013–January 2014

Perhaps the most iconic piece which represents the end of the revolutionary process was the portrait of Bassem Mohsen on the infamous corner of Tahrir Square and Mohamed Mahmoud Street, one of the final art works that also symbolized the end of the revolutionary art movement of the Egyptian uprising of 25 January 2011. Bassem Mohsen was representative of the 'child of the revolution' (Frenkel, 2013) as he embodied the hope, strength, injustice and struggle which sustained his belief that 'the revolution, in its more basic configuration of justice and dignity, was a continuing business. It was a dream, and he labored for it' (Attalah, Elmeshad, 2013). As activist Rasha Azab wrote, 'his story is the best abstraction of the revolution at large: An injury in January, a lost eye in Mohamed Mahmoud, a military trial in Morsi's time and finally, a bullet in the head' (Attalah, Elmeshad, 2013). Therefore, his death was emblematic of the rise and fall of the Egyptian revolution, and 'highlighted the difficult times faced by many Egyptian revolutionaries, as they watch the former police state return' (Frenkel, 2013).

Bassem Mohsen was shot in the eye in November 2011 in the Mohamed Mahmoud Street clashes, arrested during military rule, tried and later beaten by Muslim Brotherhood supporters in 2012, and in 2013 died from a gunshot wound to his head during a protest during a protest against the military retaking power. Bassem was, as many noted, both a 'product and victim' (Hamdy, Karl, 2013: 261) of the revolution – he was a teenager (16 years old) when the revolution began, and a teenager when he died (19 years old), towards the end of the revolution. The location of the portrait – on the street where Bassem lost his eye, and in the area (Tahrir) in which he began his journey as a revolutionary – situates the life and death of a revolutionary throughout

Figure 6.8 This is thought to be the 'final' piece in Mohamed Mahmoud Street – an iconic portrait of Bassem Mohsen (who embodied, and fought for, the original goals of the Egyptian revolution of bread, freedom and social justice throughout its three main phases), on the corner of Mohamed Mahmoud Street and Tahrir Square, symbolizing the apparent end of the revolutionary art movement. *Source*: Photo by Author.

three years of struggle within the urban epicentre of the Egyptian revolution, where it all began. Ammar, who painted this iconic piece, said that he decided to draw Bassem's portrait on the pink camouflage on 1 January 2014, as someone who represented the 'true revolution' (Ammar Abo Bakr, 2015), in that he was against all representatives (from Mubarak, to SCAF, to the Muslim Brotherhood) of the structural order which re-emerged under different ideological guises, and revolted against them with the primary goal of achieving the dignity, security and social justice that Egyptians fought and died for. The fish eye, Bassem's portrait according to Ammar, was a sign of eye opening in Egyptian culture, and its intended message is that even if the revolution is defeated, even if Bassem is gone, he will still be watching, as a sombre – and moral – reminder that many died for the revolution to live (Figure 6.8).

The king has returned

In perhaps one of the most iconic aesthetic confirmations of the revolutionary's end, and a tragic commentary on how the revolution was subverted, is the before and after of El Teneen's iconic 'checkmate' piece, painted on the iconic wall of the AUC library (which, as I mention in the next section, would be demolished), which is just a block away from Tahrir. In the first phase of the revolution, El Teneen drew a street art piece entitled 'chess game' to show how the pawns managed to overrule the king (Figure 6.9). As a reflection of the reversal of this situation, El Teneen redrew his chess game graffiti with the king enlarged, front of center, overwhelming all the other chess pieces. It was a stark visual narrative of the return to order and the end of the revolutionary process (see Figure 6.10).

Figure 6.9 El Teneen's 'checkmate', which was created shortly after the revolutionaries' ability to overthrow Hosni Mubarak's three-decade rule. However, members of the *ancien regime* – standing next to the overthrown king – still remain. *Source*: https://www.pinterest .com/pin/213076626091283961/

Figure 6.10 El Teneen's 'The King Has Returned', with the king chess piece front and centre, indicating the return to the status quo in the aftermath of El-Sisi's presidency. *Source*: https://www.researchgate.net/figure/el-Teneen-The-king-is-back-2014-Cairo-Photo-el-Teneen_fig15_315847726

The destruction of the AUC wall – September 2015

The effacement of graffiti, the whitewashing of revolutionary art and the destruction of the AUC wall on Mohamed Mahmoud Street in September 2015 – seen as one of the most iconic locations of revolutionary art during the revolution – was widely regarded as an imposition of 'order' and the permanent return to the status quo (see Figure 6.10). As Mona Abaza notes, 'the cleanup of downtown is about giving a sense of order in post-January 2011 Cairo . . . all of us are in denial. Tahrir is over, and the graffiti is part of it. We had four years of trauma – killings and euphoria – but humans need normalcy. And the normalcy is this order' (Jankowicz, 2016b).

During the proposed destruction of the AUC wall that the university claimed was part of a renovation plan, AUC held a conference on campus entitled 'Creative Cities: Re-framing Downtown.' Graffiti artist El Teneen distributed a version of the event's poster, overlaid with the phrase: 'How creative is taking down revolutionary graffiti walls?' (Jankowicz, 2015), and argued that his prank was intended to highlight the irony of hosting a 'creative cities' conference 'in the same place they are going to knock down revolutionary artwork' (Jankowicz, 2015). This location contained some of the revolution's most iconic works and the site of key revolutionary events which saw it being a space for collaborative efforts, martyr commemorations, bloody street battles and protests. This was another major turn of events which marked attempts by the authorities to stamp out any residual traces of the revolution through its art (which is, in and of itself, not only a visual aesthetic of the revolution but also a narrative of it) on urban sites and spaces, and marks the symbolic end to the revolution itself and the revolutionary art movement.

Figure 6.11 El Teneen's Facebook Post regarding his "prank" poster regarding the Creative Cities Conference at AUC. *Source*: El Teneen, Facebook post, 2015.

Figure 6.12 Ahdaf Soueif posts an image of the beginning of the destruction of the AUC wall on Mohamed Mahmoud (a site of both revolutionary art and revolutionary events), and writes "if they could, they would also destroy (or remove) the whole street and the city with it" [author's translation]. *Source*: Soueif, Twitter post, 2015.

Chapter 7

CONCLUSION

> Since the start of the Arab revolutionary process and the violence that has accompanied it, the culture and arts domain has come to play an ever more crucial role as mobilizer, witness and archivist of historical events.
>
> Hanan Toukan, Lecturer in Politics and Middle East Studies
> at Bard College Berlin, 2017.

This book examined how revolutionary art evolved and responded to changing political events within the timeline of the Egyptian revolution of 25 January 2011. I draw on the concept of liminality to ground revolutionary art within the historical process of the Egyptian uprising and to emphasize the relevance of the particular state of 'in-betweeness' in examining creative cultural expressions – themselves a method of political communication – and how different liminal moments may frame different understandings of revolutionary art.

Revolutionary art was not thought of – or created – the same way from 2011 until 2013 – it significantly evolved according to the context within which the revolutionary process was unfolding. What the liminality framework does is allow us to ground understandings of art within certain places, spaces and events, and perhaps create a more nuanced understanding of how that art is framed within a revolutionary context. For example, many of those I interviewed did not actually create revolutionary art during the utopian 18 days of the revolution. In those days, they were engaged in participating and experiencing the revolution and used scribbles on the walls and hasty stencils to show dissent, protest and warn other revolutionaries, especially when telecommunications were cut in the early days of the revolution. During this time, revolutionaries managed to disrupt the status quo and use the street as the natural location for creative expression. The second and third phases of the revolution saw revolutionaries attempt to reconstitute the experience of anti-structure that the first phase of the revolution brought about, despite being ruled by SCAF and then Mohammed Morsi of the Muslim Brotherhood. During this period, they used local cultural symbols, martyrs portraits, as well as satire (among other things) to remind the public of the original goals of the revolution, while simultaneously countering the state's false narrative of the revolutionaries as being thugs and foreign agents.

Using liminality is not intended to provide clear-cut answers; rather, it is used to unravel the historical process of the revolution through its art, and create a more nuanced lens to understand that art within a particular historical process. As Thomassen notes: 'In a perfect world, the tripartite structure of van Gennep's rites of passage would take political form via the stages of epistemic rupture and radical critique, followed by a playful liminal period of unlimited freedom and questioning of prevailing norms, reintegrated and normalized into realized political emancipation, protected by a constitution of legitimate order to the benefit of the general populace. It rarely happens like that. In effective history, the tripartite process more often resembles a long sequence of destruction that starts with desperate screams of alienation, hopeful longings for freedom and justice that continue into generalized despair, and ends in nihilism and neo-totalitarian grips of power, protected by a state of emergency. We have moved from rupture to permanent liminality' (Thomassen, 2017: 303). Looking back in retrospect, over a decade on from the beginning of the revolution on 25 January 2011, this seems a near accurate description of the revolutionary events and their aftermath which transpired in Egypt.

The Egyptian revolution managed to produce a physical and symbolic space for meaning-making in the social, cultural and political realm which was also a symbolic battlefield in which the revolutionary narrative and its meanings were contested by the authorities and revolutionaries. The further away from the ideal moment of the initial 18 days of the revolution, the greater a crisis this represented to those I interviewed. The liminal moment was characterized as the way things 'should' be versus what they are in the normative order. The struggle, from 2011 to 2013, to re-establish the initial revolutionary narrative through their art was eventually diminished in the aftermath of the Rab'a massacre, and public support for the revolution and the 'chaos' it embodied (a key linguistic repertoire in the authorities narrative) greatly waned, leading to the eventual return of the status quo with the election of a strong man and former military general Abdel Fattah El-Sisi in June 2014, who continued to stamp out any revolutionary discourse by imprisoning revolutionaries, artists, activists, journalists and protestors.

This is why the process of archiving[1] has become even more crucial in the aftermath of the revolution, to counter – and challenge – the authorities narrative of events, and to affirm its (continued) existence, as if to say 'the revolution did exist, and we will never let you forget'. Mosireen, the activist film and video collective which was formed at the beginning of the 25 January revolution, emphasized the importance of access to archives for '[m]aking things public, accessible, open, transparent, shareable – these are central qualities not only of the revolution, but of the wider drives of what we could broadly call The Left. And they are the opposite to the regime's fundamentals of secrecy, limitation and obfuscation' (Lindsey, 2018). While the revolution represents the central political figuration in which analyses of art and cultural production took place, in hindsight, a decade on from the revolution does indicate the need to go beyond Tahrir and the political events of the revolution and see the ways in which (in its aftermath) actors in dispersed spaces continue to displace normative subject-positions and constitute new ways of 'doing' art and politics within the everyday. Furthermore, as the current government attempts to erase all memories of the revolution (not least of which is the whitewashing of all traces of 'revolutionary art' on the streets and purging archive platforms of the revolution), the conversation has grown to now address the importance of the role of the artist and the archive in contemporary art in society (Downey, ed., 2015; Pinther, 2016). Major projects such as Lara Baladi's 'Vox Populi: Tahrir Archives' (2016) – described as an 'index of online archives on the 2011 Egyptian Revolution and its aftermath' (Baladi, 2016) – are setting a significant precedent in the ways in which the notion of the archive can be considered as an act of resistance, commemoration and historical signification in preserving the events, acts and expressions of the revolution. The refusal to forget is a powerful instigator in archiving, with several Facebook pages dedicated solely to documenting revolutionary art not only in Cairo but also in Egypt as a whole, the most active ones beings 'Graffiti in Egypt',[2] 'Revolutionary art in Egypt',[3] and 'Walls of Freedom: Revolutionary art of the Egyptian Revolution'[4]. In the aftermath of the Egyptian revolution, 'the prohibition on public image-making has been forcefully reasserted' (Westmoreland, 2016: 257), in lieu of severe punishments for those who create them, either in the digital or physical sphere, which makes the process of archiving – and not forgetting – even more crucial. Archiving itself is a form of resistance by other means, and ensures the historical continuity of the Egyptian revolutionaries' narrative of events which transpired during that crucial political moment in Egypt's history. Sascha Crasnow, a lecturer in Islamic arts, also emphasizes the importance of the archive process in the digital sphere in light of the regime's efforts to stamp out the memory of the revolution and its art, 'as [murals and stencils and graffiti] move through virtual spaces, their meaning and impact may or may not change as they are removed from their original context and placed into new ones' (Atta, 2021).

Art for the common good: A growing discourse in light of the Egyptian revolution?

In the aftermath of the Egyptian revolution, Hamid Dabashi argued that 'Art must respond to a renewed Arab consciousness that is aware of what is happening in the Arab World' (Dabashi, 2011), and Anthony Downey, professor of visual culture in the Middle East and North Africa, argued that artistic practices must be thought of as adhering to the 'common good' which 'must remain precisely that: common to all' (Downey, 2013: 8), in order to sustain modes of civic engagement. Although revolutionary art is but one part of the larger discourse which attempts to respond to this renewed consciousness and address the need to reassert that art and culture are not only for the elite but are for the 'common good', iconic artistic events borne in the aftermath of the revolutions such as the celebrated El-Fan Midan was effectively shut down under Sisi's presidency by security forces in October 2014 (Lewis, 2014).

As mentioned previously, El-Fan Midan, which literally translates into 'Art is a Square', was a monthly art and culture festival in Abdeen Square, founded by the Independent Culture Coalition in March 2011. Its aim was 'to bring arts and culture to the streets of Egypt' and to 'create cultural and political awareness through a street festival that would tour all governorates of Egypt' (Montasser, 2012a). The closure of El-Fan Midan symbolizes that the space for unconventional forms of creative expression constitutive of a political and cultural consciousness is gradually decreasing and is at risk since 2014. There have also been several raids by security forces against civil society organizations and not-for-profit cultural centres such as Townhouse Gallery and its affiliated building Rawabet Theater in Cairo, which one writer described as being indicative of 'a continuum of general cultural decay and state antagonism' (Jankowicz, 2016).

At the same time, however, several projects and initiatives focusing on promoting art and culture in the aftermath of the revolution have taken place, such as Mahatat for Contemporary Art, which hosts artistic projects in public spaces in more obscure residential areas and neighbourhoods areas and operates according to the notion that art should be open, accessible and decentralized (El Shimi, 2014). Although they do not make any political demands or are focused on political awareness in the same capacity as El-Fan Midan, these initiatives are indicative of a growing discourse demanding a more accessible artistic and cultural field, initiated and sustained by individuals, groups, civil society actors and not-for-profit cultural institutions alike.

Another example of the initiation of this discourse to de-centralize art and culture from the controlled cultural field of the state was a campaign started in October 2012 by Al Mawred El Thaqafy (Culture Resource) entitled 'A Culture For All Egyptians', in which they set out to 'campaign for changes to cultural laws and policies, and make culture more accessible to all sectors of society' (Montasser, 2012c). Their primary slogan, 'Culture is not only for intellectuals but for all Egyptians', reflects their

> aim [. . .] to produce a concrete policy that not only the Ministry of Culture
> but also the entire country can follow . . . the role of culture is to characterise a
> particular community or social group spiritually, physically, intellectually and
> emotionally. Culture is about art and ways of life and includes fundamental
> human rights and values, traditions and beliefs. (Montasser, 2012c)

To promote the initiative they initiated a media campaign (with a second phase launched in March 2013) with distributed print materials (in downtown Cairo, as well as popular neighbourhoods, Mansoura, Minya, Luxor and Port Said) infomercials on private and state television channels, a short documentary film and a media campaign with billboards containing slogans such as 'Culture is not in the Ministry, it is in the Neighbourhood and Street', and 'Culture is not just for the *Muthaqafeen* [intellectuals or "cultured people"]' (Culture Resource, 2013) [see Appendix 2]. Although this campaign is currently not active (as mentioned previously, Al Mawred El Thaqafy halted all activities in Egypt and moved its headquarters to Beirut), it is indicative that the Egyptian revolution had opened the door for new ways of doing politics and thinking about art and its accessibility to the public. It is even more critical now to re-ignite the conversation many cultural players in Egypt have attempted to address in regards to the role of art in a post-revolution Egypt, which touches upon crucial issues of control, relevance and accessibility in the cultural field. The very existence of this discourse for cultural production in the Arab world is crucial, because it may one day 'represent the prelude to a new phase in the cultural history of the modern Arab world, a phase that might enable new players to elaborate artistic propositions to new audiences, bypassing the mediation of "learned elites"' (Gonzales-Quijano, 2013).

Where are the artists now?

I have contacted many of those I spoke to over six years ago, and many of them unfortunately have deleted their social media accounts or are inactive (with last updates from 2014 to 2015), changed their telephone numbers or deleted their emails associated with their street artist names. When I asked the few I was able to get through how they experienced themselves now, as political agents, they responded that although they do not feel the level of optimism and political engagement they did during 2011–13, they still feel that they have been permanently altered since the revolution. As El Zeft told me, the 25th January revolution permanently changed him, as before then he 'wasn't at all interested in politics before the revolution. Before the revolution I was something and after the revolution, I was something else completely. I am raised in a very rich family. I went to a private school and a private university and in the summer I travelled to London with my friends and the summer after I travelled to Germany and the summer after to Turkey. We would think about which clubs to go to and where to go shopping – all I cared about is being happy' (El Zeft, Cairo, pers. comm., 27 April 2014). Although I was not able to get through to El Zeft recently, I was able to find his Facebook, and his last political posts were from four years ago (2018), directly criticizing and targeting the current president, Abdel Fattah El-Sisi. In reflecting on the revolution's ten-year anniversary, Ganzeer, in his most recent interview, said that

> I think the Egyptian revolution changed me in a couple of ways. One, it made it impossible for me to be okay with doing the kind of art that might be easily ignored. To me, it seems a sad waste of time to do art that doesn't have this burning urgency to it that doesn't feel like this has to get made now . . . you could say our efforts did fail in 2011 to 2013, but I don't think it's the end. (BBC World Service, 2021)

Other artists such as Alaa Awad, Ammar Abo Bakr, Hala El Sharouny and Keizer have become professional freelance artists who exhibit in private galleries and internationally, at street festivals and galleries. Keizer's last post on the Egyptian revolution, dated on its eight-year anniversary (25 January 2019), in a Facebook post (see Figure 7.1), has graffiti which says, 'if you forgot what happened I remember everything'.

Figure 7.1 Screenshot from Keizer's Facebook page, https://www.facebook.com/ KeizerStreetArt/photos/a.266935263331071/2409890655702177/

However, this kind of graffiti is no longer being created in Egypt, but exhibited abroad, or on social media platforms as most artists do not feel they have any level of freedom to exhibit in public space in Egypt. In one interview from September 2019, Ammar Abo Bakr stated blatantly that 'unfortunately, we no longer have this freedom [to create art on public spaces]. If someone tries to paint a wall with graffiti now, they are likely to be arrested' (MENASource, 2019). El Teneen argued that the internet – or exhibiting abroad – are the only spaces available for artists to showcase more political work, because within Egypt the regime only wants people to see one narrative, and so any opposing opinion is seen as a threat, which is, as he said, 'very bad news for creatives working with political themes unless they choose to promote the regime's narrative' (Duende, 2022). This is why one former street artist, Mira Shihadeh, who describes herself as a figurative artist, now focuses on making 'art that inspires joy, fun and humor. It's not easy, and my main challenge is to bring enthusiasm into what I do. I think many artists are striving in that direction' (Shihadeh, 2022).

Therefore, over ten years after the revolution began, street art has significantly decreased since 2014–15, and there is no longer the freedom to create and express opinions in public space, as Ammar Abo Bakr reflected,

At the beginning, there was space for a very large audience to start doing this. Many people from different backgrounds are now graffiti artists, and not just politically. We taught many on the streets how to be graffiti artists. There is a new generation now; eleven-year-old kids back in 2011 are now commercial graffiti artists. The political movement died after 2015, and with it, the street art. There is no longer a space for us to go and do what we used to do. (MENASource, 2019)

Yet the legacy of the Egyptian revolution continues. Organically formed collective art groups such as the Mona Lisa Brigades and Graffiti Harimi emerged, iconic images such as El Zeft's Nefertiti mask remain an enduring symbol for women as a powerful resistance force, and the idea that art should be disengaged with the formal cultural field gained traction. However, the sporadic graffiti art which now appears in the aftermath of the revolution is largely 'commercially aligned, culturally rooted and at times addresses social concerns, but is stripped of the political messaging central to its earlier avatar in the country' (Atta, 2021). Ammar Abo Bakr argued that this should not necessarily be seen in a negative light –

> most of the graffiti artists are creating their art for a commercial audience, which is very good. It is important that the culture survives and the mindsets keep changing. Many shops and restaurants in Cairo today want to use this art in decorating their spaces. Recently, we were asked by a large corporation to paint a twelve floor building for them to include in a TV commercial. The idea that they were willing to pay such a huge amount of money for the mural to be used for a couple of seconds in a commercial is something that we consider to be a very positive step. Especially that the corporation agreed to compromise by not including the brand name in this huge mural for the sake of it to stay there, shows that minds are changing and the culture is moving forward. (MENASource, 2019)

According to Othman Lazraq, the director of Fundación Alliances, although the art of the revolution has been largely commodified, the revolutions themselves allowed for an 'increase [in] the global interest for artists from the Middle East and North Africa (MENA), which are now quite popular and becoming more mainstream' (Atta, 2021).

However, others argue against the commodification of an art which was intended to push forth a revolutionary discourse to disrupt and subdue the political status quo should not be used for commercial means, as it devalues its political potency and significance. Yet many former revolutionary artists are forced to either commercialize their work or produce pro-regime art (Atta, 2021), because they have no third option available in the region, unless they permanently move abroad, such as Ganzeer (who has not returned to Egypt since he left in 2014), who is able to create – from installations to art to comics (see Figure 7.2) – with greater freedom than his counterparts in Egypt.

Conclusion

This book considers the relationship between art and revolution during the liminal moments of the Egyptian revolution, and in doing so, underlines how revolutionary art has evolved throughout the different phases of the Egyptian uprising and how this art production – whether it intends to or not – can be understood as a political communication practice. Art production as a political practice emerged during revolutionary and post-revolutionary moments, which indicates the significance

Figure 7.2 Screenshot taken from the online comic entitled 'Cairo Under the Crackdown', illustrated by Ganzeer and written by Syrian-Canadian writer, Yazan Al-Saadi. Posted in January 2019. *Source*: The Nib, https://thenib.com/cairo-under-the-crackdown/

of temporal registers of any revolution or upheaval. As Jillian Schwedler argues in her memo 'Temporality and the Arab Revolutions', different moments call for 'different narrative understandings about the event', and so '[m]any narratives, discourses, analytic frameworks, best practices, and so on, are anchored in specific temporal registers. They shape, and are shaped by, what actors do and what they understand to be happening' (Schwedler, 2016). Conceptually, the book describes these temporal registers of the revolution as liminal moments and, as such, can help us theorize more clearly the relationship between art and politics of art production as political communication practices from below. By placing emphasis on interviews, personal testimonies and lived experience of twenty-five street artists, all of whom have lived their entire, or the majority of their lives, under Hosni Mubarak's regime, this book seeks to expand the ways in which we think about art, politics and culture within the historical moment of the Egyptian revolution based on the standpoint of the artists themselves. This approach provides a nuanced examination of revolutionary art away from descriptive accounts, what Yakein Abdelmagid dubs a 'politics of representation' (Abdelmagid, 2013: 172), as it does not view revolutionary art as a homogenous, stagnant whole, but rather as a process which evolved and adapted according to the revolutionary circumstances that arose.

APPENDIX I

Profiles of cultural producers

Following are the profiles of the twenty-five individuals I interviewed for my thesis, providing a snapshot of their personal, social, professional and academic backgrounds. The names of the participants in the profiles as follows are spelt exactly as the individuals spell them, and in many cases I only use their moniker rather than their real names. Names are presented on how each participant signed my research consent form.

1) **Far3on**: An Egyptian in his twenties and a college student. Far3on's real name is Hossam (last name withheld). He is partially blind in one eye, from a rubber bullet during a protest in the revolution on 28 January 2011 outside the Mugamah (a large government institution located in Tahrir). He dabbled in art on and off as a hobby, before the uprising, but stopped for personal reasons. He started again during the uprising. His method is more of a 'draw and run', whereby he uses stencils and quickly leaves before he is caught. He usually works alone but sometimes collaborates with other artists, such as KIM or the Mona Lisa Brigades.

2) **Saiko Maino**: An Egyptian street artist, graphic designer and junior calligrapher who worked largely on art which addressed sexual harassment. He also founded the artistic organization AlMuthalath (translated as 'the triangle') in September 2015, which brings together artists of different backgrounds to collaborate on creative projects, as well as the Facebook page 'Graffiti in Egypt', which is a digital archive of photographs of street art around Egypt. https://www.behance.net/SayedGad

3) **Hany Khaled**: An Egyptian architect who graduated with a bachelor's degree in environmental design/architecture. He used to work as a graphic designer and an art director, and served his mandatory draft duty in the military in the Air Force. When I spoke to him in 2014, he said he was interested in doing his masters abroad, on the relationship of architecture to the street. https://www.linkedin.com/in/hanykhaled

4) **Hala El Sharouny**: An Egyptian expressionist artist (who goes by the moniker of 'Boshou') who graduated from Helwan University (Faculty of Art Education) in 2004 and holds a master's degree (also from Helwan University, Faculty of Art Education) in painting and drawing 2011. Hala

worked in stocks (for two years) after she became disillusioned with art due to her university education and what she said was the Ministry of Culture's rampant corruption. She then returned to practising art in the aftermath of the 2008 recession (when she quit her job as a stockbroker) and currently works as a professional freelance artist. https://www.behance.net/bosho http://hala-elsharouny.blogspot.com/

5) **Diaa Al Said:** Diaa Al Said studied media management at Misr University, a private international university in Egypt. Poor education was always an important cause for him, and he volunteered in an educational initiative in Egypt entitled 'Educate-Me', which is a nonprofit foundation established in 2010 which addresses the poor quality of education in the Egyptian public education system. For more, go to http://educateme-egypt.org/wp-content/uploads/2016/06/Educate-Me-Profile.pdf).

6) **KIM:** KIM is an Egyptian graffiti artist, calligrapher and junior graphic designer (real name Kareem) who now also runs his father's small family business, after his death. He has been interested in hip-hop graffiti since 2005 and regularly teaches graffiti workshops at various locations in Cairo, such as Qalmi Bookstore. https://www.behance.net/kimletter https://www.facebook.com/kimstreetart/

7) **Alaa Awad:** An Egyptian painter and muralist, who graduated from Luxor's Faculty of Fine Arts in 2004 (where he currently works as an assistant lecturer in the Department of Mural Painting) and in 2012 obtained his master's degree from the Faculty of Fine Arts in Helwan University in Zamalek. http://alaa-awad.com/ https://www.facebook.com/AlaaAwadArt/

8) **The Mozzah:** A street artist (from Europe) who lives and works in Cairo. She tends to avoid creating art with a direct political theme or statement and instead prefers to focus on women and their role in society. http://themozza.tumblr.com/ https://www.facebook.com/TheMozzaStreetArt/

9) **Ammar Abo Bakr:** Ammar is an Egyptian street artist and muralist. He is a former faculty member at the College of Fine Arts in Luxor who worked in cultural heritage and cultural preservation projects. https://www.facebook.com/Ammar.Abo.Bakr/

10) **Keizer:** Keizer is the pseudonym of an anonymous Egyptian street artist. I do not know much about Keizer; he divulged few personal details about his life and I do not know what he studied, his real name or anything about his early life. Although he declares most of his work is political, he says that it is intended to carry universal messages of emancipation even though it is drawn largely from local context. His recurrent symbol, the ant, is (as he informed me and what is written on his website) in reference to 'the forgotten ones, the silences, the nameless, those marginalized by capitalism'. https://www.facebook.com/KeizerStreetArt/ https://www.flickr.com/photos/keizerstreetart/

11) **Ganzeer:** Mohammad Fahmy (aka Ganzeer, which translates into 'bicycle chains') describes himself as a multidisciplinary artist who has been involved in graphic design, street art, illustration and video installations. He has

recently released a science-fiction graphic novel entitled *The Solar Grid*. He currently lives in Los Angeles, California, after having left Cairo in May 2014 amidst accusations that he was affiliated with the Muslim Brotherhood. http://www.ganzeer.com/

12) **Hend Kheera:** An Egyptian artist who studied at Egypt's Fashion & Design Center, and currently works as a fashion designer and structural engineer. She has been drawing since she was a child and loves to incorporate Egyptian cinema icons into her graffiti. Her art also focuses on addressing Egypt's patriarchal society, women's rights and questioning societal norms regarding women's roles. *Rolling Stone* magazine did a profile on her in 2013 which declared that she was 'one of the leaders of Egypt's street art boom' (Downey, 2013). https://www.linkedin.com/in/hend-kheera-71428269

13) **El Zeft:** Is an anonymous Egyptian street artist who studied business at a private university in Egypt. I did not know much about El Zeft, except that he came from a wealthy background and that his family are supporters of Sisi. When we spoke, he was still completing his draft military service.

14) **Sad Panda:** Sad Panda (Hashem) is an anonymous street artist, an art director, music producer, DJ, muralist and a freelance illustrator. He actively avoids any kind of political themes or messages in his work. https://www.facebook.com/sad.panda

15) **Mohammad Khaled:** Mohammad Khaled (aka 'The Winged Elephant') is an Egyptian street artist who studied fine arts with a painting major. Originally from Zagaziq, he now lives and works in Cairo as a freelance illustrator, filmmaker and comic artist. https://www.behance.net/WingedElephant

16) **Mira Shihadeh**: Mira is a Palestinian graffiti artist and a certified yoga instructor who has studied at the American University in Cairo and has lived and worked in Cairo most of her life. One of the main issues she addresses in her work is sexual harassment, human rights and the perception of women in society.

17) **Mohamed Alaa**: Mohammed Alaa is an Egyptian street artist and performance artist who likes to focus on the concept of 'destruction' in his work. He enjoys creating unconventional pieces which cause conversation. When I spoke to him, he was working on a book project which involves documenting the ways in which Egyptian photo studios photoshop people's photographs as a reflection of the changing sociopolitical landscape, in which he argues that during Mubarak's era the photos reflected 'social' dreams of expensive cars and houses, whereas in the aftermath of the uprising and during Sisi's time, politics has become the central discourse, as his photos tend to be photoshopped wearing the Egyptian army uniform. http://mohamedalaaartwork.blogspot.com/

18) **Heyo:** Heyo is an anonymous young Egyptian graffiti artist. He did not divulge any information on his personal life or background but said that he had been interested in graffiti long before the uprising and that he likes to work alone or collaborate on projects with KIM.

19) **Radwa Fouda:** Radwa is an Egyptian artist and the Freelance Designer at Egyptian Center for Economic and Social Rights. She is interested in graphic design, illustration and art direction. Radwa majored in painting in the Faculty of Fine Arts at the University of Helwan. http://www.radwafouda .blogspot.com/ https://www.behance.net/radz

20) **Tefa:** Tefa (Mostafa) is an Egyptian visual artist who became active in graffiti since 2010 working in Cairo, Alexandria and Upper Egypt. He currently works as a video jockey (VJ) within the Cairo Shakers collective. (http:// www.cairoshakers.com/). http://www.te-fa.com/ www.facebook.com/iTefaa www.twitter.com/iTefa www.youtube.com/iMostafatefa

21) **El Teneen:** An anonymous Egyptian street artist and graffiti artist. I do not know much about him or his real name or any details of his personal life, except that in university he studied a degree related to science. He was not interested in art before the uprising but he is now actively involved in street art. https://www.facebook.com/elteneen.teneen https://twitter.com/elteneen

22) **Mustafa El Husseiny:** Mustafa is an artist who studied at El Nahda Jesuit School (an art school in Cairo). He is originally from Zagazig but now lives in Cairo. He is one of the founders of the Mona Lisa Brigades, who started working in Giza and Cairo since 2010. Mostafa is currently serving his mandatory draft service in the Egyptian army.

23) **Amr Nazeer:** An Egyptian street artist who studied business administration at Cairo University, Amr currently works as a business developer in Axeer Studio, an Egyptian media production company. https://www.linkedin.com/ in/amr-nazeer-277b6736 and https://twitter.com/amrnazeer

24) **Layla Amr:** Layla is a 19-year-old Egyptian street artist who studied interior design. Layla said she had always been interested in politics at the behest of her parents. She noticed random street art before the uprising but said that it was the uprising itself that made her interested in becoming a type of 'citizen journalist' artist.

25) **Hanaa El Degham:** An Egyptian artist who lives and works between Egypt and Germany (where she works in an atelier). She was never involved in politics prior to the uprising but was always concerned with human rights and the issue of Egyptian identity was always a central focus of her work. http://www.hanaeldegham.com/

APPENDIX II

Al Mawred Al Thaqafy's (Culture Resource) Campaign Images for 'A Culture for All Egyptians' in 2012–13

Figure A1 'Culture is not just for the Educated' (*Source*: Al Mawred Al Thaqafy). http://www.egyptianculturepolicy.net/

Figure A2 'Culture is not a Ministry, Culture is in the Street and the Neighbourhood' (*Source*: Al Mawred Al Thaqafy). http://www.egyptianculturepolicy.net/

Figure A3 'Culture is not only in the Opera, Culture is in Tanta (a highly populated Egyptian city north of Cairo) and Shobra (one of the largest, and poorest, districts in Cairo)' (*Source*: Al Mawred Al Thaqafy). http://www.egyptianculturepolicy.net/

Figure A4 'Every human being has a right to enjoy art and culture and it is their right to present art to people' (*Source*: Al Mawred Al Thaqafy). http://www.egyptianculturepolicy .net/

NOTES

Introduction

1   The bulk of academic literature on the history and politics in the Arab world proliferated in the aftermath of the 2010 and 2011 uprisings, as scholars found that old paradigms could not adequately explain new developments, as they questioned the validity of top–down examinations of politics that focus predominantly on modernist paradigms, Marxist approaches and political economy analyses, thereby providing more nuanced examinations from a bottom–up approach, which seeks to challenge the parameters of traditional theoretical structures used to analyse the social and political fields in the Middle East (Dabashi, 2012; Beinin, Vairel, eds., 2013; Sabea in Werbner et al., 2014; Gerges, 2014; Chalcraft, 2016). The literature addressing the historical moment of the Arab uprisings (through its trajectories, histories, dynamics, possible implications, etc.) are quite extensive (e.g. Khalil, 2011; Badiou, 2012; Al-Sumait et al., 2014; Korany, El-Mahdi, eds., 2012; Abou El-Fadl, 2015).

2   Public art is not a new phenomenon in Egypt – its modern history goes back to the late nineteenth century (Karnouk, 2005; Winegar, 2006), and street art also has a history prior to the uprising in Egypt (Charbel, 2010; Jarbou, 2010; Hamdy et al., 2014, Abaza, 2016).

3   Described as a 'concrete behemoth that houses the central bureaucracy' (Murphy, 1993) and Egypt's 'most hated building' (Diab, 2016), the Mogamma is a '14-storey complex which houses some 30,000 government employees in 1,350 rooms' and visited by 100,000 citizens on a daily basis (Diab, 2016). In early January 2016, then governor of Cairo, Galal Mostafa, announced in a press release that the Mogamma would be evacuated to another location by mid-2017 (Egyptian Streets, 2016) in order to reduce traffic in Tahrir Square.

4   The protests in Egypt came in the aftermath of widespread protests in Tunisia which began in December 2010 sparked by the self-immolation of Mohamed Bouazizi, a 26-year-old fruit and vegetable street vendor, who was protesting unjust treatment he received by local officials.

5   The decolonial term SWANA (South-west Asia/North Africa) is more appropriate than the Eurocentric term Middle East (also a Western concept to differentiate between the Far East and Near East) in reflecting the multicultural and diverse character of the region. The term Arab Spring is problematic as it homogenizes SWANA, a region which encompasses several languages, ethnicities and identities. Furthermore, 'Arab Spring' was coined by Western commentators who compartmentalized 'Westernized concepts of democracy and freedom' (Hobbs, 2021) and applied it to events happening halfway across the world, without any contextualization of the unique political, social and cultural histories of the different countries who were undergoing mass protests and revolutionary acts across the region.

6   The precise origin of this term is unknown: 'The dubious credit for the term Arab
    Spring may be given to writer and academic Marc Lynch, who first used it in a
    Foreign Policy article on 6 January 2011. However, it is not clear whether Lynch was
    actually the first person to coin the term. Foreign Policy's Joshua Keating pointed
    out later that same year that the term may have been used by US conservative
    commentators in 2005 to explain movements in the MENA region towards
    democracy, most notably the Lebanese protests to oust Syrian forces from their
    country after the assassination of influential politician Rafik Al-Hariri. But, it is more
    likely that journalists and political analysts who first used the term 'Arab Spring' in
    those heady days of early 2011 did so as a nod to the 'Prague Spring', which itself was
    a nod to the 1848 'springtime of peoples' across Europe. Both 1848 and 1968 were
    years of mass political upheaval in the West' (Hobbs, 2021).

7   The political apathy of young Egyptians prior to the revolution was addressed in the
    2010 United Nations Development Programme's report on the state of young people
    in Egypt, which found that those in the 18–29 age group were the least likely to
    engage in political activity. Furthermore, it found that most young Egyptians felt they
    were being openly discouraged from taking an active role in politics at all, and were
    being encouraged instead to focus their energies on private concerns (UNDP, 2010:
    105–10).

8   This will be addressed in greater detail in Chapter 3, where I will provide a brief
    history of political and artistic dissent prior to the 2011 revolution.

9   1968 was a critical year which saw key social and political upheavals and events
    spread across Europe and the United States.

10 In retrospect, this has arguably been the case, looking at the trajectory of Egypt's
    leadership this past decade since the revolution, from 2011 to 2021, which I will make
    reference to in later chapters. Furthermore, with the same structures of power, the socio-
    economic and political situation has not significantly improved and, in many cases, have
    declined over the years since 2011 (see, e.g. Khan, Miller, 2016; Hamed, 2019).

11 Joel Beinin, professor of Middle East history at Stanford University, argued that
    although Al Jazeera and social media were 'significant tools of mobilization', their
    'discursive salience has been exaggerated because the 'Facebook youth' are like 'us' –
    employing technologies, ideologies, and products imported from the West' (Beinin,
    2009: 324; El-Mahdi, 2011), thereby echoing Rizk's claims that it is in the Western
    media's interest to promote a narrative of familiarity Western audiences can digest –
    Egyptian protestors are just like 'us', technological savvy and familiar with Western
    social media platforms.

12 The root causes of Egypt's political dissent stemmed from Western-imposed
    neoliberal policies and economic restricting programmes from the World Bank and
    the International Monetary Fund which led to greater poverty and unemployment
    during Sadat and Mubarak's era, and also saw government subsidies cuts on staple
    items such as bread, which led to major protests (see, e.g. Beinin, 2012; El-Mahdi,
    2011). According to Beinin, '[a]n IMF delegation visited in the fall of 1976 and
    suggested the government cut subsidies on basic consumer goods by up to 50 per
    cent. The nation responded to President Anwar al-Sadat's announcement of the
    reduced subsidies with widespread riots on January 18-19, 1977. The government was
    compelled to restore the subsidies and reduce them stealthily over the next 30 years.
    There were wildcat strike waves in public sector enterprises in the early 1970s, mid-
    1980s, and early 1990s, and an intensifying workers' movement since the late 1990s
    (Beinin, 1994, 2001: 142–69; 2011; El Shafei, 1995, 22–36; Posusney, 1997: 142).'

13 Ganzeer was accused of being a member of the Muslim Brotherhood, due to his critical art work of then-presidential candidate Abdel Fattah El-Sisi. Ganzeer denied the claims and le ft Egypt for the United States in May 2014, and as of 2019, is based in Houston, Texas.

14 Radwa was also the former head of the Media Unit in the Egyptian Center for Economic and Social Rights (ECESR), and currently works as a freelance graphic designer.

15 Wedeen's study was based on her research of Hafiz al-Assad's regime in Syria in the 1990s.

16 'In the liminal period we see naked, unaccommodated man, whose non-logical character issues in various modes of behavior: destructive, creative, farcical, ironic, energetic, suffering, lecherous, sub-missive, defiant, but always unpredictable' (Turner, 1968: 580).

Chapter 1

1 Although Mubarak was hailed for stabilizing Egypt in the aftermath of Anwar Sadat's assassination in 1981, his popularity was, according to some analysts, short-lived when his rule became more brutal towards the opposition, running for a record five- (four-year) presidential terms (even though the Egyptian constitution during his presidency allowed for only a maximum of two terms), and accusations of rampant corruption and crony capitalism among his party, the NDP and his sons Alaa and Gamal, both of whom are businessmen who have been accused of using their fathers presidency for their own profitable ventures.

2 Repeated calls for independent monitors and/or local nongovernmental organizations to oversee elections were regularly refused by the Presidential Election Commission, at the behest of groups such as the International Commission of Jurists (ICJ, 2005).

3 The irony in deriding Egypt as a one party state system is that the 1971 Egyptian constitution specifically established a multiparty system, and during Mubarak's rule, there was at least forty-one registered political parties, with twenty-six new political formed in the aftermath of the 2011 revolution (Carbonari, 2011). According to the Egyptian State Information Service (SIS) – which, in its website, describes itself as the 'nation's main informational, awareness and public relations agency' (SIS, 2016) – as of 2018 over 104 political parties were officially registered in the state system (Aleem, 2019).

4 'Initially this enterprise manifested itself in the establishment of a printing press, Arabic newspapers and literary translations but also the establishment of a school of translation and a modern infrastructure for secular education. Gradually the modern institutionalized culture industry expanded to other fields of cultural production including the establishment of the School of Fine Arts in 1908. Despite the fact that these modern institutions and cultural products were initially set up according to the western colonial model, they were permeated from the start with a serious effort to forge a national Egyptian image and culture' (Gershoni, 1992: 209).

5 Mohamed Naguib, an army officer, was Egypt's first president after the 1952 coup. In 1953 he took office until his forced removal by Gamal Abdel Nasser in 1954, who then proclaimed himself prime minister. From 1954 to 1956, Nasser was the de facto ruler of Egypt, and instituted a socialist Arab state which saw his popularity as a

leader rise due to the significant improvement in the lives of the average Egyptian, through land reforms, wealth distribution and socialist economic policies. Running unopposed, Nasser garnered over 99 per cent of the votes on 23 June 1956, and was subsequently elected to the office of president, where he would rule until his death from a heart attack in 1970.

6   'the change of political regime in 1952 was a continuation, and systematization of the role of the state in the production and dissemination of the expanding Egyptian culture industry' (Mehrez, 2008: 209).

7   'After 1956, government financial support and patronage were the only kind of funding the majority of artists could expect . . . as the curve of government payroll spending climbed to a record seventy-three percent in 1956, more people in the arts found themselves attached to the state' (Karnouk, 2005: 67).

8   France, the UK and Israel eventually withdrew their forces after pressure from the United States, USSR and the United Nations by 1957.

9   'President Gamal Abdel Nasser founded the Egyptian Ministry of Culture in 1958, based on the French model, but also shaped by the experiments of various Eastern Bloc countries with centralized production and dissemination of culture – meaning literature, music and other fine arts, often with an explicit message. The major goals at the time remain central to the ministry's mission today: to define the nation and national identity, to protect cultural patrimony and to uplift the so-called masses by exposing them to the arts. To these ends, the ministry employed legions of artists and literati who often did works in line with nationalist goals of the regime. Many, for example, were sent to document the building of the High Dam. The ministry also built or renovated museums and arts centres throughout the country, and, as in France, hundreds of "culture palaces" in small towns and villages. Many of today's Egyptian artists, particularly those from provincial or lower-class backgrounds, got their start in these places' (Pahwa, Winegar, 2012).

10   Sadat used the Muslim Brotherhood group to counter nationalist and Nasserite groups opposition to his rule.

11   Mehrez argues that although there was indeed a large influx of funds to the cultural field which promoted its activities, '[b]ehind the façade of state prizes, awards, stipends and costly public events in the fields of literature, theatre, music, dance, film and visual arts lurks the ghost of censorship, at all levels including self-censorship, that ensures the political field's domination and control over the cultural one' (Mehrez, 2008: 212).

12   According to famed Egyptian novelist Ahdaf Soueif during one of our conversations, because of this failed strategy, creativity became the exception, not the rule: 'From time to time you got a little burst of something energetic and creative but on the whole, the institutions are lifeless bodies using their money and their facilities as a kind of support system for themselves. I understand that something like 85 percent of their budget goes on salaries, you know, not on cultural production for example. So when you have the Ministry of Culture is going to celebrate Eid El Fan [the cultural season] you just know that you are not going to go to that, you know what it is going to be like it is going to be bland it is going to be the same old thing, there is nothing going to be energetic or alive in that. Of course this is not to say that some things don't struggle on, like the Cairo Symphony Orchestra is still trying to do good work, but that is performance that is not creation' (Ahdaf Soueif, Cairo, pers. comm., 12 August 2014).

13   Egyptian artist Ammar Abo Bakr argued that Egypt's cultural institutions and the artists they promoted were only concerned with art as a commodity and that the

artist was completely disconnected from producing any art which contained any
relevance to society – for political and economic reasons – and that it was this type of
artist that now had to be discouraged in light of the uprising:

> The artist in Egypt that draws a nice portrait of a traditional Egyptian man in his
> *jellabiyas* or a nice typical-looking Egyptian scenery in the countryside, and then sells
> it to some random person, that artist is a bastard and hopefully we will destroy and
> break him, because his role does not serve our society (Ammar Abo Bakr, Cairo, pers.
> comm., 30 April 2014).

14 Called *qusur thaqafa*, the self-proclaimed mission of these cultural palaces was to
distribute 'high' culture to the masses (i.e. 'the lower class residents of large cities
and provincial towns, rural people, women, youth, and children) to counter low
(*baladi*) levels of culture, and although the initiative began with Gamal Abdel Nasser's
presidency with the main goal of 'raising the cultural level of workers and peasants
in the interest of social equality and development', during the Mubarak era (which
saw the construction of over eighty palaces and renovation of many others) the
primary focus was to raise 'cultural levels . . . in order to fight religious ignorance
and extremism' (Winegar, 2009: 190). Although each presidents' goals were different,
their goal was ultimately the same – 'to determine the future of the Egyptian nation'
(Winegar, 2009: 190).

15 http://www.zamalekartgallery.com/en_artist.php?artistID=161

16 http://www.zamalekartgallery.com/en_artist.php?artistID=27

17 Mohammed describes a 'Piece of Bread' as being a: '30 minutes [piece] on the process of
destruction. I was just destroying a wall for 30 minutes, the intention was to talk about
the importance of destruction and how hard and tough it is to find a piece of bread. Some
people may get bored from watching the video because it is long but that is the point, to
show them that it isn't easy to get a piece of bread. There is a camera in the other room,
you see me destroying the wall on one side then you see me destroying it from the other
side, and at the end of the video you see me standing in the middle, that I am lost in the
middle, left hanging' (Mohammed Alaa, Cairo, pers. comm., 12 August 2014).

18 The April 6 movement is a youth movement founded in 2008, in the aftermath of the
workers strikes.

19 'Abdel-Aziz dismissed three respected senior culture ministry officials without
explanation: Ahmed Megahed, head of the General Egyptian Book Organization; Salah El
Meligy, head of the Applied Arts department; and Inas Abdel Dayem, head of the Cairo
Opera House, who he replaced with Badr El-Zakaziky. He unsuccessfully attempted to
fire Sameh Mahran, head of the Academy of Arts, and decided not to renew the term of
the head of the Egyptian National Library and Archives (NLA), instead replacing him
with the Islamist-leaning Arabic literature professor, Khaled Fahmy' (Jacquette, 2013).

20 Inas Abdel Daïm is an Egyptian flute player, former director of the Cairo Symphony
Orchestra, former vice president of the Academy of Arts, former dean of the Cairo
Conservatoire and the former chairperson of the Cairo Opera House. Daïm is the
current Minister of Culture of Egypt since January 2018.

Chapter 2

1 'Although sporadic and episodic, contentious action by labour has been reported in
Egypt since the beginning of the twentieth century. The first documented strike was
in 1899 by the rolled-cigarette workers, which lasted three months and resulted in

the first trade union in Egypt (Abbas 1973, p. 62). A number of labour unions known as "workers' societies" were then formed as early as 1908 and, by the end of World War I, with the rise of Marxist parties in Egypt, these unions were amalgamated into the "Workers Confederation" (Abbas 1973). Despite the changeable fortunes of these labour organisations and state attempts to clamp down on both the unions and their Socialist-Communist backers, Egypt could, by the second half of the 1940s, claim a strong independent labour movement' (El-Mahdi, 2011: 390).

2 '. . . from 1998 to 2010, well over 2 million, and probably closer to 4 million, Egyptian workers participated in some 3,400 to 4,000 strikes and other collective actions (Beinin 2011a, 191). This workers' movement was sustained with no support from the state-sponsored Egyptian Trade Union Federation (ETUF), which nominally represents about 3.8 million blue and white-collar workers out of Egypt's labor force of 26.2 million. ETUF's national officials were agents of the regime – as they have been since the federation was established in 1957' (Beinin, 2012: 326).

3 'In the 2000s, persistent workers' collective action was one of the several protest movements eroding the legitimacy of the Mubarak regime and a major component of the emergent culture of protest. However, links between workers and the pro-democracy campaigns of the middle-class intelligentsia, which were particularly salient from late 2004 to mid-2006 and in 2009–2010, were weak and episodic. Workers typically focused on immediate economic issues. Nonetheless, their movement provided numerous occasions for exercises in participatory democracy. When workers did begin to speak about politics, they did not limit themselves to formal democracy – free parliamentary elections and the rotation of power. They demanded substantive democracy: free trade unions and distributive social justice. These understandings of democracy were rarely articulated as a comprehensive political program by a recognized national leadership' (Beinin, 2009: 328).

4 'Following the Mahalla workers initial victory, which received widespread media coverage, a wave of strikes engulfed the textile sector, with workers in other mills demanding the same gains as those of Mahalla. The industrial militancy was soon to spill over into other sectors of the economy. Images of the strikes, aired via both social and mainstream media, meant millions of workers could gradually overcome their fears, and organise protests inspired by news of victories of strikes in other sectors. As a journalist covering the strike wave in 2007, I frequently heard from strikers: "We were encouraged to move after we heard of Mahalla"' (El Hamalawy, 2011).

5 El-Mahalla El-Kubra is an Egyptian city in the Nile delta, known for its textile mills. The 2008 el-Mahalla strike came amidst the wave of protests in Mahalla from 2004 to 2007, protesting (successfully) against low wages, unpaid bonuses, and unfair management which attacked the 'economic policies and political legitimacy' (Beinin, 2007) of Mubarak's rule. The 2008 strike would be an important precedent to the uprising, in that it was not only a labour strike demanding an immediate rectification of substandard wages but also directly challenged Mubarak's legitimacy. As Tripp notes, the 'portraits of President Mubarak that loomed over the textile factories of al-Mahalla al-Kubra . . . were torn down and trodden on by enraged workers. So desperate was the regime to erase this powerful message of visual defiance from public memory that, in addition to seizing and censoring all photographs of these events, they arrested and imprisoned the photographers and the publishers responsible for daring to publicize this spectacular puncturing of the myth of authority which was a vain attempt at suppression give that this image was circulated widely via social media' (2013: 188).

6   Axeer Studio is an Egyptian media production company.
7   Khaled Said (see Figure 2.2) was a 28-year-old middle-class Egyptian who lived in the
    Egyptian coastal city Alexandria, where he was dragged from an internet café by two
    policeman for allegedly sharing a video of police officers dividing up narcotics and
    money from a drug deal, who then subsequently beat him to death. The government
    incensed the public by trying to cover up the incident and saying that Khaled Said
    allegedly swallowed and choked on a packet of drugs.
8   According to Reem Saad, the 'We are all Khaled Said' Facebook page channelled the
    anger at Khaled Said's brutal death at the hands of police 'into political action whose
    discourse and practice were novel, refreshing, and inclusive'; thus '[t]he picture of
    the tortured face of Khaled Said became an icon of this movement and, later, of the
    Egyptian revolution' (Saad, 2012: 64).
9   For more on this topic, see, for example, Salwa Ismail (2012).
10 These protests were primarily called for online by the April 6 Youth Movement and
    the *Kulina Khaled Said* ('We are all Khaled Said') Facebook page, run by former
    Google employee Wael Ghonim.
11 This is a national holiday in Egypt which celebrates the resistance efforts of police
    against British occupation forces in Egypt. The reason this date was chosen was an
    irony of sorts – a day meant to celebrate the police became the chosen date where
    they would be put on 'public trial' (Ismail, 2012: 435).
12 A chapter of the International Federation of Independent Revolutionary Art founded
    by André Breton in 1938 promoting unhindered cultural expression against the
    increasing cultural repression of the state.
13 One of the most revolutionary aspects of these exhibitions was the unprecedented
    inclusion of women whose works were featured prominently, at a time when they
    were largely marginalized from the cultural field. One such prominent woman was
    Egyptian painter and women's activist Inji Alflatoun (LaCoss, 2009-10: 30; Karnouk,
    2005: 74–5).
14 One of the groups of artists, not mentioned in the main body of the text but worth
    mentioning for its impact in the design field, was the 'Group of Art & Life' founded
    by Hamed Said, an Egyptian artist. One of its most prominent members was Hassan
    Fathi, the Egyptian architect who sought to establish a form of architecture which
    was not reliant on modern design and expensive materials, but rather one that was
    structurally, economically and aesthetically sustainable and compatible with Egypt's
    environment (Karnouk, 2005: Ch. 4).

Chapter 3

1   One notorious example of this is the closure of the infamous Townhouse Gallery,
    a not-for-profit art space located in downtown Cairo. Established in 1998, it
    'emerged onto a scene dominated by the Egyptian Ministry of Culture and its private
    affiliates' as 'one of the first independent art spaces in Cairo' (Townhouse, 2021).
    On 29 December 2015, Townhouse was shut down by interagency administrative
    officials (one month prior to the Egyptian revolution five-year anniversary on
    25 January 2016, which usually sees large-scale protests in downtown Cairo) from
    the Censorship Authority, Tax Authority, National Security Agency and the local
    office of the Ministry of Manpower (Neuendorf, 2015). When Townhouse reopened

briefly in February 2016, its director, William Wells, warned that the gallery faces 'unprecedented censorship' after the gallery had 'been given two weeks to comply with new legal restrictions, some of which amounted to state control of its work' which, he argued, was ultimately seen 'as a means to control freedom of expression' (Batty, 2016). Townhouse did not reopen again until September 2016, under stricter regulation imposed by the government.

2   'You have to submit what it is you're going to hold a workshop on, what the discussion will be about – ultimately we're looking at forms of control. It's a matter of being able to control the activities and programming that take place – music, performance, talks, visual art' – William Wells, director of Townhouse (Batty, 2016).

3   Egyptian society is, for the most part, a conservative society, and social norms in public are generally quite strict, however, it also largely depends where in Egypt you are (e.g. within the megacity of Cairo itself, there are huge discrepancies between more affluent areas such as Zamalek versus, e.g. poorer areas such as Bulaq, whose residents tend to be more conservative).

4   *Hajj* is one of the five central pillars of Islam, the other four being *shahada* (the profession of faith), *salah* (prayer, of which there are five obligatory prayers during the day), *zakat* (almsgiving to those in need) and *sawm* (fasting) during the Holy month of Ramadan, which falls on the ninth month of the Islamic lunar calendar.

5   The first building, or 'House of God', built for the worship of Allah, which lies in the centre of Islam's holiest mosque, *Al-Masjid Al-Haram*, in Mecca, Saudi Arabia.

6   In a 2013 United Nations report found that a staggering nine out of ten Egyptian women have been sexually assaulted, from verbal and physical harassment to rape, which 'demonstrates a real problem that requires rapid and sustainable solutions, policies, and advocacy work. There has been extensive public discussion on the topic for the last couple of years, and the state has denied the breadth and severity of the problem' (Abdelaal, 2021).

7   This would include, over the course of 2011, hundreds of other members, from artists, performers, to poets and musicians (Adel, 2011).

8   A non-exhaustive list of examples of these exhibitions are *This is Not Graffiti*, which had works from nine artists in Townhouse Gallery, Hany Rashed's *Toys* exhibition in Mashrabia Gallery (a contemporary art gallery located in downtown Cairo, and founded in the mid-1970s), Ahmed Hefnawy's art installations at the abandoned Viennoise Hotel in downtown Cairo, and Huda Lutfi's *Cut and Paste* exhibition in Townhouse Gallery.

Chapter 4

1   Ganzeer was briefly arrested for putting up posters and stickers of the 'Mask of Freedom' in the Spring of 2011, an image which represented the army crackdown down on revolutionaries sit-ins and continued calls to remain in Tahrir.

2   Islam was a martyr of the revolution, an 18-year-old who was killed on the Friday of Rage (28 January 2011) after he was brutally run over by a security truck.

3   Former field marshal Mohamed Hussein Tantawi was the Minister of Defense and commander-in-chief of the Egyptian Armed Forces. Tantawi was temporarily the Head of State in the aftermath of Hosni Mubarak's ouster, and was derided for his previous close ties to the former president, military trials of thousands of civilians

in the aftermath of the revolution, as well as the violent and brutal tactics used by the military to suppress protests in the winter of 2011/2012.

4　After Mohammed Khaled's first drawing was defaced, he and his friends formed the Mona Lisa Brigades, as a mocking reference to the Badr Brigades.

5　Bahia Shehab is an Egyptian-Lebanese artist and historian, and associate professor of design and founder of the graphic design programme at the American University in Cairo (AUC).

6　'The *wilad sis* are young men who might be described as working class, though most are unemployed, underemployed, unskilled and semi-skilled, doing occasional jobs that change every day (though on most days, there is no "work"). They are often marked by a particular dress code and hairstyle that often involves copious quantities of gel (the word *sis* alludes to the attention they often pay to their appearance, considered by other Egyptians as almost effeminate)' (Ryzova, 2011a).

7　'It is claimed [that Central Security Forces], have targeted protesters' heads – it has been reported that more than 80 people have lost eyes and many more have sustained head and neck injuries since the protests in January [2011]. . . . Claims by protesters that the targeting was more pronounced in the November clashes are backed up by Ghada Shahbender of the Egyptian Organisation for Human Rights, who says she heard a high-ranking CSF officer instructing soldiers to aim at the protesters' heads as she passed through their ranks on 19 November' (Tomlin, 2011).

8　The Freedom and Justice Party of the Muslim Brotherhood won an overwhelming majority of the votes – 47.2 per cent – when the final results came out on 21 January 2012 (Hamdy, Karl, 2013: 130).

9　Fatwas are legal opinions or an official statement/ruling issued by an Islamic leader.

10　The Institute of Egypt, located near Tahrir Square, was established in the eighteenth century by Napoleon Bonaparte – it contained priceless manuscripts, most of which were destroyed when the institute was burned down on 17 December 2011 (Associated Press in Cairo, 2011).

11　'The blocking of Qasr Al-Aini Street, a vital Cairo artery, has made normal perambulation in downtown impossible. It appears as if the powers that be have a master plan to torment all the capital's denizens – pedestrians and car drivers, rich and poor (this is democracy) – via the tactic of "detouring"' (Abaza, 2013c).

12　During Mad Graffiti Week, 'three youths are reported to have been arrested – one in Banha City and two in Mahalla City – for acts of "vandalism." These youths were reportedly detained, questioned and then released on the same day' (Charbel, 2012).

13　A *trompe l'oeil* (direct translation, to 'deceive the eye') is a technique which uses realistic imagery to create a type of optical illusion to trick the viewer into seeing two dimensional objects, such as a wall, as three dimensional.

14　See Jerzak, 2013, for how the Ultras became a revolutionary force.

15　Many witnesses reported that the steel doors of the stadium were bolted shut (Al Arabiya, 2012; Doward, 2012; Fayed, Perry, 2012), and reports of police officers inciting the attacks could be heard. Indeed, twin brothers who play for the home team Al Masry 'claim[ed] the violence was encouraged by the police with the backing of the army' (Doward, 2012).

16   The *buraq* refers to the steed which Prophet Muhammad rode on in his journey
     to Al-Aqsa Mosque in Jerusalem in *Isra'a wa'l Miraj* (the Night of Ascension), as
     mentioned in the Holy Qu'ran.

Chapter 5

1   The infamous 'Battle of the Camel' of 2 February 2011 in Tahrir Square refers to an
    'armed attack by groups of armed Egyptian civilians and Mubarak supporters against
    underamed Egyptian civilians . . . carried out in medieval fashion; camels, horses and
    knives were deployed. Nearly a dozen people were killed and more than a thousand
    were injured. The Fact Finding Mission concluded that figures [such as Ahmad Shafiq]
    from the ruling regime were behind the attack' (Hamamou, S., 2016).
2   Ammar made the decision to relocate from Luxor to Cairo during the revolution as he
    felt that he had to be in the epicentre of events with the people and work in the streets
    permanently. This very much had to do with his previous experiences being embedded
    in – and documenting – the *mulids*.

Chapter 6

1   Hisham Rizk was a 19-year-old member of the Revolution Artists Union (RAU) and
    a graffiti artist who was found a week after his disappearance in a morgue in late June
    2014 (Abaza, M., 2015). Issa was a revolutionary artist who was also killed during the
    period of my fieldwork, though the circumstances and context of his death were not
    known to me.

Chapter 7

1   There are many notable archives of the Egyptian revolution which are still active
    and functioning, such as the 858 archive, https://858.ma/, which 'vast collection
    that documents famous and tragic events as well as more mundane ones – a
    collage of scenes and moments that add up to an incomplete but rich and moving
    people's history. Activists have worked for years to make this material free in every
    sense. The archive draws its name from the number of hours of video available
    upon its creation – though it is designed to allow more material to be added. The
    members of the anonymous collective behind the archive, whom Al-Fanar Media
    interviewed by email, chose not to identify themselves, both for their personal
    safety and to emphasize the collective nature of the project, which does not belong
    to anyone. The archive is a challenge to the current Egyptian regime, which has
    arrested many of the activists who led the protests and has rewritten the recent
    history they made. In the current official version, the Arab Spring was a foreign
    and/or Islamist plot; protesters were misguided if not downright seditious; and the
    police and the military have never committed human-rights abuses but only did
    what was necessary to defend order and the authority of the state. The disparity
    between events on the ground and the official narrative was a great impetus to the
    original effort to collect video of the revolution. During the 18 days of protest in

Tahrir Square, activists set up a Media Tent, where they collected video evidence of state violence against protesters. The footage was collected under the principle of creative commons' (Lindsey, 2018).

2 https://www.facebook.com/Graffiti.in.Egypt/?pnref=lhc
3 https://www.facebook.com/WallsOfFreedom/?fref=ts
4 https://www.facebook.com/StreetARTnEgypt/?fref=ts

BIBLIOGRAPHY

Abaza, M., 2011. 'On Egypt, Public Space and Media'. *Theory, Culture, & Society*. Available online at: http://www.theoryculturesociety.org/mona-abaza-on-egypt-public-space -and-media/ [Accessed 3 July 2012].

Abaza, M., 2012a. 'An Emerging Memorial Space? In Praise of Mohammed Mahmoud Street'. *Jadaliyya*, 10 March. Available online at: http://www.jadaliyya.com/pages/index /4625/an-emerging-memorial-space-in-praise-of-mohammed-merging-memorial -space-in-praise-of-mohammed-m [Accessed 29 April 2013].

Abaza, M., 2012b. 'The Revolution's Barometer'. *Jadaliyya*, 12 June. Available online at: http://www.jadaliyya.com/pages/index/5978/the-revolutions-barometer [Accessed 27 February 2013].

Abaza, M., 2012c. 'Walls, Segregating Downtown Cairo and the Mohammed Mahmud Street Graffiti'. *Theory, Culture, & Society*, 30(1), pp. 122–39.

Abaza, M., 2013a. 'Cairo Diary: Space Wars, Public Visibility and the Transformation of Public Space in Post-Revolutionary Egypt'. In: Berry, C., Harbord, J, Moore, R.O., (eds), *Public Space, Media Space*. London: Palgrave Macmillan, pp. 88–109.

Abaza, M., 2013b. 'The Dramaturgy of a Street Corner'. *Jadaliyya*, 25 January. Available online at: http://www.jadaliyya.com/pages/index/9724/the-dramaturgy-of-a-street -corner [Accessed 13 May 2014].

Abaza, M., 2013c. 'Mourning, Narratives and Interactions with the Martyrs through Cairo's Graffiti'. 7 October. Available online at: http://www.e-ir.info/2013/10/07/ mourning-narratives-and-interactions-with-the-martyrs-through-cairos-graffiti/ [Accessed 20 April 2015].

Abaza, M., 2014. 'Post January Revolution Cairo: Urban Wars and the Reshaping of Public Space'. *Theory, Culture, & Society*, 31(7/8), pp. 163–83.

Abaza, M., 2015. 'Is Cairene Graffiti Losing Momentum?' *Jadaliyya*, 25 January. Available online at: http://cci.jadaliyya.com/pages/index/20635/is-cairene-graffiti-losing -momentum [Accessed 8 February 2015].

Abaza, M., 2016. 'The Field of Graffiti and Revolutionary Art in Post-January 2011 Egypt'. In: Ross, J.I., (ed.), *Routledge Handbook of Graffiti and Revolutionary Art*. Abingdon, Oxon and New York: Routledge, pp. 318–33.

Abdalla, N., 2012. 'Social Protests in Egypt Beforeand after the 25 January Revolution:Perspectives on the Evolution of Their Forms and Features'. *The European Institute of the Mediterranean (IEMed)*. Available online at: https://www.iemed.org /publication/social-protests-in-egypt-before-and-after-the-25-january-revolution -perspectives-on-the-evolution-of-their-forms-and-features/.

Abdelaal, H., 2021. 'Sexual Harassment Laws in Egypt: Does Stricter Mean More Effective?' *The Tahrir Institute for Middle East Policy*. Available online at: https://timep .org/commentary/analysis/sexual-harassment-laws-in-egypt-does-stricter-mean-more -effective/.

Abdel Kouddous, S., 2013. 'What Led to Morsi's Fall – and What Comes Next?'. *The Nation*, 5 July. Available online at: https://www.thenation.com/article/what-led-morsis -fall-and-what-comes-next/ [Accessed 18 June 2014].

Abdelmagid, Y., 2013. 'The Emergence of the Mona Lisa Battalions: Graffiti Art Networks in Post-2011 Egypt'. *Review of Middle East Studies*, 47(2), pp. 172–82.

Abo Bakr, A., 2015. 'Art Revolution – Egypt: Walls of Freedom'. Tea after Twelve, Issue 1, Chapter 2. Available online at: http://www.tea-after-twelve.com/all-issues/issue-01/issue-01-overview/chapter2/art-revolution/ [Accessed 29 June 2017].

Abou Bakr, T., 2013. 'In Pictures: Walls of Freedom Documents Egyptian Revolutionary Art'. *Daily News Egypt*, 16 July. Available online at: https://dailynewsegypt.com/2013/07/16/in-pictures-walls-of-freedom-documents-egyptian-street-art/ [Accessed 28 November 2013].

Abu-Lughod, L., 1986. *Veiled Sentiments: Honor and Poetry in a Bedouin Society*. Berkeley: University of California Press.

Abu-Lughod, L., 1993. *Writing Women's Worlds: Bedouin Stories*. Berkeley: University of California Press.

Abu-Lughod, L., 2005. *Dramas of Nationhood: The Politics of Television in Egypt*. Chicago, IL: University of Chicago Press.

Adel, D., 2012. 'Egypt's Revolutionary Artists Return to Their Spot in Tahrir'. *Ahram Online*. Available online at: https://english.ahram.org.eg/NewsContent/5/25/16358/Arts--Culture/Visual-Art/Egypts-Revolutionary-Artists-return-to-their-spot-.aspx.

Adorno, T.W., 2002. *Aesthetic Theory*. Adorno, G., Tiedemann, R., (eds), Kentor, R.H., (trans.). London and New York: Continuum.

Adorno, T.W., 2007. 'Commitment'. In: Adorno, T.W., et al. (eds), *Aesthetics and Politics*. London: Verso, pp. 177–95.

Agamben, G., 1988. *Homo Sacer. Sovereign Power and Bare Life*. Stanford, CA: Stanford University Press.

Agence-France Press, 2011. 'Ahmed Harara, the Blind Hero of Egypt's Revolution'. *The National*, 28 November. Available online at: https://www.thenational.ae/world/mena/ahmed-harara-the-blind-hero-of-egypt-s-revolution-1.448157 [Accessed 19 June 2017].

Ahram Online, 2012. 'Tahrir Protesters Commemorate "Day of Rage"'. 28 January. Available online at: http://english.ahram.org.eg/NewsContent/1/64/33104/Egypt/Politics-/Tahrir-protesters-commemorate-Day-of-Rage.aspx [Accessed 14 March 2013].

Ahram Online, 2013a. 'Court Postpones Retrial of Khaled Said "murderers"'. 6 July. Available online at: http://english.ahram.org.eg/NewsContent/1/64/75836/Egypt/Politics-/Court-postpones-retrial-of-Khaled-Said-murderers.aspx [Accessed 8 June 2014].

Ahram Online, 2013b. 'Hundreds Protest Release of "Killers" of Egypt Revolution Icon, Khaled Said'. 1 June. Available online at: http://english.ahram.org.eg/NewsContent/1/64/72869/Egypt/Politics-/Hundreds-protest-release-of-%E2%80%98killers%E2%80%99-of-Egypt-rev.aspx [Accessed 9 June 2014].

Ahram Online, 2014. *Egypt's Illiteracy Rates Increase in 2013: CAPMAS Report*. 7 September. Available online at: http://english.ahram.org.eg/NewsContent/1/64/110142/Egypt/Politics-/Egypts-Illiteracy-rates-increase-in--CAPMAS-report.aspx [Accessed 29 January 2015].

Alaa, M., 2011. *Protestors Signing 50-metre Parchment*. [image]. Available online at: http://mohamedalaaartwork.blogspot.co.uk/?view=snapshot [Accessed 9 January 2012].

Aleem, A., 2019. 'More than Half of Egypt's Political Parties Join one Alliance'. *Al-Monitor*. Available online at: https://www.al-monitor.com/originals/2019/01/egypt-60-political-parties-join-hands-in-upcoming-elections.html#ixzz7aMJsBCPS.

Al Arabiya, 2011. 'Egypt Cultural Scene Gets Facelift after Revolution'. 22 February. Available online at: https://www.alarabiya.net/articles/2011/02/22/138763.html [Accessed 19 September 2012].

Al Arabiya, 2012. 'Egypt's Inquiry Blames Fans, Police for Stadium Deaths; Ultras Call for "retribution"'. 13 February. Available online at: http://english.alarabiya.net/articles/2012/02/13/194278.html

Alfred, C., 2014. 'Revolutionary Art Just Got More Dangerous in Egypt, But Artists Are Getting More Creative'. *Huffington Post*, 8 May. Available online at: http://www.huffingtonpost.com/2014/05/08/egypt-street-artists_n_5148542.html [Accessed 18 September 2014].

Al Ghoul, A., 2013. 'Is Egypt's Media Inciting Hatred Against Palestinians?' *Al-Monitor*, 17 July. Available online at: http://www.al-monitor.com/pulse/en/originals/2013/07/egypt-media-incitement-palestinians.html [Accessed 16 August 2013].

Al Mawred Al Thaqafy, 2013. *Images of Culture Campaign*. Available online at: http://www.egyptianculturepolicy.net/ [Accessed 5 February 2014].

Al Sharouny, H., 2013. 'Graffiti and Posters (Vienna, Gaza, Cairo'. *Behance*, 31 January. Available online at: https://www.behance.net/gallery/6937223/Graffiti-and-Posters-(ViennaGazaCairo [Accessed 4 April 2013].

@AlSisi, 2014. *Twitter*. 12 May. Available online at: https://twitter.com/alsisiofficial/status/465870568135593984?refsrc=email [Accessed 3 January 2015].

Al Sumait, F., Lenze, N., Hudson, M.C. (eds), 2014. *The Arab Uprisings: Catalysts, Dynamics, and Trajectories*. Lanham, MD: Rowman & Littlefield.

Amaria, K., 2011. 'The 'Girl in the Blue Bra'. *NPR*, 21 December. Available online at: http://www.npr.org/sections/pictureshow/2011/12/21/144098384/the-girl-in-the-blue-bra [Accessed 15 March 2017].

Amin, S., 2014. 'Egypt's Nascent Revolutionary Art Movement under Pressure'. *Index*, 22 August. Available online at: https://www.indexoncensorship.org/2014/08/egypts-nascent-graffiti-movement-threat/ [Accessed 6 September 2014].

Amin, S., 2015. 'Artistic Freedom of Expression Shrinks in "new" Egypt'. *Al Monitor*. Available online at: https://www.al-monitor.com/originals/2020/01/january-25-anniversary-freedom-of-expression.html#ixzz7be39FUH7.

Amin, S., 2016. 'Egypt Five Years after the Revolution: Artistic Freedom is Stifled'. *Freemuse*, 25 January. Available online at: http://artsfreedom.org/?p=10696 [Accessed 21 February 2016].

Amnesty International, 2012. 'Egypt: President Morsi Changes to the Constitution Trample Rule of Law'. 23 November. Available online at: https://www.amnesty.org.uk/press-releases/egypt-president-morsi-changes-constitution-trample-rule-law [Accessed 7 February 2017].

Andeel, 2015. '"Take it" Back Please, Ramy Essam'. *Mada Masr*, 8 February. Available online at: http://www.madamasr.com/sections/culture/take-it-back-please-ramy-essam [Accessed 29 June 2015].

Anis, M., 1967. 'Hawl Qadiyyat al-Taghayyur al-Thaqaf i'. *Al-Hilal*, LXXV(9), p. 5.

Arendt, H., 1998. *The Human Condition*. Chicago, IL: University of Chicago Press.

Armbrust, W., 1996. *Mass Culture and Modernism in Egypt*. Cambridge: Cambridge University Press.

Armbrust, W., 2013a. 'The Ambivalence of Martyrs and the Counter-revolution'. *Hot Spots, Cultural Anthropology Website*, 8 May. Available online at: https://culanth.org/fieldsights/213-the-ambivalence-of-martyrs-and-the-counter-revolution [Accessed 11 March 2017].

Armbrust, W., 2013b. 'The Trickster in the January 25th Revolution'. *Comparative Studies in Society and History*, 55(4), pp. 834–64.

Armbrust, W., 2015. 'The Iconic State: Martyrologies and Performance Frames in the 25 January Revolution'. In: Abou-El-Fadl, R., (ed.). *Revolutionary Egypt: Connecting Domestic and International Struggles*. Kindle ed. London: Routledge, pp. 83–112.

Armbrust, W., 2017. 'Trickster Defeats the Revolution: Egypt as the Vanguard of the New Authoritarianism'. *Middle East Critique*, 26(3), pp. 221–39.

Arnold, M., [1867] 1960. *Culture and Anarchy*. Cambridge: Cambridge University Press.

Atta, F., 2021. 'Speaking in Colour: What is the Legacy of Egypt's Revolutionary Art?'. *MENA Solidarity Network*. Available online at: https://menasolidaritynetwork.com /2021/06/16/speaking-in-colour-what-is-the-legacy-of-egypts-revolutionary-art/.

Attalah, L., Elmeshad, M., 2013. 'Good-bye, Bassem'. *Mada Masr*, 23 December. Available online at: https://www.madamasr.com/en/2013/12/23/feature/politics/good-bye -bassem/ [Accessed 12 April 2017].

'Awad, Luis, 1968. 'Cultural and Intellectual Developments'. In: Vatikiotis, P.J., (ed.). *Egypt since the Revolution*. New York and Washington: Frederick A. Praeger, Publishers, pp. 143–61.

Azoulay, A., 2010. 'Getting Rid of the Distinction between the Aesthetic and the Political'. *Theory, Culture, & Society*, 27(7–8), pp. 239–62.

Azoulay, A., 2012. *Civil Imagination: A Political Ontology of Photography*. London, New York: Verso.

Babcock, J., 2012. 'Ancient Egyptian Ostraca: A Reevaluation'. *The Metropolitan Museum of Art*, 10 October. Available online at: http://www.metmuseum.org/blogs/now-at-the -met/features/2012/ancient-egyptian-ostraca [Accessed 16 June 2014].

Badiou, A., 2012. *The Rebirth of History: Times of Riots and Uprising*. London, New York: Verso Books.

Badran, M., 2014. 'Dis/Playing Power and the Politics of Patriarchy in Revolutionary Egypt: The Creative Activism of Huda Lutfi'. *Postcolonial Studies*, 17(1), pp. 47–62.

Baker, R., 2013. 'Egypt's Coup Does Not Bode Well for Palestinians'. *The Guardian*, 10 July. Available online at: https://www.theguardian.com/commentisfree/2013/jul/10/egypt -coup-palestinians-morsi-gaza [Accessed 8 August 2013].

Baker, M., (ed.), 2016. *Translating Dissent: Voices From and With the Egyptian Revolution*. New York: Routledge.

Bal, M., 2003. 'Visual Essentialism and the Object of Visual Culture'. *Journal of Visual Culture*, 2(1), pp. 5–32.

Baladi, L., 2016. 'Archiving a Revolution in the Digital Age, Archiving as an Act of Resistance'. *IBRAAZ*, 28 July. Available online at: http://www.ibraaz.org/usr/library/documents/main/ archiving-a-revolution-in-the-digital-age.pdf [Accessed 12 August 2016].

Baroud, R., 2013. 'Hated in Egypt: How the Palestinian Bogeyman Resurfaced Like Never Before'. *RamzyBaroud.Net*, 30 July. Available online at: http://www.ramzybaroud.net/ hated-in-egypt-how-the-palestinian-bogeyman-resurfaced-like-never-before/?print =pdf [Accessed 30 November 2013].

Batty, D., 2016. 'Cairo Gallery Bemoans Unprecedented Censorship as it Prepares to Reopen'. *The Guardian*. Available online at: https://www.theguardian.com/world/2016/ feb/22/egypt-cairo-art-gallery-townhouse-unprecedented-censorship.

Baxandall, L., Morawski, S., 1973. *Marx & Engels on Literature & Art: A Selection of Writings*. St. Louis, MO: Telos Press.

Bayat, A., 1997. *Street Politics: Poor People's Movements in Iran*. New York: Columbia University Press.

Bayat, A., 2010. *Life as Politics: How Ordinary People Change the Middle East*. Stanford, CA: Stanford University Press.

Bayat, A., 2013. *Life as Politics: How Ordinary People Change the Middle East*. Second Revised Edition. Stanford, CA: Stanford University Press.

Bayat, A., 2015. 'Revolution and Despair'. *Mada Masr*, 25 January. Available online at: http://www.madamasr.com/opinion/revolution-and-despair [Accessed 24 February 2015].

BBC World Service, 2021. 'Egyptian Street Artist Ganzeer - Arab Spring 10 Years on - BBC World Service'. *BBC News*, 8 July. Available online at: https://www.youtube.com/watch?v=s1TKRFa_3Aw.

Beaumont, P., 2012. 'Mohamed Morsi Signs Egypt's New Constitution into Law'. *BBC News*, 26 December. Available online at: https://www.theguardian.com/world/2012/dec/26/mohamed-morsi-egypt-constitution-law [Accessed 4 February 2013].

Beinin, J., 1994. 'Will the Real Egyptian Working Class Please Stand Up?'. In: Lockman, Z. (ed.), *Workers and Working Classes in the Middle East: Struggles, Histories, Historiographies*. Albany: State University of New York Press, pp. 247–70.

Beinin, J., 2001. *Workers and Peasants in the Modern Middle East*. Cambridge: Cambridge University Press.

Beinin, J., 2007. 'The Militancy of Mahalla al-Kubra'. *Middle East Report*. Available online at: http://merip.org/mero/mero092907 [Accessed 29 September 2012].

Beinin, J., 2011. 'A Workers' Social Movement on the Margin of the Global Neoliberal Order, Egypt 2004–2009'. In: Beinin, J., Vairel, F. (eds), *Social Movements, Mobilization, and Contestation in the Middle East and North Africa*. Stanford: Stanford University Press.

Beinin, J., 2012. 'Egyptian workers and January 25th: a social movement in historical context'. *Social Research*, vol. 79, no. 2, summer 2012, pp. 323+. Gale Academic OneFile, Available online at: https://www.link.gale.com/apps/doc/A304051119/AONE?u=anon~88ac603d&sid=googleScholar&xid=b14b51b2 [Accessed 15 October 2022].

Beinin, J., 2012. 'The Rise of Egypt's Workers'. *Carnegie Endowment for International Peace*. Available online at: https://carnegieendowment.org/2012/06/28/rise-of-egypt-s-workers-pub-48689.

Beinin, J., Vairel, F., 2013. *Social Movements, Mobilization, and Contestation in the Middle East and North Africa*. Stanford: Stanford University Press.

Benjamin, W., 1978. *Reflections*. New York: Schocken Books.

Benjamin, W., 1988. 'The Author as Producer'. In: Boston, A., (trans.), *Understanding Brecht*. London and New York: Verso, pp. 85–103.

Benjamin, W., [1934] 2007. 'The Work of Art in the Age of Mechanical Reproduction'. In: Arendt, H., (ed.), Zohn, H., (trans.). *Illuminations*. New York: Schocken Books, pp. 217–51.

Bennett, T., 1992. 'Putting Policy into Cultural Studies'. In: Grossberg, L., Nelson, C., Treichler, P.A., (eds), *Cultural Studies*. New York: Routledge, pp. 23–37.

Berànek, O., 2005. 'The Surrealist Movement in Egypt in the 1930s and the 1940s'. *ARCHIV ORIENTÁLNÍ*, 73, pp. 203–22.

Beyes, T., 2010. 'Uncontained: The Art and Politics of Reconfiguring Urban Space'. *Culture and Organization*, 16(3), pp. 229–45.

Bishara, A., Winegar, J., 2009. 'Culture Concepts in Political Struggle: Introduction'. *Review of Middle East Studies*, 43(2), pp. 164–7.

Bohstedt, J., 2014. 'Food Riots and the Politics of Provisions in World History'. *Institute of Development Studies*, Working Paper 44. Available online at: http://onlinelibrary.wiley.com/doi/10.1111/j.2040-0209.2014.00444.x/pdf [Accessed 31 July 2015].

Boraïe, S., 2012. *Wall Talk: Graffiti of the Egyptian Revolution*. Cairo: Zeitouna Press.

Bourdieu, P., 1994. 'Rethinking the State: Genesis and Structure of the Bureaucratic Field'. *Sociological Theory*, 12(1), pp. 1–18.

Boyatzis, R.E., 1998. *Transforming Qualitative Information*. Thousand Oaks, CA: Sage.

Bradley, M., Abdellatif, R., 2013. 'Egypt Army Issues Ultimatum'. *The Wall Street Journal*, 2 July. Available online at: http://www.wsj.com/articles/SB10001424127887323297504578578991289439784 [Accessed 28 September 2013].

Braun, V., Clarke, V., 2006. 'Using Thematic Analysis in Psychology. Qualitative Research in Psychology'. *Qualitative Research in Psychology*, 3(2), pp 77–101.

Browne, B., Moffett, L., 2014. 'Finding Your Feet in the Field: Critical Reflections of Early Career Researchers on Field Research in Transitional Societies'. *Journal of Human Rights Practice*, 6(2), pp. 223–37.

Carbonari, J., 2011. *Map of Egyptian Political Parties*. Available online at: https://www.europarl.europa.eu/meetdocs/2009_2014/documents/dmas/dv/dmas20120125_02_/dmas20120125_02_en.pdf.

Carpentier, N., Cammaerts, B., 2006. 'Hegemony, Democracy, Agonism and Journalism: An Interview with Chantal Mouffe'. *Journalism Studies*, 7(6), pp. 964–75.

Certeau de, M., 1984. *The Practice of Everyday Life*. Berkeley, CA: University of California Press.

Chaffee, L.G., 1993. *Political Protest and Revolutionary art: Popular Tools for Democratization in Hispanic Countries*. Westport, CT: Greenwood Press.

Chalcraft, J., 2014. 'Egypt's 25 January Uprising, Hegemonic Contestation, and the Explosion of the Poor'. In: Gerges, F.A., (ed.), *The New Middle East: Protest and Revolution in the Arab World*. Cambridge: Cambridge University Press, pp. 155–79.

Chalcraft, J., 2016. *Popular Politics in the Making of the Modern Middle East*. Cambridge: Cambridge University Press.

Charbel, J., 2010. 'A Cry on the Walls'. *Daily News Egypt*, 3 March. Available online at: http://www.dailynewsegypt.com/2010/03/03/a-cry-on-the-walls/ [Accessed 12 March 2012].

Charbel, J., 2011. '1,000s Commemorate Khaled Said, & Confront Police Brutality'. 6 June. Available online at: http://she2i2.blogspot.com/2011/06/protesters-commemorate-anniversary-of.html [Accessed 6 November 2011].

Charbel, J., 2012. 'Graffiti Week Returns with Calls to Resume Revolution'. *Egypt Independent*, 25 January. Available online at: http://www.egyptindependent.com/graffiti-week-returns-calls-resume-revolution/ [Accessed 19 November 2012].

Cole, J., 1993. *Colonialism and Revolution in the Middle East: Social and Cultural Origins of Egypt's 'Urabi Movement*. Princeton, NJ: Princeton University Press.

Colla, E., 2011. 'The Imagination as Transitive Act: An Interview with Sonallah Ibrahim'. *Jadaliyya*, 12 June. Available online at: http://www.jadaliyya.c.jadaliyya.com/pages/index/1811/the-imagination-as-transitive-act_an-interview-wit [Accessed 9 November 2011].

Cooke, Miriam, 2007. *Dissident Syria: Making Oppositional Arts Official*. Durham, NC: Duke University Press.

Crabbs, J.J., 1975. 'Politics, History, and Culture in Nasser's Egypt'. *International Journal of Middle East Studies*, 6(4), pp. 386–420.

Creswell, R., 2011. 'Egypt: The Cultural Revolution'. *The New York Times*, 10 February. Available online at: http://www.nytimes.com/2011/02/20/books/review/Creswell-t.html?_r=0 [Accessed 3 September 2011].

Cronin, S., (ed.), 2007. *Subalterns and Social Protest: History from Below in the Middle East and North Africa*. New York: Routledge.

Cull, N.J., Cullbert, D.H., Welch, D., 2003. *Propaganda and Mass Persuasion: A Historical Encyclopedia, 1500 to the Present*. Santa Barbara, CA: ABC-CLIO.

Culture Resource, 2013. 'Second Phase of the "Cultural Policy for All Egyptians" Campaign to be Launched in Cairo and Other Egyptian Governorates'. Available

online at: http://mawred.org/press-room/second-phase-of-the-cultural-policy-for
-all-egyptians-campaign-to-be-launched-in-cairo-and-other-egyptian-governorates/
[Accessed 9 September 2014].

Dabashi, H., (ed.), 2006. *Dreams of a Nation: On Palestinian Cinema*. New York: Verso.

Dabashi, H., 2011. 'Art as the Politics of the Impossible'. *Al Jazeera English*, 20 December. Available online at: http://www.aljazeera.com/indepth/opinion/2011/12/20111218113
148105494.html [Accessed 30 May 2015].

Dabashi, H., 2012. *The Arab Spring: The End of Colonialism*. London and New York: Zed Books.

Daraghi, B., 2013. 'Egypt's Immigrants Flee as Xenophobia Rears its Head'. *Financial Times*, 18 December. Available online at: http://www.ft.com/cms/s/0/b469fb74-52a3
-11e3-8586-00144f eabdc0.html#axzz4CVa285GN [Accessed 29 December 2013].

Dawson, B., 2003. *Street Graphics Egypt*. New York: Thames & Hudson Inc.

Demos, T.J., 2013. *The Migrant Image: The Art and Politics of Documentary during Global Crisis*. Durham, NC: Duke University Press.

Deutsche, R., 1996. *Evictions: Art and Spatial Politics*. Cambridge: The MIT Press.

Diab, K., 2016. 'Mogamma: Egypt's Other Great Pyramid'. *Al Jazeera*, 18 January. Available online at: https://www.aljazeera.com/opinions/2016/1/18/mogamma-egypts-other
-great-pyramid [Accessed 30 May 2021].

di Vincenzo, M., 2011. 'Mohamed Alaa – The Egyptian "Schugnizzo"'. 21 May. Available online at: https://vincenzomattei.com/mohamed-alaa-the-egyptian-schugnizzo/street
-art-wishes-and-dreams-of-all-egyptians-lll/ [Accessed 9 January 2014].

Doward, J., 2012. 'Egyptian Police Incited Massacre at Stadium, Say Angry Footballers'. *The Guardian*, 5 February. Available online at: https://www.theguardian.com/world
/2012/feb/05/egypt-football-massacre-police-arab-spring [Accessed 18 November 2012].

Downey, A., 2011. 'Beyond the Former Middle East: Aesthetics, Civil Society, and the Politics of Representation'. *IBRAAZ*, 1 June. Available online at: http://www.ibraaz
.org/usr/library/documents/essay-documents/beyond-the-former-middle-east
-aesthetics-civil-society-and-the-politics-of-representation.pdf [Accessed 17 April 2012].

Downey, A., 2013. 'For the Common Good: Artistic Practices, Collective Action and Civil Society in Tunisia'. *IBRAAZ*, 28 February. Available online at: http://www.ibraaz
.org/usr/library/documents/essay-documents/for-the-common-good.pdf [Accessed 7 December 2013].

Downey, A., 2014a. *Art and Politics Now*. Farnborough: Thames & Hudson.

Downey, A., (ed.), 2014b. *Uncommon Grounds: New Media and Critical Practices in North Africa and the Middle East*. London: I.B. Tauris.

Downey, A., (ed.), 2015. *Dissonant Archives: Contemporary Visual Culture and Contested Narratives in the Middle East*. London: I.B. Tauris.

Duende, 2022. 'El-Teneen, A Cairo Artist Off-The-Wall'. *L'Eclectique*. Available online at: https://leclectique-mag.com/el-teneen-a-cairo-artist-off-the-wall/

EAWorldview, 2011. 'Egypt (and Beyond) LiveBlog: Black Hole or Another Day of Revolution'. 28 January. Available online at: http://www.enduringamerica.com/home
/2011/1/28/egypt-and-beyond-liveblog-black-hole-or-another-day-of-revol.html
[Accessed 5 March 2017].

Egyptian Streets, 2014. 'Three Arrested in Egypt for Speaking English'. *Egyptian Streets*, 15 December. Available online at: http://egyptianstreets.com/2014/12/15/three
-arrested-in-egypt-for-speaking-english/ [Accessed 27 December 2014].

Egyptian Streets, 2016. 'Egypt to Shut Down "Most Hated" Building: The Mugamaa'.
7 January. Available online at: https://egyptianstreets.com/2016/01/07/egypt-to-shut
-down-most-hated-building-the-mugamaa/ [Accessed 28 May 2021].

Egypt Independent, 2012. '60 Released in Mohamed Mahmoud Clashes, Violence
Continues'. *Egypt Independent*, 24 November. Available online at: http://www
.egyptindependent.com/60-released-mohamed-mahmoud-clashes-violence-continues/
[Accessed 10 June 2013].

Eid, H., 2013. 'Why is the Egyptian Regime Demonizing Palestinians?'. *Mondoweiss*,
19 August. Available online at: http://mondoweiss.net/2013/08/why-is-the-egyptian
-regime-demonizingpalestinians/#sthash.NwXAJK1r.dpuf [Accessed 9 September
2013].

El Ansary, H., 2014. 'Revolutionary art: Complicating the Discourse'. *Jadaliyya*,
1 September. Available online at: http://www.jadaliyya.com/pages/index/
19033/revolutionary-street-art_complicating-the-discours [Accessed 26 November
2014].

El-Aref, N., 2015. 'Interview: Egypt's Culture Minister Helmy El-Namnam Talks about
his Vision, Plans'. *Ahram Online*, 14 October. Available online at: http://english.ahram
.org.eg/NewsContent/5/35/155935/Arts--Culture/Stage--Street/INTERVIEW-Egypts
-Culture-Minister-Helmy-ElNamnam-t.aspx [Accessed 9 December 2015].

El Attar, A., 2009. 'Sonallah Ibrahim: Odd Man Out'. *Bidoun Magazine*, Issue 18.
Available online at: http://bidoun.org/articles/sonallah-ibrahim [Accessed
3 September 2011].

El Cheikh, H., 2016. 'Art in Public Space in Egypt'. *A Restless Art*, 8 April. Available online
at: https://arestlessart.com/2016/04/08/art-in-public-space-in-egypt-by-heba-el
-cheikh/ [Accessed 9 May 2016].

El-Din, M., 2013. 'Sisi in his Own Words'. *Mada Masr*, 26 March. Available online at:
http://www.madamasr.com/sections/politics/sisi-his-own-words [Accessed 9 July
2013].

El Hamalawy, H., 2011. 'How Palestine's Uprising Inspired Egypt's'. *Electronic Intifada*.
Available online at: https://electronicintifada.net/content/how-palestines-uprising
-inspired-egypts/9253.

El-Hibry, H., 2014. 'Arab Revolutions: Breaking Fear: The Cultural Logic of Visibility in
the Arab Uprisings'. *International Journal of Culture and Communication*, 8(18), pp.
835–52.

El-Husseiny, B., 2014. 'Culture, the State, and the Culture of the State'. *Mada Masr*,
7 January. Available online at: http://www.madamasr.com/opinion/culture-state-and
-culture-state [Accessed 9 April 2014].

El-Mahdi, R., 2011. 'Labour Protests in Egypt: Causes and Meanings'. *Review of African
Political Economy*, 38(129), pp. 387–402. http://www.jstor.org/stable/23055362.

El-Mahy, A., 2012. 'Egypt's Popular Committees: From Moments of Madness to NGO
Dilemmas'. Middle East Report 42.

El Nabawi, M., 2013. 'Inside the Culture Ministry: A Stalemate between Cultural Policy
and Protest'. *Mada Masr*, 29 June. Available online at: http://www.madamasr.com/
sections/culture/inside-culture-ministry [Accessed 3 July 2013]

El Shafei, O., 1995. 'Workers, Trade Unions, and the State in Egypt: 1984–1989'. *Cairo
Papers in Social Science*, 18(2), pp. 1–42.

El Shahed, M., 2011. 'Tahrir Square: Social Media, Public Space'. *The Design Observer
Group*, 27 February. Available online at: https://placesjournal.org/article/tahrir-square
-social-media-public-space/ [Accessed 3 September 2012].

ElShamy, M., 2012. 'Photo Essay: In Remembrance of Mohamed Mahmoud'. *Atlantic Council*, 19 November. Available online at: http://www.atlanticcouncil.org/blogs/menasource/photo-essay-in-remembrance-of-mohamed-mahmoud [Accessed 12 May 2014].

El Shazly, Y., 2014. 'The Origins of the Rebellious Egyptian Personality'. In: Hamdy, B., Karl, D., (eds). *Walls of Freedom: Revolutionary art of the Egyptian Revolution*. Berlin, Germany: From Here To Fame Publishing, pp. 6–8.

El Shimi, R., 2014. 'Local Initiative Mahatat Brings Arts to City Streets Around Egypt'. *Ahram Online*. Available online at: https://english.ahram.org.eg/NewsContent/5/0/112484/Arts--Culture/0/Local-initiative-Mahatat-brings-arts-to-city-stree.aspx.

El Teneen, 2015. *Facebook Post*. 5 November. Available online at: https://www.facebook.com/photo.php?fbid=910887715658903&set=pcb.910889918992016&type=3&theater [Accessed 5 February 2016].

El Wakil, M., 2011. 'Imagining a Different Ministry of Culture'. *Al Masry Al Youm*, 2 March. Available online at: http://www.egyptindependent.com/news/imagining-different-ministry-culture [Accessed 11 May 2012].

El Zeft, 2012a. 'Nefertiti'. *Facebook*. 12 September. Available online at: https://www.facebook.com/pg/el.zeft.7/posts/?ref=page_internal [Accessed 7 March 2013].

Fayed, S., Perry, T., 2012. 'Egyptians Incensed after 74 Die in Soccer Tragedy'. *Reuters*, 2 February. Available online at: https://www.reuters.com/article/us-egypt-soccer-violence/egyptians-incensed-after-74-die-in-soccer-tragedy-idUSTRE81022D20120202 [Accessed 4 May 2017].

Fisk, R., 2011. 'Robert Fisk: Why Does Life in the Middle East Remain Rooted in the Middle Ages?' *The Independent*, 23 October. Available online at: https://www.independent.co.uk/voices/commentators/fisk/robert-fisk-why-does-life-in-the-middle-east-remain-rooted-in-the-middle-ages-1763252.html [Accessed 2 June 2021].

Foster, H., 2002. *Design and Crime (And Other Diatribes)*. London: Verso.

Foucault, M., 1977. 'Nietzsche, Geneology, History'. In: Bouchard, D.F., (ed.), *Language, Counter-Memories, Practice: Selected Essays and Interviews*. Oxford: Blackwell, pp. 139–64.

Frenkel, S., 2013. 'Egyptian Activist Hailed As "Child Of The Revolution" Laid To Rest'. *Buzzfeed News*, 23 December. Available online at: https://www.buzzfeed.com/sheerafrenkel/egyptian-activist-hailed-as-child-of-the-revolution-laid-to?utm_term=.rc7604B9o#.mgJEyWz5K [Accessed 19 August 2017].

Fyfe, G., Law, J., 1988. *Picturing Power: Visual Depiction and Social Relations*. London: Routledge.

Ganzeer, 2014a. 'Concept Pop'. *The Cairo Review of Global Affairs*, 6 July. Available online at: https://www.thecairoreview.com/essays/concept-pop/ [Accessed 17 October 2014].

Ganzeer, 2014b. 'Who's Afraid of Art?' Available online at: http://www.ganzeer.com/post/85826356062/whos-afraid-of-art [Accessed 1 August 2014].

Ganzeer, 2017. 'Martyr Murals 2011'. Available online at: http://www.ganzeer.com/post/158030041274/title-martyr-murals-date-2011-description-a [Accessed 2 March 2017].

Geertz, C., 1973. 'Religion As a Cultural System'. In: Geertz, C., (ed.), *The Interpretation of Cultures*. New York: Basic Books, pp. 87–125.

Gennep, A.V., [1909] 1960. *The Rites of Passage*. Chicago: University of Chicago Press.

Gerges, F.A., (ed.). *The New Middle East: Protest and Revolution in the Arab World*. Cambridge: Cambridge University Press.

Gershoni, I., 1992. 'Imagining and Reimagining the Past: The Use of History by Egyptian Nationalist Writers, 1919–1952'. *History and Memory*, 4(2), pp. 5–37.

Gonzalez-Quijano, Y., 2013. 'Rap, an Art of the Revolution or a Revolution in Art?'. *Orient-Institut Studies*, 2. Available at: http://www.perspectivia.net/content/ publikationen/orient-institut-studies/2–2013/gonzalez-quijano_rap [Accessed 2 March 2014].

Graham, G., 1997a. *Philosophy of the Arts: An Introduction to Aesthetics*. London and New York: Routledge.

Graham, G., 1997b. 'The Marxist Theory of Art'. *British Journal of Aesthetics*, 37(2), pp. 109–17.

Gramsci, A., 1971. *Selections from the Prison Notebooks*. Hoare, Q., Smith, G.N., (eds and trans.). New York: International Publishers.

Gramsci, A., 2000. *The Gramsci Reader: Selected Writings, 1916–1935*. Forgacs, D., (ed.). New York: New York University Press.

Gregory, D., 2013. 'Tahrir: Politics, Publics and Performances of Space'. *Middle East Critique*, 22(3), pp. 235–46.

Gresh, A., 2014. 'I was Arrested for Chatting in a Cairo Cafe'. *Al Jazeera*, 15 November. Available online at: http://www.aljazeera.com/indepth/opinion/2014/11/i-was-arrested -chatting-cairo-20141114175012955778.html [Accessed 12 December 2014].

Gribbon, L., 2014. 'New Coat, Same Colors: Ilka Eickhof on Funding and Cultural Politics'. *Mada Masr*, 7 April. Available online at: http://www.madamasr.com/sections/culture /new-coat-same-colors-ilka-eickhof-funding-and-cultural-politics [Accessed 9 June 2015].

Gröndahl, M., 2012. *Revolution Graffiti: Revolutionary Art of the New Egypt*. Cairo: The American University in Cairo Press.

Gruber, C., Haugbolle, S., (eds), 2013. *Visual Culture in the Modern Middle East: Rhetoric of the Image*. Bloomington: Indiana University Press.

Guyer, J., 2014. 'Picturing Egypt's Next President'. *The New Yorker*, 22 May. Available online at: http://www.newyorker.com/news/news-desk/picturing-egypts-next -president [Accessed 10 August 2014].

Hafez, S., 2012. 'No Longer a Bargain: Women, Masculinity, and the Egyptian Uprising'. *American Ethnologist*, 39(1), pp. 37–42.

Hall, S., 1959. *The Silent Language*. New York: Doubleday/Fawcett.

Hall, S., 1969. *The Hidden Dimension*. Garden City, NY: Anchor Press/Doubleday.

Hall, S., 1997. 'The Work of Representation'. In: HALL, S., (ed.), *Representation: Cultural Representations and Signifying Practices*. London: Sage Publications & Open University, pp. 13–64.

Hamamou, S., 2016. 'The Only Weapon We Have Is Memory: Remembering The Camel Battle'. *Huffington Post*. Available online at: https://www.huffingtonpost .com/sabah-hamamo/the-only-weapon-we-have-i_b_9167332.html [Accessed 7 February 2017].

Hamed, Y., 2019. 'Egypt's Economy Isn't Booming. It's Collapsing'. *Foreign Policy*, 7 June. Available online at: https://foreignpolicy.com/2019/06/07/egypts-economy-isnt -booming-its-collapsing-imf-abdel-fattah-sisi-poverty/ [Accessed 13 May 2021].

Hamdy, B., Karl, D., (eds), 2013. *Walls of Freedom: Revolutionary Art of the Egyptian Revolution*. Berlin, Germany: From Here To Fame Publishing.

Hanauer, D.I., 2011. 'The Discursive Construction of the Separation Wall at Abu Dis: Graffiti as Political Discourse'. *Journal of Language and Politics*, 10(3), pp. 301–21.

Hanine, H., 2013. 'Why are Egyptian Media Demonizing Palestinians?'. *The Electronic Intifada*, 23 July. Available online at: https://electronicintifada.net/content/why-are -egyptian-media-demonizing-palestinians/12632 [Accessed 9 August 2013].

Hart, D., 2012. 'The Eye Patch as a Symbol of Resistance in Egypt'. 1 January. http://davidmhart.com/blog/C20120101094113/E20120101094200/index.html.

Haugbolle, S., Bandak, A., 2017. 'The Ends of Revolution: Rethinking Ideology and Time in the Arab Uprisings'. *Middle East Critique*, 26(3), pp. 191–204.

Hauslohner, A., 2011. 'Profiles of Protesters: Why I Protest: Ahmed Harara of Egypt'. *Time Magazine*, 14 December. Available online at: http://content.time.com/time/specials/packages/article/0,28804,2101745_2102138_2102236,00.html [Accessed 30 September 2012].

Hawkins, H., 2012. 'Geography and Art. An Expanding Field: Site, the Body and Practice'. *Progress in Human Geography*. Available at: http://phg.sagepub.com/cgi/doi/10.1177/0309132512442865 [Accessed 8 May 2013].

Hellyer, H.A., 2013. 'How Morsi let Egyptians Down'. *Foreign Policy*, 2 August. Available online at: http://foreignpolicy.com/2013/08/02/how-morsi-let-egyptians-down/ [Accessed 4 September 2013].

Hemingway, A., 2006. *Marxism and the History of Art: From William Morris to the New Left*. London: Pluto Press.

Hobbs, S.D., 2021. 'Why the Phrase "Arab Spring" Should be Retired'. *The Cairo Review of Global Affairs*, 4 February. Available online at: https://www.thecairoreview.com/essays/why-the-phrase-arab-spring-should-be-retired/ [Accessed 13 July 2021].

Hollingsworth, M., 1986. 'Education in Egypt's Development: The Need for a Wider System of Appraisal'. *Project Appraisal*, 1(4), pp. 246–55, doi:10.1080/02688867.1986.9726577.

Holstein, J.A., Gubrium, J.F., 1995. *The Active Interview*. London: Sage.

Homer, W.I., 1998. 'Visual Culture: A New Paradigm'. *American Art*, 12(1), pp. 6–9.

Hooper-Greenhill, E., 2000. *Museums and the Interpretation of Visual Culture*. London: Routledge.

Huffington Post, 2014. 'This Graffiti Art Shows How Egypt's Revolution Came Full Circle'. 11 February. Available online at: http://www.huffingtonpost.com/2014/02/11/graffiti-art-egypt-revolution_n_4762431.html [Accessed 1 March 2017].

Iskandar, R., al-Malakh, K., al-Sharuni, S., 1991. *Eighty Years of Art (Thamanun sana min al-fann)*. Cairo: Al-hay'a al-misriyya al-'amma lil-kitab.

Ismail, A., 2011. 'Eye-Patched Protesters March in Solidarity with Those Who Lost Their Eyes'. *Egypt Independent*, 1 December. Available online at: http://www.egyptindependent.com/eye-patched-protesters-march-solidarity-those-who-lost-their-eyes/ [Accessed 8 April 2012].

Ismail, S., 2012. 'The Egyptian Revolution against the Police'. *Social Research*, 79(2), pp. 435–62. Available online at: http://www.jstor.org/stable/23350072.

Ismail, S.F., 2013. 'Revolutionizing Art'. *Mada Masr*, 15 October. Available online at: http://www.madamasr.com/opinion/culture/revolutionizing-art [Accessed 9 February 2014].

Jacquette, E., 2013. 'Taking a Stand for Culture'. *Atlantic Council*, 6 June. Available online at: http://www.atlanticcouncil.org/blogs/menasource/taking-a-stand-for-culture [Accessed 17 January 2014].

Jankowicz, M., 2016a. 'Against Helplessness in the Arts'. *Mada Masr*, 24 May. Available online at: http://www.madamasr.com/sections/culture/against-helplessness-arts [Accessed 17 June 2016].

Jankowicz, M., 2016b. '"Erase and I Will Draw Again": The Struggle Behind Cairo's Revolutionary Graffiti Wall'. *The Guardian*, 23 March. Available online at: https://www.theguardian.com/cities/2016/mar/23/struggle-cairo-egypt-revolutionary-graffiti [Accessed 23 June 2016].

Jarbou, R., 2010. 'The Seeds of a Graffiti Revolution'. In: Hamdy, B., Karl, D., (eds), *Walls of Freedom: Revolutionary art of the Egyptian Revolution*. Berlin, Germany: From Here To Fame Publishing, pp. 9–12.

Jerzak, C., 2013. 'Ultras in Egypt: State, Revolution, and the Power of Public Space'. *Interface*, 5(2), pp. 240–62.

Johnson, H.M., 1962. *Sociology: A Systematic Introduction*. London: Routledge & Kegan Paul.

Johnson, J.M., 1975. *Doing Field Research*. New York: Free Press.

Johnston, J., 2016. 'Democratic Walls?: Revolutionary Art as Public Pedagogy'. In: Baker, M., (ed.), *Translating Dissent: Voices From and With the Egyptian Revolution*. New York: Routledge, pp. 178–96.

Jones, B., 2013. 'How Morsi Became The New Mubarak'. *Business Insider*, 2 July. Available online at: http://www.businessinsider.com.au/how-morsi-became-the-new-mubarak -2013-7 [Accessed 9 January 2014].

Kane, P., 2013. *The Politics of Art in Modern Egypt: Aesthetics, Ideology, and Nation-Building*. New York: I.B. Tauris.

Karl, D., Zoghbi, P., 2011. *Arabic Graffiti*. Berlin, Germany: From Here To Fame Publishing.

Karnouk, L., 1988. *Modern Egyptian Art: The Emergence of a National Style*. Cairo: American University in Cairo Press.

Karnouk, L., 1995. *Contemporary Egyptian Art*. Cairo: American University in Cairo Press.

Karnouk, L., 2005. *Modern Egyptian Art, 1910–2003*. Cairo: American University in Cairo Press.

Keesing, R.M., 1974. 'Theories of Culture'. *Annual Review of Anthropology*, 3, pp. 73–97.

Kelada, M., 2015. 'Social Change Between Potentiality and Actuality: Imagination in Cairo's Alternative Cultural Spaces'. *International Journal of Sociology*, 45(3), pp. 223–33.

Kennedy, M., 2015. 'Egypt Raids 2 Major Independent Cultural Institutions In 2 Days'. *NPR*, 29 December. Available online at: http://www.npr.org/sections/thetwo-way/2015 /12/29/461401135/egypt-raids-2-major-independent-cultural-institutions-in-2-days [Accessed 4 February 2016].

Khaled, H., 2011. 'Down with Hosni Mubarak'. *Facebook*, 25 January. Available online at: https://www.facebook.com/photo.php?fbid=10152747301430637&set=a .10151122868630637.788726.875815636&type=3&theater [Accessed 9 February 2012].

Khalil, A., 2011. 'Route to Revolution'. *Index on Censorship*, 40(1), pp. 62–4. doi:10.1177/0306422011399690.

Khan, M., Miller, E., 2016. 'The Economic Decline of Egypt after the 2011 Uprising'. *Atlantic Council*, 14 June. Available online at: https://www.atlanticcouncil.org/in-depth -research-reports/report/the-economic-decline-of-egypt-after-the-2011-uprising-2/ [Accessed 17 May 2021].

Khatib, L., 2012. *Image Politics in the Middle East: The Role of the Visual in Political Struggle*. London: I.B. Tauris.

Khattab, N., 2015. 'Theater, Performance, and Affect'. *International Journal of Sociology*, 45(3), pp. 234–45.

Khodr, M., 2012. 'Down with the Cultural Elite! Long Live the Cultural Elite!'. *Al-Monitor*, 16 February. Available online at: http://www.al-monitor.com/pulse/ar/culture/2012/02/ the-crisis-of-the-egyptian-intel.html [Accessed 9 March 2013].

Khorshid, S., 2013. 'Mohamed Morsi Has Turned his Back on Egypt's Revolution'. *The Guardian*, 27 July. Available online at: https://www.theguardian.com/commentisfree /2013/jun/27/mohamed-morsi-turned-back-egypt [Accessed 8 July 2017].

Kingsley, P., 2013. 'Eye Sniper of Tahrir Square is in Jail, but Has Anything Changed?' *The Guardian*, 6 March. Available online at: https://www.theguardian.com/world/shortcuts /2013/mar/06/eye-sniper-tahrir-egypt-jailed [Accessed 14 April 2017].

Kingsley, P., 2014. 'Abdel Fatah al-Sisi won 96.1% of Vote in Egypt Presidential Election, Say Officials'. *The Guardian*, 3 June. Available online at: https://www.theguardian.com /world/2014/jun/03/abdel-fatah-al-sisi-presidential-election-vote-egypt [Accessed 8 February 2017].

Kirkpatrick, D.D., 2012. 'Egyptian Judges Challenge Morsi Over New Power'. *Boston Globe*, 25 November. Available online at: https://www.bostonglobe.com/news/world /2012/11/25/resistance-emerges-egypt-against-morsi/EbxlWkBmlb6vDSjpE1TncN/ story.html [Accessed 18 December 2012].

Korany, B., El-Mahdi, R. (eds), 2012. *Arab Spring in Egypt: Revolution and Beyond*. American University in Cairo Press. Available online at: http://www.jstor.org/stable/j.ctt15m7mbm.

Kraidy, M., 2016. *The Naked Blogger of Cairo: Creative Insurgency in the Arab World*. Cambridge, MA: Harvard University Press.

Kurzman, C., 2012. 'The Arab Spring Uncoiled'. *Mobilization: An International Journal*, 17(4), pp. 377–90.

Laachir, K., Talajooy, S. (eds.), 2013. *Resistance in Contemporary Middle Eastern Cultures: Literature, Cinema and Music*. New York and London: Routledge.

Labovitz, C., 2011. 'Egypt Loses the Internet'. *Arbor Networks*, 28 January. Available online at: https://www.arbornetworks.com/blog/asert/egypt-loses-the-internet/ [Accessed 28 February 2017].

LaCoss, D., 2009–2010. 'Art and Liberty: Surrealism in Egypt'. *Communicating Vessels*, 21, pp. 28–33.

LaCoss, D., 2010. 'Egyptian Surrealism and "Degenerate Art" in 1939'. *Arab Studies Journal*, 18(10), pp. 79–118.

Lampert, M., 2016. 'Beyond the Politics of Reception: Jacques Rancière and the Politics of Art'. *Continental Philosophy Review*, 50(2), pp.1–20.

Latuff, C., 2012. 'My Khaled Said Cartoon in the Hands of a Protester in #Egypt Yesterday'. 8 June. Available online at: https://latuffcartoons.wordpress.com/2012/06/08/my -khaled-said-cartoon-in-the-hands-of-a-protester-in-egypt-yesterday/ [Accessed 19 February 2013].

Lau, L., 2012–2013. 'The Murals of Mohammad Mahmoud Street: Reclaiming Narratives of Living History for the Egyptian People'. *WR: Journal of the CAS Writing Program*, 5. Available online at: http://www.bu.edu/writingprogram/journal/past-issues/issue-5/lau/.

Lears, T.J.J., 1985. 'The Concept of Cultural Hegemony: Problems and Possibilities'. *The American Historical Review*, 90(3), pp. 567–93.

Lefebvre H., 1970. *The Urban Revolution*. Minneapolis: University of Minnesota Press.

Lenssen, A., 2007/2008. 'Book Review: Creative Reckoning: The Politics of Art and Culture in Contemporary Egypt'. *The Arab Studies Journal*, 15/16(2/1), pp. 225–7.

Lewis, S., 2014. 'My Pragmatist Friend Surrenders'. *Mada Masr*, 4 December. Available online at: http://www.madamasr.com/sections/culture/my-pragmatist-friend -surrenders [Accessed 11 January 2015].

Lewisohn, C., 2008. *Revolutionary Art: The Graffiti Revolution*. New York: Abrams.

Lifshitz, M., 1938. *The Philosophy of Art of Karl Marx*. Great Britain: Lowe & Brydone Printers Limited.

Lindsey, U., 2013. 'The Cult of Sisi'. *The New York Times*, 12 September. Available online at: http://latitude.blogs.nytimes.com/2013/09/12/the-cult-of-sisi/?_r=0 [Accessed 4 December 2014].

Lindsey, U., 2018. 'An Online Archive of the Egyptian Revolution'. *Al-Fanar Media*.
Available online at: https://www.al-fanarmedia.org/2018/02/online-archive-egyptian
-revolution/.

Lynch, S., 2014. 'For Egypt's Graffiti Artists, the Writing is No Longer on the Wall'. *USA
TODAY*, 23 June. Available online at: http://www.usatoday.com/story/news/world/2014
/06/23/egypt-street-art-freedom-of-expression/11255419/ [Accessed 30 November
2014].

MacFarquhar, N., 2011. 'Hosni Mubarak's Shadow Still Falls Over Egypt'. *The New York
Times*, 25 March. Available online at: http://www.nytimes.com/2011/03/26/world/
middleeast/26egypt.html?pagewanted=all&_r=0 [Accessed 19 February 2012].

Marcuse, H., 1972. *Counterrevolution and Revolt*. Boston: Beacon Press.

Marcuse, H., 1978. *The Aesthetic Dimension: Towards a Critique of Marxist Aesthetics*.
Boston: Beacon Press.

Marcuse, H., 2007. *Art and Liberation: Collected Papers of Herbert Marcuse*, Vol. 4. Kellner,
D., (ed.). London and New York: Routledge.

Maslamani, M., 2013. *Graffiti of the Egyptian Revolution*. Beirut: Arab Centre for Research
and Policy.

Massey, D., Rose, G., 2003. *Personal Views: Public Art Research Project*. Milton Keynes: The
Open University.

Matar, D., 2012a. 'Contextualising the Media and the Uprisings: A Return to History'.
Middle East Journal of Culture and Communication, 5(1), pp. 75–9.

Matar, D., 2012b. 'Rethinking the Arab State and Culture: Preliminary Thoughts'. In: Sabry,
T., (ed.), *Arab Cultural Studies: Mapping the Field*. London: I.B. Tauris, pp. 123–36.

Matar, D., 2014. 'A Critical Reflection on Aesthetics and Politics in the Digital Age'. In:
Downey, A., (ed.), *Uncommon Grounds: New Media and Critical Practices in North
Africa and the Middle East*. London: I.B. Tauris, pp. 163–8.

Matar, D., Harb, Z., 2013. *Narrating Conflict in the Middle East: Discourse, Image and
Communication Practices in Lebanon and Palestine*. London: I.B. Tauris.

Mattern, M., 1999. 'John Dewey, Art and Public Life'. *The Journal of Politics*, 61(1), pp.
54–75.

McLagan, M., McKee, Y., 2012. *Sensible Politics: The Visual Culture of Nongovernmental
Activism*. New York: Zone Books.

Mehrez, S., 2008. *Egypt's Culture Wars: Politics and Practice*. London and New York:
Routledge.

Mehrez, S., (ed.), 2012a. *Translating Egypt's Revolution: The Language of Tahrir*. Cairo:
American University in Cairo Press.

Mehrez, S., 2012b. 'Watching Tahrir'. *Global Dialogue Newsletter, International Sociological
Association*, 2(3), February. Available online at: http://isa-global-dialogue.net/wp
-content/uploads/2013/07/v2i3-english.pdf [Accessed 8 March 2017].

MENASource, 2019. 'Art of the Egyptian Revolution'. Available online at: https://www
.atlanticcouncil.org/blogs/menasource/egypts-protests-art-of-the-revolution/.

Merrill, S., 2015. 'Keeping it Real? Subcultural Graffiti, Revolutionary Art, Heritage and
Authenticity'. *International Journal of Heritage Studies*, 21(4), pp. 369–89.

Metwaly, A., 2013a. 'Opera and Co'. *Al-Ahram Weekly*, 6 June. Available online at: http://
weekly.ahram.org.eg/News/2895/17/Opera-and-Co.aspx [Accessed 23 October 2013].

Metwaly, A., 2013b. 'From Opposing Culture Minister to Fighting for Egypt's "identity"'.
Ahram Online, 14 June. Available online at: http://english.ahram.org.eg/NewsContentP
/1/73960/Egypt/From-opposing-culture-minister-to-fighting-for-Egy.aspx [Accessed
9 August 2013].

Mikdadi, S., 2004. 'Egyptian Modern Art'. *The Metropolitan Museum of Art*, October. Available online at: http://www.metmuseum.org/toah/hd/egma/hd_egma.htm [Accessed 3 June 2014].

Miles, M., 1997. *Art, Space and the City*. London: Routledge

Mitchell, W., (ed.), 1992. *Art and the Public Sphere*. Chicago, IL: The University of Chicago Press.

Mitchell, W.J.T., 1995. 'Interdisciplinarity and Visual Culture Studies'. *Art Bulletin*, 77, pp. 540–4.

Mitchell, W.J.T., 2012. 'Image, Space, Revolution: The Arts of Occupation'. *Critical Inquiry*, 39(1), pp. 8–32.

Mohsen, M., 2013. 'Health Ministry Raises Death Toll of Wednesday's Clashes to 638'. *Daily News Egypt*, 16 August. Available online at: http://www.dailynewsegypt.com /2013/08/16/health-ministry-raises-death-toll-of-wednesdays-clashes-to-638/ [Accessed 15 November 2013].

Mollerup, N., Gaber, S., 2015. 'Making Media Public: On Revolutionary Street Screenings in Egypt'. *International Journal of Communication*, 9, pp. 2903–21.

Montasser, F., 2012a. 'A Year of El-Fan Midan Egypt'. *Ahram Online*, 10 April. Available online at: http://english.ahram.org.eg/NewsContent/5/0/38785/Index.aspx [Accessed 23 August 2013].

Montasser, F., 2012b. 'Al-Mawred Al-Thaqafy Gears up for Campaign to Save Egyptian Culture'. *Ahram Online*, 12 November. Available online at: http://english.ahram.org.eg /NewsContentPrint/5/0/57936/Arts--Culture/0/AlMawred-AlThaqafy-gears-up-for -campaign-to-save-E.aspx [Accessed 14 May 2013].

Montasser, F., 2012c. '"The Future of Culture" Seeks Solution to "identity Confusion"'. *Ahram Online*, 24 February. Available online at: http://english.ahram.org.eg/ NewsContent/5/35/35290/Arts--Culture/Stage--Street/The-Future-of-Culture-seeks -solution-to-identity-c.aspx [Accessed 9 March 2013].

Morayef, S., 2013. 'Angels Caught in a Tightening Noose'. *Open Democracy*, 13 November. Available online at: https://www.opendemocracy.net/arab-awakening/soraya-morayef/ angels-caught-in-tightening-noose [Accessed 10 December 2014].

Morayef, S., 2015. 'Pharaonic Street Art: The Challenge of Translation', In: Baker, M., 1st ed. In *Translating Dissent Voices From and With the Egyptian Revolution*. London: Routledge, pp. 194–207.

Morgan, D., 2005. *The Sacred Gaze: Religious Visual Culture in Theory and Practice*. Berkeley: University of California Press.

Mouffe, C., et al., 2001. 'Every Form of Art Has a Political Dimension'. *MIT Press Journals: Grey Room*, 2, pp. 98–125.

Mouffe, C., 2007. 'Artistic Activism and Agonistic Spaces. Art & Research: A Journal of Ideas'. *Contexts and Methods*, 1(2), pp. 1–5.

Mousa, S., 2014. 'Ammar Abo Bakr: Committing Murder, Then Marching in the Funeral Procession'. *Jadaliyya*, 27 January. Available online at: http://www.jadaliyya.com/pages /index/16192/ammar-abo-bakr_committing-murder-then-marching-in- [Accessed 13 March 2017].

Mousa, S., 2015. 'Egypt: Making Art Public'. *Al Jazeera*, 25 August. Available online at: http://www.aljazeera.com/indepth/opinion/2015/08/egypt-making-art-public -150822104944575.html. [Accessed 29 November 2015].

Murphy, K., 1993. 'Column One: Woe Awaits in Tower of Babble: Cairo Residents Hate to Enter the Concrete Behemoth That Houses the Central Bureaucracy. Frustrated Patrons Have Leaped from Windows. Visits Inside Evoke Images of Kafka at the DMV'.

LA Times. Available online at: https://www.latimes.com/archives/la-xpm-1993-05-24 -mn-39315-story.html.

Naji, A., 2014. 'Culture in the Age of Sisi'. *The Tahrir Institute for Middle East Policy*, 12 March. Available online at: http://timep.org/commentary/culture-in-the-age-of-sisi/ [Accessed 30 September 2014].

Neunedorf, H., 2015. 'Egyptian Arts Non-Profit Shut Down By State Censorship Authority'. *Artnet News*. Available online at: https://news.artnet.com/market/egypt -townhouse-gallery-shut-down-censorship-399770.

Nickolas, M., 2014. *Nefertiti's Daughters*. [film]. USA, EGYPT: Mosaic Films, NYC.

Oweidat, N., et al. 2008. *The Kefaya Movement: A Case Study of a Grassroots Reform Initiative*, 1st ed. RAND Corporation. JSTOR. Available online at: http://www.jstor.org/ stable/10.7249/mg778osd [Accessed 11 August 2022].

Pahwa, S., Winegar, J., 2012. 'Culture, State, and Revolution'. *Middle East Report*, 42. Available online at: http://www.merip.org/mer/mer263/culture-state-revolution [Accessed 9 February 2013].

Panikkar, K.N., 2009. 'Culture as a Site of Struggle'. *Economic and Political Weekly*, 44(7), pp. 34–41.

Patton, M.Q., 2002. *Qualitative Research and Evaluation Methods*, 3rd ed. Thousand Oaks, CA: Sage Publications.

Perec, G., 1997. *Species of Spaces and Other Pieces*. London: Penguin.

Peteet, J. 1996, 'The Writing on the Walls: The Graffiti of the Intifada'. *Cultural Anthropology*, 11(2), pp. 139–59.

Peterson, M.A., 2012. 'In Search of Antistructure: The Meaning of Tahrir Square in Egypt's Ongoing Social Drama'. Paper given at the International Conference 'The Egyptian Revolution, One Year On: Causes, Characteristics and Fortunes', 18–19 May 2012 at the Department of Politics and International Relations, Oxford University.

Peterson, M., 2015a. 'In Search of Antistructure: The Meaning of Tahrir Square in Egypt's Ongoing Social Drama'. In: Horváth, Á., Thomassen, B., Wydra, H., (eds), *Breaking Boundaries: Varieties of Liminality*. New York: Berghan Books, pp. 164–82.

Peterson, M., 2015b. 'Re-envisioning Tahrir: The Changing Meanings of Tahrir Square in Egypt's Ongoing Revolution'. In Abou-El-Fadl, R., (ed.), *Revolutionary Egypt: Connecting Domestic and International Struggles*. Kindle ed. London: Routledge, pp. 164–82.

Pieprzak, K., 2010. 'Book Review: Creative Reckonings: The Politics of Art and Culture in Contemporary Egypt'. *Comparative Studies of South Asia, Africa and the Middle East*, 30(3), pp. 662–3.

Pinder, D., 2008. 'Urban Interventions: Art, Politics and Pedagogy'. *International Journal of Urban and Regional Research*, 32, pp. 730–6.

Pinther, K.S., 2016. 'Artists' Archives and the Sites of Memory in Cairo and Algiers'. *World Art*, 6(1), pp. 169–85.

Posusney, M.P., 1997. *Labor and the State in Egypt: Workers Unions, and Economic Restructuring, 1952–1996*. New York: Columbia University Press.

Prawer, S.S., 2011. *Karl Marx and World Literature*. London and New York: Verso.

Preston, J., 2011. 'Movement Began With Outrage and a Facebook Page That Gave It an Outlet'. *The New York Times*, 11 February. Available online at: http://www.nytimes.com /2011/02/06/world/middleeast/06face.html?_r=0 [Accessed 2 June 2013].

Rancière, J., 1991. *The Ignorant Schoolmaster: Five Lessons in Intellectual Emancipation*. Ross, K., (trans.), Stanford, CA: Stanford University Press.

Rancière, J., 1999. *Disagreement: Politics and Philosophy*. Ross, J., (trans.). Minneapolis: University of Minnesota Press.

Rancière, J., 2001. 'Ten Theses on Politics'. *Theory and Event*, 5(3). Available online at: http://www.colorado.edu/humanities/ferris/Courses/1968/Ranciere/Ten%20Theses /Ranciere_Ten%20Theses%20on%20Politics_Theory%20and%20Event5.3_2001.pdf [Accessed 29 November 2012].

Rancière, J., 2004. *The Politics of Aesthetics: The Distribution of the Sensible*. Rockhill, G., (trans.). London: Continuum.

Rancière, J., 2005. 'From Politics to Aesthetics?'. *Paragraph*, 28(1), pp. 13–25.

Rancière, J., 2009a. *Aesthetics and its Discontents*. Corcoran, S., (trans.). Cambridge: Polity Press.

Rancière, J., 2009b. *The Emancipated Spectator*. Elliot, G., (trans.). New York: Verso.

Rancière, J., 2010. *Dissensus: On Politics and Aesthetics*. Corcoran, S., (ed., trans.). New York: Continuum.

Rancière, J., 2011. *Reading Rancière*. Bowman, P., Stamp, R., (eds.). London and New York: Continuum.

Rashed, W., 2013. 'Egypt's Murals Are More Than Just Art, They Are a Form of Revolution'. *Smithsonian Magazine*, May. Available online at: http://www.smithsonianmag.com /arts-culture/egypts-murals-are-more-than-just-art-they-are-a-form-of-revolution -36377865/?no-ist [Accessed 18 August 2013].

Rashwan, N.H., 2011. 'No Hope for Left-Eye of Injured Revolutionary Ahmed Harara'. *AhramOnline*, 26 December. Available online at: http://english.ahram .org.eg/NewsContent/1/64/30197/Egypt/Politics-/No-hope-for-lefteye-of-injured -revolutionary-Ahmed.aspx [Accessed 18 January 2012].

Reza, S., 2007. 'Endless Emergency: The Case of Egypt'. *New Criminal Law Review: An International and Interdisciplinary Journal*, 10(4), pp. 532–53.

Riessman, C.K., 2000. 'Analysis of Personal Narratives'. Available online at: http://alumni .media.mit.edu/~brooks/storybiz/riessman.pdf [Accessed 11 March 2013].

Riggle, N.A., 2010. 'Revolutionary art: The Transfiguration of the Commonplaces'. *The Journal of Aesthetics and Art Criticism*, 68(3), pp. 243–57.

Rizk, P., 2014. '2011 is not 1968: An Open Letter from Egypt'. *ROAR Magazine*, 25 January. Available online at: https://roarmag.org/essays/egyptian-revolution-working-class/ [Accessed 12 March 2014].

Rizzo, H.M., 2015. 'How Culture and Politics Intersect in Post-January 2011 Egypt'. *International Journal of Sociology*, 45(3), pp. 171–5.

Rodriguez, A., Clair, R.P., 1999. 'Graffiti as Communication: Exploring the Discursive Tensions of Anonymous Texts'. *Southern Communication Journal*, 65, pp. 1–15.

Rommel, C., 2015. *Revolution, Play and Feeling: Assembling Emotionality, National Subjectivity and Football in Cairo, 1990–2013*. PhD dissertation, University of London, School of Oriental and African Studies.

Rose, M.A., 1984. *Marx's Lost Aesthetic: Karl Marx and the Visual Arts*. Cambridge: Cambridge University Press.

Ross, J.I., (ed.), 2015. *Routledge Handbook of Graffiti and Revolutionary Art*. London and New York: Routledge.

Roulston, K., 2001. 'Data Analysis and "theorizing as Ideology"'. *Qualitative Research*, 1(3), pp. 279–302.

Russell, M., (ed.), 2013. *Middle East in Focus: Egypt*. Santa Barbara, CA: ABC-CLIO.

Ryzova, L., 2011a. 'The Battle of Cairo's Muhammad Mahmoud Street'. *Al Jazeera*, 29 November. Available online at: http://www.aljazeera.com/indepth/opinion/2011/11 /201111288494638419.html [Accessed 14 February 2017].

Ryzova, L., 2011b. 'The Battle of Muhammad Mahmud Street: Teargas, Hair Gel, and Tramadol'. *Jadaliyya*, 28 November. Available online at: http://www.jadaliyya.com/ Details/24723/The-Battle-of-Muhammad-Mahmud-Street-Teargas,-Hair-Gel,-and -Tramadol [Accessed January 19 February 2017].

Ryzova, L., 2015. 'The Image Sans Orientalism: Local Histories of Photography in the Middle East'. *Middle East Journal of Culture and Communication*, 8(2–3), pp. 159–71.

Saad, R., 2012. 'The Egyptian Revolution: A Triumph of Poetry'. *American Ethnologist*, 39(1), pp. 63–6.

Sabea, H., 2013. 'A "Time out of Time": Tahrir, the Political and the Imaginary in the Context of the January 25th Revolution in Egypt'. *Hot Spots*, Cultural Anthropology website, 9 May. Available online at: https://culanth.org/fieldsights/211-a-time-out-of -time-tahrir-the-political-and-the-imaginary-in-the-context-of-the-january-25th -revolution-in-egypt [Accessed January 18 2014].

Sabea, H., 2014. 'I Dreamed of Being a People: Egypt's Revolution, the People and Critical Imagination'. In: Webner, P., Webb, M., Spellman-Poots, K. (eds), *Beyond the Arab Spring: The Political Aesthetics of Global Protest*. Edinburgh University Press, pp. 67–92.

Sabea, H., 2014. 'Still Waiting: Labor, Revolution and the Struggle for Social Justice in Egypt'. *International Journal of Working Class History*, 86, pp. 1–5.

Sabry, T., 2010. *Cultural Encounters in the Arab World: On Media, the Modern, and the Everyday*. London: I.B. Tauris.

Sabry, T., (ed.), 2012. *Arab Cultural Studies: Mapping the Field*. London: I.B. Tauris.

Said, E., 1983. *The World, The Text, and the Critic*. Cambridge, MA: Harvard University Press.

Sailer, M., 2013. 'Egypt's Military Regime Tolerates Xenophobia'. *DW*, 16 July. Available online at: http://www.dw.com/en/egypts-military-regime-tolerates-xenophobia/a -16952496 [Accessed 26 August 2013].

Salih, R., Richter-Devroe, S., 2014. 'Cultures of Resistance in Palestine and Beyond: On the Politics of Art, Aesthetics, and Affect'. *Arab Studies Journal*, XXII (1), pp. 8–28.

Sanders IV, L., 2015. 'Egypt's Artists Face Nuanced Challenges in Post-Revolution Climate'. 14 May. Available online at: http://www.dw.com/en/egypts-artists-face-nuanced -challenges-in-post-revolution-climate/a-18449322 [Accessed 20 June 2015].

Sartwell, C., 1992. 'Process and Product: A Theory of Art'. *The Journal of Speculative Philosophy*, 6(4), pp. 301–16.

Schielke, S., 2017. 'There Will be Blood: Expectation and Ethics of Violence during Egypt's Stormy Season'. *Middle East Critique*, 26(3), pp. 205–20.

Schwedler, J., 2016. 'Taking Time Seriously: Temporality and the Arab Uprisings'. Available online at: https://pomeps.org/2016/06/10/taking-time-seriously-temporality -and-the-arab-uprisings/ [Accessed 8 July 2017].

Selim, A., 2014. 'Toward an Art That Hides Behind Nothing'. *Mada Masr*, 3 August. Available online at: http://www.madamasr.com/sections/culture/toward-art-hides -nothing-behind [Accessed 19 October 2014].

Sharaf, R.O., 2015. 'Graffiti as a Means of Protest and Documentation in the Egyptian Revolution'. *African Conflict and Peacebuilding Review*, 5(1), pp. 152–61.

Sharp, J., Pollock, V., Paddison, R., 2005. 'Just Art for a Just City: Public Art and Social Inclusion in Urban Regeneration'. *Urban Studies*, 42(5/6), pp. 1001–23.

Shaw, A., 2013. 'Egypt's Art World Rallies to Defend Freedom of Expression'. *Institute of Museum Ethics*, 24 January. Available online at: http://www.museumethics.org/2013/01/egypts-art-world-rallies-to-defend-freedom-of-expression/ [Accessed 24 March 2013].

Shehab, B., 2016. 'Translating Emotions: Graffiti as a Tool for Change'. In: Baker, M., (ed.), *Translating Dissent: Voices From and With the Egyptian Revolution*. New York: Routledge, pp. 163–77.

Shenker, J., 2011. 'Egypt's Uprising Brings DIY Spirit out on to the Streets'. *The Guardian*, 19 May. Available online at: https://www.theguardian.com/world/2011/may/19/egypts-uprising-diy-art-cairo-streets [Accessed 12 February 2014].

Shihadeh, 2022. 'Interview with Mira Shihadeh'. *Artist Closeup*, 24 February, Available online at: https://www.artistcloseup.com/blog/interview-mira-shihadeh.

Shorbagy, M., 2007. 'The Egyptian Movement for Change—Kefaya: Redefining Politics in Egypt'. *Public Culture*, 19(1), pp. 175–96. doi:10.1215/08992363-2006-029.

Shoureap, S.A., 2014. 'Al-Fan Midan Revolutionary Art Festival Shut Down by Security Forces'. *The Cairo Post*, 8 April. Available online at: http://thecairopost.youm7.com/news/105596/news/al-fan-midan-street-art-festival-shut-down-by-security-forces [Accessed 14 June 2014].

Singerman, D., 1996. *Avenues of Participation: Family, Politics, and Networks in Urban Quarters of Cairo*. Princeton, NJ: Princeton University Press.

Singerman, D., 2009. *Cairo Contested: Governance, Urban Space, and Modernity*. Cairo: American University in Cairo Press.

Singerman, D., Amar, P., 2006. *Cairo Cosmopolitan: Politics, Culture, and Urban Space in the New Globalized Middle East*. Cairo: American University in Cairo Press.

Singh, S., 2014. 'Historical Realities of Concept Pop: Debating Art in Egypt'. *Jadaliyya*, 17 December. Available online at: http://www.jadaliyya.c.jadaliyya.com/pages/index/20305/historical-realities-of-concept-pop_debating-art-i [Accessed 9 January 2015].

Smith, C., 2015. 'Art as a Diagnostic: Assessing Social and Political Transformation Through Public Art in Cairo, Egypt'. *Social & Cultural Geography*, 16(1), pp. 22–42.

Smith, M., 2008. *Visual Culture Studies*. London: Sage Publications Ltd.

Sooke, A., 2013. 'Egypt's Powerful Revolutionary Art Packs a Punch'. *BBC News*, 9 May. Available online at: http://www.bbc.co.uk/culture/story/20130508-egypts-street-art-revolution [Accessed 12 October 2013].

Soueif, A., 2015. *Twitter Post*. 17 September. Available online at: https://twitter.com/asoueif/status/644511374555652099 [Accessed 19 December 2015].

Souri, H.T., 2012a. 'The Necessary Politics of Palestinian Cultural Studies'. In: Sabry, T., (ed.), *Arab Cultural Studies: Mapping the Field*. London: I.B. Tauris, pp. 137–61.

Souri, H.T., 2012b. 'It's Still About the Power of Place'. *Middle East Journal of Culture and Communication*, 5(1), pp. 86–95.

Sreberny, A., Torfeh, M., (eds), 2013. *Cultural Revolution in Iran: Contemporary Popular Culture in the Islamic Republic*. International Library of Iranian Studies. London: I.B. Tauris.

Sreberny-Mohammadi, A., Mohammadi, A., 1994. *Small Media, Big Revolution: Communication, Culture, and the Iranian Revolution*. Minneapolis: University of Minnesota Press.

Stanglin, D., 2011. 'Egyptian Court Orders Mubarak's Name, Image Removed from Public Places'. *USA TODAY*, 21 April. Available online at: http://content.usatoday.com/communities/ondeadline/post/2011/04/egyptian-court-orders-mubaraks-name-image-removed-from-public-places/1#.V8iRJrXfdBU [Accessed 9 September 2012].

Stein, R., Swedenburg, T., (eds.), 2005. *Palestine, Israel, and the Politics of Popular Culture.* Durham, NC: Duke University Press.

Suzeeinthecity, 2011. 'The Revolution Continues . . . And So Does Graffiti'. 3 December. Available online at: https://suzeeinthecity.wordpress.com/2011/12/03/the-revolution -continues-and-so-does-graffiti/ [Accessed 4 March 2012].

Suzeeinthecity, 2012a. 'January 25 – The Anniversary: Graffiti'. 26 December. Available online at: https://suzeeinthecity.wordpress.com/2012/01/26/january-25-the -anniversary-graffiti/ [Accessed 17 November 2013].

Suzeeinthecity, 2012b. 'In the Midst of Madness: Graffiti of the Ultras on Mohamed Mahmoud Street'. 8 February. Available online at: https://suzeeinthecity.wordpress.com /2012/02/08/in-the-midst-of-madness-graffiti-of-the-ultras-on-mohamed-mahmoud -street/ [Accessed 18 November 2013].

Suzeeinthecity, 2012c. 'Return to Tahrir: Two Years and Graffiti of the Martyrs'. 29 December. Available online at: https://suzeeinthecity.wordpress.com/2012/12/29/ return-to-tahrir-two-years-and-graffiti-of-the-martyrs/ [Accessed 9 June 2013].

Suzeeinthecity, 2012d. 'Revolutionary Art on Mohamed Mahmoud – Photos'. 25 March. Available online at: https://suzeeinthecity.wordpress.com/2012/03/25/street-art-on -mohamed-mahmoud-photos/ [Accessed 18 March June 2014].

Suzeeinthecity, 2013. 'Street Art and Morsi – Cairo Artists Continue the Fight'. 1 May. Available online at: https://suzeeinthecity.wordpress.com/2013/05/01/street-art-and -morsi-cairo-artists-continue-the-fight/ [Accessed 18 June 2017].

Szakolczai, A., 2000. *Historical Reflexive Sociology.* London: Routledge.

Szakolczai, A., 2009. 'Liminality and Experience: Structuring Transitory Situations and Transformative Events'. *International Political Anthropology*, 2(1), pp. 141–72.

TahrirNews, 2011. 'Tamer from Ghamra and Kentucky – The Coverage of the 25 January Revolution on Egypt's State Television is Different' [translated by author from Arabic]. Available online at: http://www.tahrirnews.com/posts/374519/%C2%AB%D8%AA%D8 %A7%D9%85%D8%B1+%D9%85%D9%86+%D8%BA%D9%85%D8%B1%D8%A9+ %D9%88%D9%83%D9%86%D8%AA%D8%A7%D9%83%D9%8A%C2%BB..+%D8 %AB%D9%88%D8%B1%D8%A9+25+%D9%8A%D9%86%D8%A7%D9%8A%D8 %B1+%D9%81%D9%8A+%D8%A7%D9%84%D8%AA%D9%84%D9%8A%D9%81 %D8%B2%D9%8A%D9%88%D9%86+%D8%A7%D9%84%D9%85%D8%B5%D8%B1 %D9%8A+%C2%AB%D8%BA%D9%8A%D8%B1%C2%BB [Accessed 4 April 2017].

Tantawi, G., Rizk, M., 2016. 'Egypt Takes Harsh Line Towards Artists and Authors'. *BBC News*, 20 April. Available online at: http://www.bbc.co.uk/news/world-middle-east -36039529 [Accessed 2 May 2016].

The Mosireen Collective, 2013. 'Never Forget. Always Remember'. *YouTube*, 17 November. Available online at: https://www.youtube.com/watch?v=gvop9dL36lI [Accessed 23 August 2017].

The Telegraph, 2013. 'Egypt Protests: President Morsi Vows to Lay Down Life for Revolution'. 3 July. Available online at: https://www.telegraph.co.uk/news/worldnews /africaandindianocean/egypt/10156619/Egypt-protests-President-Morsi-vows-to-lay -down-life-for-revolution.html [Accessed 7 June 2017].

Thomassen, B., 2009. 'The Uses and Meaning of Liminality'. *International Political Anthropology*, 2(1), pp. 5–28.

Thomassen, B., 2012. 'Notes Toward an Anthropology of Political Revolutions'. *Comparative Studies in Society and History*, 54(3), pp. 679–706.

Thomassen, B., 2014. *Liminality and the Modern: Living through the In-between.* London: Routledge.

Thomassen, B., 2017. 'Endnotes: Wandering in the Wilderness or Entering the Promised Land?'. *Middle East Critique*, 26(3), pp. 297–307.

Toenjes, A., 2015. 'This Wall Speaks: Graffiti and Transnational Networks in Palestine'. *Jerusalem Quarterly*, 61(1), pp. 55–68.

Tomlin, J., 2011. 'How Eyepatches Became a Symbol of Egypt's Revolution'. 19 December. Available online at: http://www.julietomlin.co.uk/wordpress/how-eyepatches-became-a-symbol-of-egypts-revolution/ [Accessed 19 December 2013].

Trew, B., Abdalla, M., Feteha, A., 2013. 'Walled in: SCAF's Concrete Barricades'. *AhramOnline*, 9 February. Available online at: http://english.ahram.org.eg/NewsContent/1/64/33929/Egypt/Politics-/Walled-in-SCAFs-concrete-barricades-.aspx [Accessed 14 March 2017].

Tripp, C., 2013a. 'Art of the Uprisings in the Middle East'. *Brown Journal of World Affairs*, 19 (2), pp. 185–99.

Tripp, C., 2013b. *The Power and the People: Paths of Resistance in the Middle East.* Cambridge: Cambridge University Press.

Trotsky, L., 2009. *Art and Revolution: Writings on Literature, Politics, and Culture.* Siegel, P.N., (ed.). Canada: Pathfinder Press.

Turner, V.W., 1957. *Schism and Continuity in African Society: A Study of Ndembu Village Life.* New York: Humanities Press.

Turner, V.W., 1986[1967]. *The Forest of Symbols: Aspects of Ndembu Ritual.* Ithaca: London: Cornell University Press.

Turner, V., 1968. 'Myth and Symbol'. In: Sills, D. (ed.), *International Encyclopedia of the Social Sciences*, Vol. 10. New York: Macmillan, pp. 576–82.

Turner, V.W., 1969. *The Ritual Process: Structure and Anti-Structure.* Chicago: Aldine.

Turner, V., 1974. 'Liminal to Liminoid in Play, Flow, and Ritual: An Essay in Comparative Symbology'. *Rice University Studies*, 60(3), pp. 53–92.

Turner, V.W., 1988. *The Anthropology of Performance.* New York: PAJ Publications.

United Nations Development Programme (UNDP), Regional Bureau for Arab States, 2009. 'Arab Human Development Report 2009: Challenges to Human Security'. Available online at: http://www.undp.org/content/dam/undp/library/corporate/HDR/ahdr2009e.pdf [Accessed 28 March 2012].

United Nations Development Programme (UNDP), 2010. 'Egypt Human Development Report 2010. Youth: Building Our Future'. Handoussa, H., ed. Available online at: http://hdr.undp.org/sites/default/files/reports/243/egypt_2010_en.pdf [Accessed 5 February 2012].

United Nations Entity for Gender Equality and the Empowerment of Women (UN Women), Egypt's National Council for Women, 2013. 'Study on Ways and Methods to Eliminate Sexual Harassment in Egypt'. Available online at: http://www.dgvn.de/fileadmin/user_upload/DOKUMENTE/English_Documents/Sexual-Harassment-Study-Egypt-Final-EN.pdf [Accessed 5 December 2014].

Wedeen, L., 1999. *Ambiguities of Domination: Politics, Rhetoric, and Symbols in Contemporary Syria.* Chicago, IL: University of Chicago Press.

Weinbaum, G.M., 1985. 'Egypt's "Infitah" and the Politics of US Economic Assistance'. *Middle Eastern Studies*, 21(2), pp. 206–22.

Werkmeister, O.H., 1973. 'Marx on Ideology and Art'. *New Literary History*, 4, pp. 501–19.

Westmoreland, M.R., 2016. 'Street Scenes: The Politics of Revolutionary Video in Egypt'. *Visual Anthropology*, 29(3), pp. 242–62.

Williams, R., 1958. *Culture and Society 1780–1950.* London: Chatto & Windus.

Williams, R., 1961. *The Long Revolution.* New York: Columbia University Press.

Williams, R., 1977. *Marxism and Literature*. Oxford and New York: Oxford University Press.

Williams, R., 1981. *Culture*. London: Fontana Paperbacks.

Wilms, M., 2014. *Art War*. [film]. Germany: HELDEN FILM.

Winegar, J., 2006. *Creative Reckonings: The Politics of Art and Culture in Contemporary Egypt*. Stanford, CA: Stanford University Press.

Winegar, J., 2009. 'Culture is the Solution: The Civilizing Mission of Egypt's Culture Palaces'. *Review of Middle East Studies*, 43(2), pp. 189–97.

Winegar, J., 2011. 'Taking Out the Trash: Youth Clean Up Egypt After Mubarak'. Middle East Report 259. Available online at: https://anthropology.northwestern.edu/documents/people/TakingOuttheTrash_Winegar.pdf.

Winegar, J., 2014. *Facebook Post*. Available online at: https://www.facebook.com/jessica.winegar.9?fref=ts [Accessed 2 June 2015].

Wolff, J., 1981. *The Social Production of Art*. London: Macmillan.

Woltering, R., 2013. 'Unusual Suspects: "Ultras" as Political Actors in the Egyptian Revolution'. *Arab Studies Quarterly*, 35(3), pp. 290–304.

INDEX

Lightning Source UK Ltd.
Milton Keynes UK
UKHW020016170123
415455UK00005B/252